SWAMI KRIYANANDA

As We Have Known Him

SWAMI
KRIYANANDA

As We Have Known Him

Asha Praver

Crystal Clarity Publishers
Nevada City, California

Printed in Canada
1 3 5 7 9 10 8 6 4 2

Design by Tejindra Scott Tully
*Thanks to all the photographers, known and unknown,
who have contributed to this book.*

Crystal Clarity Publishers
14618 Tyler Foote Road
Nevada City, CA 95959 USA

Tel: 800.424.1055 or 530.478.7600
clarity@crystalclarity.com
email: www.crystalclarity.com

Library of Congress Catalog-in-Publication Data available

CONTENTS

Vivid in My Heart

The first time I saw Swami Kriyananda was in a tent set up behind the Beta Chi fraternity house on the campus of Stanford University, in Palo Alto, California. It was late November 1969. He was in his early forties. I was twenty-two years old.

Usually the tent served as an expanded venue for the parties for which the fraternity was famous. It was the '60s, though, and every-thing was changing. Someone thought it would be interesting to invite a swami to speak.

I had attended Stanford University, but had dropped out after only one year. I had hoped to find teachers there who were not only knowledgeable, but also *wise*. It soon became apparent to me that my professors, though brilliant in their own fields, were groping in the dark for happiness even as I was. So I left.

Soon after, I discovered the *Bhagavad Gita* and the teachings of Sri Ramakrishna. Even as a child, I had the feeling that something far more important was going on in life than most people were aware of. At first, I thought the adults around me were all in on the secret and were just holding it back from me as a kind of elaborate practical joke. "Soon," I thought, "they will reveal it to me." Only slowly did I come to know that this was not the case. My parents and teachers were good people, intelligent, honorable, and kind. For the most part, though, they accepted life as it appeared to be and expected me to do the same.

Once I discovered Eastern religion, at least I had a name for what I was seeking: Self-realization. Still, I had no idea how to turn these high ideals into an actual way of life. I read about the saints of many religious traditions, hoping to find in their example a way to bridge the gap between theory and practice.

Their stories were deeply inspiring and I devoured book after book. The circumstances of their lives, though, were so different from my own. Catholic monasteries, Indian ashrams, Himalayan caves, leper colonies in the middle of the jungle—their example proved to be of little practical value. My life was becoming one of quiet desperation.

Then Swamiji walked into that tent and everything changed.

I was in the last row of the bleachers, way up toward the top of the tent. I had wanted to be closer to the stage, but my companions insisted on this faraway perch. The choice proved felicitous, I daresay, God-inspired, for I was directly across from the entrance and high enough to have a unobstructed view of Swami Kriyananda when he walked in.

Swami means teacher. *Ji* is a suffix denoting both affection and respect. From the moment I saw him he was *Swamiji* to me. The image of Swamiji coming through that doorway is as vivid in my heart today as it was the moment it happened.

He was dressed in the traditional orange robes of an Indian Swami: a long loose fitting shirt and a sarong-like garment called a *dhoti*. He had a neatly trimmed beard and long hair, brownish in color, which hung straight and thin down his back.

He was slender, a little less than six feet tall. He moved with a certain grace and gave the impression of great strength, although more like a dancer than an athlete. Later I heard the phrase "lion-like Swami." It described him perfectly.

The instant I saw him, the thought flashed in my mind, *He has what I want.* With a determined step and what I came to recognize as his characteristic posture—straight spine, slightly raised chest so as to meet life "heart-first"—he covered the short distance from the doorway to the stage at the center of the tent. By the time he reached the platform, before I even heard the sound of his voice, I had forged with Swamiji a lifelong bond.

He gave a lecture, but I don't remember a word of what he said. All I remember is that when he finished, I thought, "This is the most intelligent man I have ever met."

Somehow I picked up a few facts. Swamiji is an American, although he was born in Europe, and spent his childhood there. He is a direct disciple of Paramhansa Yogananda. He had been part of Self-Realization Fellowship (SRF), the organization Yogananda founded, but now he was on his own. He lived in San Francisco and taught classes all over the Bay Area to earn money for a community he was starting in the Sierra Nevada foothills, about four hours away. He called the community *Ananda.*

I owned a copy of Yogananda's classic *Autobiography of a Yogi*, but I had never read more than a few pages. The devotional tone and the plethora of miracles had not appealed to me. On page 9, the yogi Lahiri Mahasaya materializes in a wheat field to deliver a spiritual message to Yogananda's father. I don't think I even got to page 10.

Now, with renewed interest, I tried again. If Swamiji was devoted to this book and its author, I had to give it another try. This time, I was enthralled. I couldn't understand why *Autobiography of a Yogi* had not held my interest before. Later I understood that my first meeting with Swamiji opened my heart not only to him, but to Paramhansa Yogananda as well.

It wasn't long before I threw my lot in with Swamiji and moved to Ananda.

The idea of writing this book came very early in my time with Swamiji. I have always had a deep longing to help others, but until I met him, I didn't feel I had anything meaningful to give. Now I was eager to pass on to others all that I was learning.

I began giving classes for guests at our retreat, which I filled with stories about Swamiji. I longed, though, to make a more lasting contribution. Though I hardly felt qualified to write a book, I began to write down my experiences with Swamiji. When I spoke to him about it, he was reassuring.

"You don't have to do it now," he said, "you can do it later when you feel ready. I will help you."

In the many years that passed between the first time we spoke of it and when I actually began to write this book, Swamiji referred to it only occasionally. It was always in my mind, though, and, I believe, also in his, for I see now all the ways in which he helped me, just as he said he would.

He included me in so many situations where I didn't really belong except that to be there helped me understand the breadth of his work and the depth of his consciousness. Whenever his attitudes or actions were obscure to me, he would patiently explain what he was doing and why. Whatever I asked, he would answer. In this way, again and again I was able to test my intuition against his explanations, until gradually I gained the confidence to write this book.

What follows is not a biography in the conventional sense. You will learn about many of the significant events and achievements of Swamiji's life, but it is not a comprehensive account. There is no chronology or sequence to the stories that follow. Sometimes events from different time periods and different locations are included in the same vignette. It is a biography of *consciousness*—Swami Kriyananda as we have known him.

Many people have shared their stories with me. Some names are included; others have preferred to appear in the book only as "an Ananda devotee." When there is no other attribution, the first person accounts are my own experiences. I have also described the experiences of others as I observed them, or learned about them from Swamiji himself. Names that appear first with an asterisk (*) are pseudonyms.

Unless it is clear from the context that the individuals involved are from India, devotees referred to by a single Sanskrit name are Europeans or Americans upon whom Swamiji has bestowed these names as a spiritual blessing. Swamiji's appointed spiritual successor, for example, is *Jyotish*, which means *inner light*. Jyotish's wife and partner in leading Ananda is *Devi*, which is a name for *Divine Mother*. My name, *Asha*, means *hope*.

The name *Master* refers only to Paramhansa Yogananda.

~ 1 ~

MOMENTS OF TRUTH

"Softer than the flower,
where kindness is concerned;
stronger than the thunder,
where principles are at stake."

Vedic definition of a man of God

It Must Be Lonely

Adjacent to the lobby of the hotel where Swamiji and a few of us were staying there was a small jewelry store. For hours every day, a woman sat alone behind the counter.

"I never see any customers in there," Swamiji said.

There was nothing in the shop that Swamiji wanted to buy, but the next day we went in. "Every day I see you sitting here," he said. "There are so few customers, what do you do all day? It must be lonely."

She seemed startled to be addressed in such a personal way, then touched by his kindness.

"I read," she said. "I have a little paperwork to do." Her voice trailed off. "It *is* lonely," she said. Her eyes filled with tears.

Swamiji offered no words of comfort; he was silent and still. I was standing next to him, and suddenly I was enveloped in an expanding sense of joy, emanating from him. He was reaching out to her with his spirit. Suddenly her eyes shone with happiness. When Swamiji saw she had received what he had come to give her, he wished her well, and we left the shop.

After that, whenever he went by, Swamiji would greet her through the window. Often, then, she would come to the doorway and watch him until he was out of sight. Just seeing Swamiji seemed to ease her loneliness.

The Love of One Devotee

During the hours when Swamiji was having open-heart surgery, I led a prayer vigil in the temple of the Ananda Sacramento community where I lived. A few others joined me, but mostly I prayed alone.

Swamiji was in a hospital nearby, and afterwards I wanted to go see him. Each time I tried, however, so many others were there before me that I couldn't get in.

When he got out of the hospital, he came to our community to rest for a few days before returning to Ananda Village. The operation was a major one; they had placed an artificial valve in his heart.

Before I could tell Swamiji about the prayer vigil, or how disappointed I was not to be able to see him sooner, he asked to speak to me.

"I am so sorry you weren't able to visit me in the hospital," he said. "But I felt your love."

Swamiji was so weak and in so much pain he could barely speak above a whisper, yet he used the little energy he had to reassure me. People all over the world had been praying for him, and still, in the midst of it, he sensed my tiny consciousness. I was so moved I couldn't even reply.

~ From Lalita ~

Soul to Soul

By the time I got to Swamiji's lecture it was standing room only and I had to sit on the floor of the middle aisle. It didn't matter where I was in the room, when Swamiji began to speak, I felt as if he were inside my spine, speaking directly to my soul. I don't know how else to explain it.

And many of the things he talked about were issues I was facing right at that time, as if his whole lecture was just for me.

"My lectures are really conversations," Swamiji says. "It is the consciousness of the audience that determines what I say. I never prepare in advance. I just pray to Divine Mother, 'Use me as your instrument. Inspire me to say what You want this audience to hear.'"

When the lecture was over, I stood at the edge of a group gathered around Swamiji. Our eyes met and I said simply, "Thank you for everything."

"I am so glad you came and we could have this time together," he replied.

Even with so many people present, Swamiji was still conscious of us as individual souls.

~ From Liladevi ~

Called on the Carpet

I always tended to be a rebel, getting into arguments with teachers, neighbors, and anyone in authority. Even at Ananda I decided, "No one will boss me but God!" For a while I got away with it. No one interfered with my way of doing things. Then Swamiji appointed a new director for our community in Italy. As soon as I saw him, I knew I was in for a hard time.

It wasn't long before we got into a big fight, not with our fists but with words. I didn't hide my resentment and he threw his uncharitable opinion of me right back in my face. We argued at high volume even in front of others. It was a bad scene and I came close to leaving.

Then Swamiji came to Italy for a visit. Someone told him what was going on and he sent word that he wanted to see me. Once again, I thought, I was being called on the carpet. I expected a big scolding and was ready to battle for my beliefs.

To my surprise, Swamiji was kind to me. He invited me to sit on the couch and served me a cup of tea. We chatted a little about this and that. Then he said, "We don't want 'Yes-men' at Ananda. You should always think for yourself." I was so surprised! I had expected him to say, "Get in line, or else!"

He then added, "Just keep this in mind. Negativity has its own momentum. If you keep on criticizing others, your negativity will carry you right out of Ananda, and Ananda is where I think your heart wants to live."

When he spoke those words I felt so much love from him, it was like a wave that flattened me against the couch. I couldn't move. It was, for me, a moment in Eternity. Finally Swamiji said gently, "I think it is time for you to go." I backed out of his house, without ever turning away from him: hardly my usual way of treating someone in authority!

I resolved, "I won't be so stupid as to let myself be taken away from a place of such harmony as Ananda."

It took time for me to change, however. I still hadn't altered enough when, one day, Swamiji said to me, "You are a jewel." What a surprise! Then he said to the director, "He is very sincere." It didn't flatter my ego for Swamiji to say these things. What it told me was that he saw behind my argumentative manner to the shy, self-doubting little boy I really was.

Love is more powerful than fighting. I would never have believed it if I hadn't experienced it myself. Swamiji tamed me.

~ From Jayadev ~

Lou Gehrig's Disease

My husband was forty years old when he was diagnosed with ALS, more commonly known as Lou Gehrig's disease. He was a carpenter —a big, robust man. We have four children; the youngest was three. I knew the medical facts but I still found it impossible to imagine that my husband would never get better, that this disease would weaken him, paralyze him, and then take his life.

A couple of years later, reality had set in with a vengeance and I was beginning to see what I was up against. Every week I drove my husband to the doctor. He had long since lost the ability to drive himself. Afterwards we would stop at a local bakery and have coffee and a treat. If he felt well enough, we'd sit inside. If not, I'd bring things out in a bag and we'd eat in the car.

On this day, he wasn't feeling well and I went in alone to place the order. As it happened, Swamiji was standing in line in front of me. I was about at the end of my rope. Every part of me was screaming, "This is too much. I can't do this! Nobody could do this. I want to be a wife, not a nurse. I want a husband to help me raise these children, not an invalid I have to push around in a wheelchair." I am not proud of how I was feeling, but, well, there it is.

When I saw Swamiji I thought, "Maybe he could talk to Somebody!" God? Master? I didn't care Who, I just wanted Somebody to *do* something. There were so many things I wanted to say to Swamiji, but all that came out was, "I don't think I can do this."

Swamiji looked at me with such compassion and said simply, "You'll get stronger." In other words, don't try to swallow the whole thing at once. Just take one teaspoon at a time. It was the perfect advice for me. I know how to put one foot in front of the other.

Several years after the diagnosis, when my husband was really sick, he asked Swamiji, "How should I pray?" The question behind it was, "Should I accept this as God's will or should I ask to be healed?"

Swamiji answered, "Don't pray *for* anything. Just pray. Be in a state of openness and communion with God. Put your life in His hands."

Swamiji's answer was a huge relief. Adding to the difficulty of the disease itself was the lingering thought in my husband's mind that he had to *do* something about it. Now Swamiji was telling him, "Just be with God."

I did get stronger, as Swamiji said I would. And the last years of my husband's life were the sweetest years of our marriage.

~ From Hassi ~

An Unhappy Couple

Once when Swamiji was traveling with Lawrence* in Europe, they went out to dinner with a married couple who are friends of Swamiji's, but not connected with Ananda. Afterwards, Lawrence exclaimed, "What a relief to get away from those two! The negativity between them was so thick you could cut it with a knife."

"It was?" Swamiji said. "I didn't notice."

Lawrence was incredulous. "How could you not notice?" He rattled off several examples of the unkind and disrespectful way they had treated each other. "It is a wonder they are still married."

Swamiji was silent for a moment, then he said, "I never saw them in that light. I don't like to give energy even to the *thought* of negativity. But I see now that I did respond to it. As I think back, I see that all my comments were directed toward trying to create harmony and understanding between them. I hope it helped."

BUSINESS REPLY MAIL

FIRST-CLASS MAIL PERMIT NO. 414 NEVADA CITY, CA

POSTAGE WILL BE PAID BY ADDRESSEE

CRYSTAL CLARITY PUBLISHERS
14618 TYLER FOOTE RD
NEVADA CITY CA 95959-9989

Dear Friends,

In today's world, peace and tranquility can be difficult to find. **Crystal Clarity Publishers** and **Clarity Sound & Light** seek to support you in your efforts. Our products are created with one thought in mind—to help every individual find a sense of harmony within and with the world around them.

We hope these products bring you joy and peace!

Many blessings to you,

The staff of
Crystal Clarity

Yes, I would like to receive:

☐ A free catalog of **books, music, audios** and **videos**.

☐ FREE e-mail newsletter with articles, discounts and special offers.

☐ Brochure about the **Ananda Course in Self-Realization**.

☐ Retreats and Programs at **The Expanding Light** retreat center in northern California.

Or call: **800-424-1055**, or visit our website at:
www.crystalclarity.com

Name:_____

Address:_____

City:_____State_____Zip_____

Phone: (____) _____

E-mail address:_____

A Kiss

The child was retarded, and the unaccustomed energy of having Swamiji and our whole tour group staying in her home as guests of her mother was making her loud and unruly.

She was about fourteen years old and a formidable force in the middle of the kitchen where we were trying to make breakfast. I had no idea how to react; I just wanted to get away from her. Swamiji, however, knew just what to do. He put his hands on her shoulders and planted a huge kiss right on her cheek.

Instantly, she calmed down—and so did I.

That simple act by Swamiji taught me more than words can ever say. Faced with disharmony and chaos, my impulse had been to run away. Swamiji's instinctive response in *all* circumstances is to *give* energy and love.

~ From an Ananda devotee ~

Puzzled

After the earthquake in Assisi, Italy in 1998, tourism dropped off for awhile. Many small businesses went bankrupt. The Ananda community there is twenty miles outside of town on a rural road. A small restaurant, serving mostly coffee and sweets, opened on that road just after the earthquake happened.

"When so many businesses are closing," Swamiji said, "it took courage to go ahead and open anyway. I'd like to help the owner make a success of his business." Whenever Swamiji drove to town he made a point of stopping at that restaurant for a coffee and something to eat, greeting the owner like an old friend.

Swamiji had recorded many of his songs in Italian and he brought one of those CDs for the owner to hear. "Perhaps your customers would enjoy it if you played music like this," Swamiji said.

Once when Swamiji went in, the owner had fresh strawberries and ice cream as the specialty of the day. Swamiji's enthusiasm for the dish seemed to boost the owner's spirits. Often Swamiji and his group were the only customers in the restaurant.

The owner played Swamiji's CD whenever he came in, but it is doubtful that he played it at any other time. "His mind is too restless to listen to my music," Swamiji said later.

A friend accompanied Swamiji to the restaurant once and afterwards remarked, "It is obvious that the owner likes you, but I think he doesn't quite know what to make of you. He looks at you in such a puzzled way, as if he were trying to figure you out."

Swamiji laughed and said, "Years ago, a young man at Ananda Village traveled with me on a lecture tour. He was a nice man, but complex, with many crosscurrents of ego. Every morning at breakfast he would stare at me in just the way you describe. Finally, after a week, he said in exasperation, *'I just can't figure you out!'*

"I told him, 'To figure someone out means to understand his motives. You can't figure me out because the only motive I have is to serve God.'"

Single Mom

With no job, and two children to support, I felt all alone and in desperate need of spiritual guidance and inspiration. A friend had recently moved to Ananda and she suggested I come there for Spiritual Renewal Week. I knew nothing about Master, and had never met Swami Kriyananda, but I had promised God I would walk through every door He opened for me, so I said yes.

Usually I sit in the back of any crowd, but for Swamiji's first class, I sat right in the front row, virtually at his feet. Directly in front of me there was a large photograph of Master.

Swamiji spoke about the need to "open the heart." That phrase struck a deep chord within me. I stared into Master's eyes and he—not the photograph, but the living presence behind it—stared back at me.

I was intensely aware of Swamiji's presence, too, but his words had become a musical hum and I no longer followed the meaning. The three of us—Master, Swamiji, and I—formed a triangle of energy. My heart filled to overflowing with an inexplicable sweetness. I knew I had found my home.

In two weeks, I packed up all our belongings, rented out our house, and came to Ananda. The only housing available was a converted shed, which at that time didn't even have indoor plumbing.

My daughters, eight and eleven years old, were appalled by our sudden change in circumstances, and often spoke longingly of the comfortable home and the friends they had left behind. It took every ounce of my energy to earn a living, take care of my children, and keep my attitude upbeat so as to lead by example. It was a difficult transition.

New Year's Day is my birthday and Swamiji was holding an open house for the community. My children were away visiting their father—we had been divorced for many years—so I was free to go. I decided to walk the two miles to Swamiji's home.

It had been snowing for days. The forest was magical, pure white and silent, except for the occasional *whoosh* as a branch released its accumulated load of snow. It could have been a beautiful walk with God, but I was feeling sorry for myself, and all alone on my birthday. Inwardly, I prayed to Master.

"I am so grateful to be at Ananda," I said, "but you know it hasn't been easy. I'm not asking for a husband, but sometimes I feel so alone. I long for someone just to hold my hand."

Swamiji was standing in the doorway of his house, greeting the community members as they streamed in. When he saw me, he reached out, took me by the hand and drew me to stand next to him. He didn't say anything, or even look at me. He just went on greeting his guests, holding my hand, the way I hold my children when we walk through a crowded place and I want to be sure they don't wander away from me.

After about five minutes, when everyone had arrived, Swamiji turned and smiled at me so sweetly, as if to say, "Don't worry. You are not alone." Then he let go of my hand and we went into the living room so he could begin the satsang.

~ From Helen Purcell ~

The Heart of a Child

I have always appreciated the way Swamiji relates to children. He doesn't patronize them, as some adults do. The soul is ageless, even if the body is young. But the consciousness of a child is different. Swamiji recognizes that and takes it into account.

My son Rama was nine when we went to visit Swamiji in Assisi, Italy. We were having dinner with Swamiji at a local restaurant. My son was the only child at the table and he desperately wanted to be part of what was going on, but the conversation was too adult for him to join in.

On the table in front of us was a basket of two-foot long breadsticks that they often serve in Italy. Suddenly Swamiji grabbed one of those breadsticks, pointed it at Rama like a sword, and called out, "On guard!"

Instantly, Rama seized a "weapon" of his own and a battle royal began! It went on for several moments until, with one daring stroke, Rama broke Swamiji's "sword" in half and was declared the winner.

A few days later at the Sunday Service, Rama got in line for the blessing. When Swamiji is blessing, he doesn't relate to you as a personality. It is a sacred soul contact.

In his arms, Rama carried "Minkey the Monkey", a stuffed animal who was his constant companion, as real to him as any other friend.

Swamiji touched Rama at the spiritual eye and solemnly blessed him. Then, with just the hint of a smile, Swamiji put his finger at the spiritual eye of Minkey the Monkey and blessed him, too.

"Swamiji makes people happy," Rama said. "When I grow up, I want to be just like him."

~ From Sara Cryer ~

Head to Heart

I was born at Ananda and have lived here all my life. When I was six years old, Swamiji was in the dining room at the Retreat, and for some reason all the children started going up and hugging him.

At first, I held back—I didn't want to do it just because everyone else was. Finally I decided my feelings were sincere and I went up and put my arms around him.

Swamiji was standing up. My head was resting on his heart and my little arms went only halfway around him.

I remember thinking, "Hugging Swamiji is different than hugging anyone else!" It caught me off guard. Waves of peace and joy were coming out of him and going into me. I was so happy just standing there with my head against his heart. I've never forgotten that hug.

~ From Peter Kretzmann ~

Age Difference

Swamiji is 21 years older than I. When I became his secretary, I was just 25. Despite my youth and inexperience, I held strong views on many subjects and didn't easily give in, even if it was Swamiji who disagreed with me. Decades later, when I began to work with strong-minded young people, I appreciated how respectfully Swamiji had treated me.

"I want to thank you, Sir," I said to him one day, "for the kindness, patience, and respect you have always shown me. Never once in all these years have you referred to my age."

"I've never thought about it," Swamiji said. "I don't see even children in terms of their age. Age is just a passing phase of the body. The soul is ageless."

I've made the mistake of thinking that Swamiji *disciplines* himself to behave correctly. I've come to understand, however, that his behavior is not an act of will. It is the pure reflection of his *consciousness.*

Revolving Door

Swamiji was the guest of honor at an Ananda elementary school event. A little girl, nine years old, asked him, "How old are you?"

Swamiji replied, "Let's put it this way: When I was your age, you were an old woman."

For a moment she looked at him wonderingly. Then she seemed to understand and walked thoughtfully away.

Are You Saved?

I was one of fifty people from Ananda on a pilgrimage with Swamiji to Israel in 1985. One day we went to Nazareth and, after visiting the holy sites, we were moving through the lively street scene. Swamiji was enjoying the passing show when suddenly a young Arab man, apparently a Christian, accosted him with considerable fervor: "Do you believe Jesus Christ died for your sins?"

How would Swamiji answer that one? He couldn't sincerely say "Yes," but to say "No," could invite a harangue, or even damage the young man's faith—which Swamiji no doubt considered an even worse outcome. I thanked my lucky stars the question hadn't been directed toward me!

Swamiji wasn't troubled at all, however. In a kindly yet penetrating manner, he simply asked, "How can God die?"

The young man wobbled in shocked silence for a few moments, then departed.

~ From Gyandev ~

Circles

When the formal interview was done, Steven, the journalist, began to ask Swamiji some personal questions of his own.

"I am a Gemini," Steven said, "and am curious about everything. It's hard for me to stick to just one spiritual path. I feel like I might be missing something, so I keep jumping from one to another.

"Each time I meet a new teacher and start a new set of practices, I feel like I'm accomplishing so much. But spiritually I keep ending up right back where I started."

"Going in circles," Swamiji said, "does give one a certain sense of accomplishment. The bigger the circle, the greater the sense of accomplishment."

"What is the answer then to all my doubts?" Steven asked.

"Peace," Swamiji said. "The *experience* of peace resolves all doubts. There are many true paths. Choose one and go deeply into it. Until you do that, your mind will always be restless."

Analysis or Devotion

"I'm not making the spiritual progress I hoped for," an over-intellectual devotee said to Swamiji. "I think I need to improve my powers of *analysis*."

"*No!*" Swamiji said, forcefully, as if to remove from the devotee's mind—and even from the air between them—every trace of that word.

Then again, more quietly, he said, "No. Analysis won't help you. Love God. What you need is to develop more devotion."

I Need Time

A man in the community was about to make a serious mistake. His judgment was clouded by desire and he could no longer tell what was spiritually right for him.

When Swamiji heard about it, he called the man on the phone. "Please don't do anything until we have a chance to talk," Swamiji said.

Reluctantly, the man agreed—on one condition. "The situation is complicated," he said to Swamiji, "and I'll need at least half an hour to explain it to you."

"You can have as much time as you need," Swamiji replied.

Later, however, Swamiji said to me, "The truth can be spoken in a minute. It is *self-justification* that takes a long time."

A Way of Life

Swamiji was one of several guest teachers sitting on the raised dais at a large yoga center waiting his turn to speak. It was a casual event and the speakers were all in rocking chairs.

The room was hot and stuffy and the talks were a little dull. Swamiji was gently rocking back and forth with an abstracted air. Still, watching him was more interesting to me than listening to the speakers, so I was astonished when suddenly he simply disappeared!

Unbeknownst to him, the chair had been rocking not only forward and back, but also slowly across the platform until it simply fell off the edge with Swamiji in it.

Even though it was a total surprise to suddenly be tumbling off the stage, Swamiji didn't make a sound. He just hit the ground, got up, lifted the chair back into place, sat down, and resumed rocking. It all happened so fast, only a few people even noticed.

On another occasion, this time at Ananda Village, Swamiji and his chair also fell off the stage. He was giving a lecture, sitting in a chair which had been placed so close to the edge of the raised platform, that a vigorous gesture by Swamiji sent it toppling over.

This time, everyone's eyes were on him, and the whole audience gasped in dismay. Swamiji, however, made no exclamation of alarm or gesture of surprise. In fact, he barely paused in his lecture, but stood up immediately and continued talking as if nothing had happened, even while others lifted the chair into place so he could sit down again.

In and of itself, falling off a stage is not a significant spiritual event, except that these incidents illustrate an interesting quality in Swamiji's nature: He lives in the "now" and is not unsettled, therefore, by sudden, unexpected changes. Rather, to him, such changes are just part of the natural flow, and not worth exclaiming over.

Master said, "What comes of itself, let it come." For Swamiji, this is more than an aphorism—it is a way of life.

"Take care of the minutes," Master said, "and the incarnations will take care of themselves."

~ From an Ananda devotee ~

Buying a Car

The event was a "new age" ecumenical gathering called *Meeting of the Ways*. It was held in San Francisco and included leaders from the most prominent yoga and meditation groups in America. The day before the public program started, there was a reception for the spiritual leaders and a handful of their students so they could meet one another.

A few of us came with Swamiji in his car, an old, well-used Chevrolet that he had bought for $75 through a government surplus auction. The paint was faded, but the car ran well. It was spacious inside, and had a large trunk—important features, since Swamiji seldom traveled alone.

The reception was held at a large home in one of San Francisco's more elegant neighborhoods. We were a little late, and most of the guests had already arrived. Both sides of the street were lined with parked cars. There were several Mercedes, a Rolls Royce or two, and even a chauffeured limousine. The majority were late model cars of no special distinction. Swamiji's car, compared to even the humblest of them, was a sorry sight.

As we walked toward the house, Swamiji said, "I have to get a new car. For myself, I don't care. In India they understand renunciation and would respect me for driving a car like mine. When I met the Shankaracharya of Kanchipuram, whose position might be compared to that of the Pope, he was receiving people out of doors, seated on the ground under a palm tree.

"In America, however, where money is easily come by, when people see me driving a car like that, they think, 'If he can't afford a better car, there must be something wrong with his teachings.' I don't want anything fancy. That, too, would give the wrong impression. Just something nice enough so people don't form a negative impression of us."

Soon after, Swamiji received a large donation and used it to buy a new Chevrolet. About a decade later, when that car needed to be replaced, he went to a local auto mall. One car he rather liked was a certain American model; I think it was a Buick. The ride was smooth and quiet, the trunk was large, and the seats were very comfortable. Swamiji had trouble with his hips, and comfort was important for him. The only drawback was, it was marketed as a *luxury* car, even though it wasn't that expensive. The advertising was meant to flatter the ego.

"In the brochure they gave me about the car," Swamiji said, "all the people looked so unpleasant. Puffed up with pride as if to say, 'Now I have *arrived*.' I don't want to be one of them."

So he bought a Nissan.

"It isn't as comfortable as the other one," Swamiji said, "but I feel more comfortable driving it."

Saving the Planet

Several people dedicated to ending war and banning nuclear weapons came to Ananda to try and enlist Swamiji's support for their cause. Their presentation included a graphic description of what would happen if a nuclear bomb hit an American city. Using charts, graphs, and full-color illustrations, they explained how people would be vaporized, incinerated, burned, scorched, and, if that didn't get them, poisoned by radiation.

Using fear to motivate people is not a tactic Swamiji admires. When you increase fear, you create more of the very consciousness you are trying to eradicate.

When the anti-war advocates finally paused long enough for Swamiji to get a word in, he said, "A hundred years from now almost no one who is on the planet now will still be here. Whether we dribble off a few at a time over the next century or all go out at once in one big bang, once we are in the astral world, it won't make any difference."

Then more seriously he said, "When cataclysms come, as my Guru said they will, those who die will be the lucky ones. The real suffering will come to those who live through it." He paused a moment to let his words sink in.

"I know you are trying to do a good thing," Swamiji said sympathetically, "and I don't want to dampen your enthusiasm. But the only way to change the world is by changing consciousness—above all, by changing your own consciousness. Everything else is just a symptom. I prefer to work on the cause, which is consciousness itself."

On another occasion, a man presented Swamiji with a long list of ecological disasters that had happened or would happen soon unless something was done to prevent them. He wanted Swamiji to put the resources of Ananda into solving these problems.

Swamiji listened patiently then said, "We are already doing exactly what you ask. All the problems you describe are caused by wrong consciousness. If everyone in the world lived the way we do at Ananda, these problems would simply cease to exist."

Growing Pains

I meant well, but I was too immature to handle the assignment. Eventually I had to admit defeat and go back to Ananda Village. I felt like a complete failure.

Soon after I returned, Swamiji had a party at his home, Crystal Hermitage. I was in such turmoil I didn't feel like being with people, so I stayed just long enough to greet Swamiji. Then I slipped out the door unnoticed and went up the hill to meditate in the chapel. Everyone else was at the party so I had it all to myself.

My mind was churning. "Where did I go wrong? What could I have done differently?" After about an hour, I felt a presence beside me. When I opened my eyes, Swamiji was sitting there. I don't know how he even found me.

Part of my turmoil was the thought that I had let Swamiji down. He had trusted me to make the situation better; instead I had made it worse. He reached over and touched me consolingly on the hand. Then he looked deeply into my eyes and offered a few simple words of advice. "Don't take it inside, just let it go. These things happen."

I felt a ray of hope penetrating the grim interior of my mind where I had been wrestling for days with my failure. In his eyes, there was neither judgment nor disappointment, just compassion for my suffering and the promise of his unconditional friendship.

~ From Sudarshan ~

Full Prostration

The night before, one of the retreat guests had shaved his head. Now he was hidden in the bushes, stark naked, carrying his clothes in a small bundle. Swamiji was giving a class in the outdoor Temple of Leaves and the man's intention was to lay himself and all he possessed at Swamiji's feet.

He came out of the bushes behind Swamiji. A collective gasp went up from the crowd. Swamiji, however, went on with his discourse, unaware of the unfolding drama.

Then the man stepped in front of Swamiji, placed his clothes on the ground and made a full prostration at Swamiji's feet. Immediately, two men on the Retreat staff started moving forward, intending to lift the man and lead him away. With a small gesture, Swamiji made it clear: "Let him stay."

To the audience, Swamiji said in a matter-of-fact way, "Sometimes on the spiritual path, these things happen," meaning, that a person may get carried away by excessive zeal. Then, with the man lying at his feet, covered now by a blanket someone had tossed over his nakedness, Swamiji went on with his lecture as if nothing had happened.

If the man had remained quiet and still, Swamiji would have let him stay there until the class was finished. Instead, however, he began inching forward, sobbing with ever increasing volume and intensity, until his head was resting on Swamiji's feet.

At this point, Swamiji leaned forward and said quietly, "Please put your clothes back on." Then he indicated to the staff members to help the man move away.

Without missing a beat, even as the man was being escorted off the scene, Swamiji went on with his lecture.

Fortunately, the man soon recovered and resumed a more normal relationship to the spiritual path.

Brother Donkey

When an opportunity came to go to Ananda Assisi for a few months and work in the retreat kitchen, I jumped at the chance. For twelve years, I had been a critical care nurse. Now I wanted to get into a more holistic kind of healing. I also had some body problems of my own to solve—mainly a painful lower back that was beginning to get me down.

Swamiji was living in Assisi at the time and I got to see him more than I ever had before—not that we had much free time even to attend his programs. Meals had to be ready just when the satsangs ended, so when Swamiji was in the Temple, usually I was in the kitchen. But I didn't mind. It was good work and we had lots of fun.

Swamiji's house was a kilometer away from the Retreat center. When he came to the Temple, he parked his car on a little hill about 25 yards from the back door of the kitchen. Whenever we saw him pull in, the whole kitchen crew would come out the back door, wave our arms, flap our aprons, and call his name.

"Ciao, Swamiji!" The joyful cry echoed across the distance between us. It was a little undignified, but Swamiji never seemed to mind. He called back in the same exuberant fashion. "Ciao tutti!"—"Hello everyone!"

One Sunday morning I was able to go to Service. Swamiji was a little unwell, and the only part of the Service he did was the inspirational talk. When that was over, he quietly exited. The *Festival of Light* was about to begin, but I felt drawn to leave the Temple and be with Swamiji the few minutes it would take him to walk to his car.

I caught up with him just a few steps outside the door. To my surprise, he was alone. Usually someone escorts him. Just as I got there, for no apparent reason, Swamiji stumbled and started to fall. My nursing instincts kicked in and I caught him in my arms, saving him from a nasty spill.

"Perhaps that's why I felt to come out here," I thought to myself. But God had more in store for me.

Swamiji began to talk with me about some of what his body was going through. Bronchitis, irregular heartbeat, confusion with his medications that made him weak and light headed. Nothing surprised me. In my years of nursing I'd seen it all. What was unusual, though, was the way Swamiji spoke about it. He was so impersonal, as if the body he referred to belonged to someone else. It wasn't just his manner of speaking. It was his whole vibration, as if he were looking down on himself from a distance away.

Nurses take care of physical bodies. No matter how holistic we try to be, nursing gives you an intensely physical perspective on life.

"Brother Donkey," Swamiji commented then with a smile, "that's how St. Francis referred to his body, just a beast of burden to carry around his consciousness. In the end, what does the body matter? The only thing that endures is our love for God."

By that point in the conversation we had reached his car and Swamiji got in and drove away. I had come to Assisi in part to figure out what to do with my body. I hadn't explained that to Swamiji but without my even asking he had solved the problem for me. He didn't cure my back problem. He showed me how to relate to it.

Yes, it is tiresome to have a body that doesn't work properly. Even Swamiji feels that way. But what I also saw in him was just the quality I needed: detachment.

Brother Donkey. Use the body, care for it appropriately, but never forget: You are not your body. You are one with the Infinite Spirit.

~ From Madhavi ~

My Choice

I was in a bad mood. When the phone rang in the Ananda publishing office where I worked, I answered it in a less than cordial manner. Whoever it was, I made it clear that I didn't want to hear from him.

Of course, it was Swamiji. Others have told me he has a knack for catching a person at moments like this.

In an abrupt, not very friendly tone—reflecting back to me the way I had greeted him—Swamiji asked if the manager was in. She was not. He was all business and seemed to be in a hurry, but before hanging up, he inquired more gently, "How are you?"

I saw the choice before me: To remain in a bad mood or put out the energy to rise above it. With all the positive force I could muster, I said, "*Very* good, Sir!"

For a moment, Swamiji was silent. Then he said sweetly, "Good girl."

~ From an Ananda devotee ~

Yes

Whenever I cooked for Swamiji, even if others helped me, I kept strict control of the final product. But once when I was cooking dinner for Swamiji and for a dozen guests, a woman helping me asked to take charge of the two main dishes. I didn't think she had the skill, but I didn't want to hurt her feelings, so I said yes. As I feared, the result was not, in my opinion, up to my usual standard.

We sat down at the table and sang grace. Swamiji had his spoon in hand, but he hadn't tasted a single bite. He hadn't even dipped his spoon into the food, when he said, "Asha, over the years you have made many memorable dinners, but this is the *best* meal you have ever cooked."

"Sir, we made it together."

"I know that," he said. "It is the best meal *you* have ever cooked."

I knew the magic ingredient in this meal, which made it better than any of the others, was my sensitivity to the feelings of others.

Saintly Sweetness

No one was home at Swamiji's house, so Tim placed the bowl of pudding in the refrigerator. It was a gift to Swamiji from a spiritual teacher known as Shree Ma. Rather than write a note, Tim decided he would explain it to Swamiji later.

But before Tim could tell him about it, Swamiji found the pudding himself. He took a big spoonful.

"This pudding was made by a saint," Swamiji exclaimed. "It is delicious. Who made it?" A few friends were in the kitchen with him, but no one knew.

The next day, of course, the story came out. But with one bite, Swamiji had already grasped the essentials.

Melody for a Prayer

I had suffered a severe disappointment and was living under a cloud of sadness I couldn't seem to shake. I found comfort in the words of St. Teresa of Avila: "Let nothing disturb you, nothing afright you. All things will pass, but God changes not."

Teresa is a popular saint at Ananda, and several people had set those words of hers to music. But the melodies expressed the sadness of life, not the underlying joy.

I was talking to Swamiji about my disappointment and my love for Teresa's prayer. "I want to chant it as well as say it," I said. "But the melodies we have are depressing."

"Would you write down the words?" he said. I was touched by his concern for my little desire.

We were sitting in his living room and his coffee table was covered with papers and correspondence awaiting his attention. I wrote down the words, but as I added my piece of paper to that heap I thought, "It will be a long time before he gets to this."

Imagine my surprise and gratitude the next morning when Swamiji called at 8am. It was my birthday, and he said, "I have something for you." Then, over the phone, he sang St. Teresa's prayer with the lilting, joyful, *perfect* new melody he had written.

Singing that prayer, and feeling Swamiji's love behind it, helped turn the tide. The cloud of sadness soon melted away.

~ From an Ananda devotee ~

Valentine Cookies

A devotee prayed to Master, "How can I thank Swamiji for all he has done to help me?" The thought came, "It will soon be Valentine's Day. You could make him some cookies."

"It was just a small thing, a plateful of cookies," she said. "But I felt the inspiration came from Master and it was important to me that I do this for Swamiji." In her little cabin, she had only a hotplate, so she arranged to use the oven at the community market. Early in the morning, on Valentine's Day, she gathered up her supplies and went to do her baking.

But there had been a misunderstanding, and the oven was in use. A few hours later, she returned there, but the oven still wasn't available. When the same thing happened a third time, she decided sadly, "I guess it wasn't meant to be. The whole day has passed, and I have nothing to give Swamiji. Master, you'll have to find a way to thank him for me."

Two days later, she received a note from Swamiji, which began, "Thank you for the Valentine cookies..."

Hello—Again

"When I see people again after a long separation," Swamiji said, "sometimes at first I don't recognize them. Then their eyes come into focus and I remember who they are."

The "separation" Swamiji refers to is not only within one lifetime, but also from one incarnation to the next.

"When I introduced myself to Swamiji at our first meeting," Santoshi said, "He brushed aside my introduction as an unnecessary formality between old friends. 'I know you,' he said, 'I recognize you by your eyes.'"

"The first time I went to a satsang at Swamiji's house in Assisi," Premi said, "he smiled in welcome and said, 'Many years have passed since we last saw each other.' I had known him only a few months and this was just our second meeting. I knew he was referring to past incarnations."

"The first time I met Seva," Swamiji said, "was at a class I gave in San Francisco in 1967. As soon as I saw her in the room, I knew she was an old friend." Seva was instrumental in getting Ananda started.

"Swamiji has known me for years," Rick Bonin said, "but we live in different communities and meet infrequently. So I wasn't surprised when I greeted him one day and he just stared at my face without saying a word. It was clear he didn't know who I was. I didn't take it personally; Swamiji meets thousands of people. I was about to remind him of my name, when his eyes locked onto mine and he looked deeply into me.

"'Rick,' he said warmly, 'how nice to see you,' as if I had just appeared on the scene, which, in a sense, I had."

Sometimes Swamiji recognizes a person even before they meet. After he moved to India, someone casually mentioned to him the name of a person who was visiting the retreat in America. "He belongs here in India," Swamiji said. When the message reached the man, he immediately agreed.

Once Swamiji held an unopened letter in his hand, from a woman he didn't know. "She is unhappy," he said. "Ananda is her lifeline. She belongs here with us." Then he added a few other comments about her life and personality, all of which proved true.

~ 2 ~

GOD ALONE

"Thou hast made us for Thyself
and our hearts are restless until
they find their rest in Thee."

St. Augustine

You'll Get It Right

The satsang with Swamiji had been particularly deep and inspiring. His body was right in front of me, but his consciousness seemed to embrace a sphere far larger than the living room of his dome and the fifty of us sitting there.

After the closing prayer he looked lovingly at us and, as if from a great distance, said, "You are going to get it right sooner or later. Why waste millions of years?"

A Calm Heart

I had a difficult decision to make. Desperately I prayed to God, "What do You want me to do?" But no matter how much I prayed I couldn't get an answer.

I asked to speak to Swamiji about it. When we met, he was sitting in an armchair and I was on the floor in front of him, with an ottoman between us. As I began to explain my dilemma, I was so overcome with emotion I collapsed against the ottoman, buried my head in my hands, and began to sob.

Through my tears, I said to Swamiji, "It is so hard to know what God wants."

Swamiji looked at me calmly and said simply, "No, it's not."

We sat together for a few moments longer, but it was soon clear he had nothing else to say to me, so I left.

"It may not be hard for *him* to know," I thought, as I made my way back home, "but it is hard for me." Swamiji's answer, however, had not referred to either one of us. He spoke of the simplicity of the task itself.

Later I prayed, "*Why* is it hard for me?"

Instantly the answer came: "Because you don't want to know. You are afraid that God's will may contradict other desires of your heart."

The first time I heard Swamiji speak, I thought, "He is the most intelligent man I have ever met." That impression has been more than confirmed by all my experiences in the years since. I had often wondered, "What is the secret of his remarkable intelligence?"

"Reason follows feeling," Master said. Whatever the predisposition of the heart, the mind will follow. Most people are predisposed in favor of their desires, attachments, and the fear of facing an unknown challenge. All these block one's ability to perceive reality.

Swamiji's only "predisposition" is to know the truth. He is not plagued by what Master calls the "thwarting cross-currents of ego." He has a single desire: To know God's will.

Swamiji leads with his heart. From the side, he looks like a strung bow: straight spine, outwardly curving chest. The clarity of his mind comes from the courage of his heart.

"In teaching meditation," Swamiji said, "people speak of the need to calm the *mind*. In fact, it is the *heart* that needs to be calmed. That is why devotion is fundamental to success in meditation. When the heart is calm and one-pointed in its focus on God, the mind is also still, because there are no restless feelings to disturb it.

"Patanjali defines the state of yoga, meaning 'union with God,' as *'Yogas chitta vrittis nirodh.'* Yoga is the 'neutralization of the whirlpools of feeling.' These whirlpools—*chitta*—reside in the heart.

"Jesus put it this way, 'Blessed are the pure in heart, for they shall see God.' Purity means the absence of any other desire except the desire for God. This is our natural state. It is not something we have to acquire. All we have to do is remove the impurities of the heart which keep us from knowing ourselves as we truly are: One with God."

That simple exchange with Swamiji—my anguished cry, "It is so hard to know God's will," and Swamiji's calm, three-word answer "No it's not."—was one of the most influential encounters I have ever had with him.

Whenever I find myself struggling to know God's will, instead of crying repeatedly, "What do You want me to do?" as if God had to be persuaded to tell me, I pray instead, "What am I afraid of?"

Whether the answer comes in a flash of intuition, or after long and sometimes painful introspection, once the fear is removed, Swamiji is right. It may still be hard for me to *follow* God's will, but it is not hard to know.

Asking Master

"I am at a crossroad," a woman wrote Swamiji. "I have to choose between two alternatives, and the decision will affect my life for years to come. I have prayed and prayed to Master, but I don't get any guidance. What should I do?"

"Master is pleased simply because you have asked him," Swamiji replied. "Choose either one. It won't matter, so long as you offer whatever you do in devotion and service to God."

I Get Along Easily

I had to work closely with a woman I found overbearing and opinionated. Since I, too, have strong opinions, we often had a personality conflict. I asked Swamiji for advice.

"She is the same way with me," he said, "but I get along with her easily. When I am with her, I just don't bother to have a personality of my own, so there is nothing to conflict with hers."

I took this to mean that I should let go of my likes and dislikes, especially the thought that she needed to be different from what she was. I tried it, and found we got along much better. This thought also helped me in several other relationships.

"Suffering is the result of wanting things to be other than they are," Swamiji says.

Years later, I mentioned to Swamiji how helpful his statement had been: "When I am with her, I just don't bother to have a personality of my own."

He seemed puzzled by his own remark. "Well, I just *don't* have a personality," he said. What for me was an affirmation of right attitude was, for Swamiji, his natural state of consciousness.

"I never identify myself as 'Swami Kriyananda,'" he says. "To me, Kriyananda is just an event for which I am responsible."

~ From an Ananda devotee ~

God Remembrance

I was with Swamiji having dinner with the family of an Ananda friend. They were educated, refined people, but not devotees, so the conversation was about art, language, politics—everything but God. It was interesting, but part of me kept thinking, "Here I am sitting next to Swamiji. How nice it would be if we could speak more freely about the things that are closest to our hearts."

At that moment Swamiji turned to me and softly hummed one of my favorite chants: "Lord I am Thine. Be Thou mine."

I felt he was telling me, "No matter what you are doing outwardly, your consciousness can always be with God."

~ From Jayadev ~

I Did This

One night, Swamiji was walking through an area of the community near his home. It was a picturesque scene—lights twinkling in the windows of several residences and faintly in the distance the sound of someone chanting.

"For the only time in Ananda's history," Swamiji said later, "the thought crossed my mind, '*I* did this. Formerly, there was only forest here. Now there is a community.'

"It felt so *limiting*, though, to bring everything we have done together to a personal focus in me. Instantly, I repudiated the thought and it has never occurred to me again. I prefer the truth and the inner freedom it brings: God is the doer."

Someone once asked Swamiji, "You receive so much praise and appreciation, yet I see no trace of pride in you. How do you manage it? I would think the temptation to feel pleased with yourself *must* crop up now and then."

"Pride comes," Swamiji replied, "when you place importance on what you *receive* from others. When your energy is focused wholly on giving, you forget yourself and simply *do*. Then the question of pride never arises."

With Divine Mother's Help

In the summer of 1980, Swamiji spent most of his time in San Francisco helping to establish an Ananda Center there. Even with him spearheading the energy, it was hard going. The San Francisco Bay area, however, is the population hub of northern California. Swamiji felt we must establish some presence there, for the sake of the work we were doing.

One evening, Swamiji drove an hour north of the city to give what he thought was a free introductory lecture for an upcoming class series. When he arrived he found there was no introductory lecture; it was the first class of the paid series and only three people had come.

"I raised the money to build Ananda by giving classes," Swamiji said to those responsible for the mistake. "One thing I learned is *always* to give a free introductory lecture."

Trying to put a positive spin on the whole experience, someone said, "Maybe Divine Mother wanted just these three people to be here."

"*Please*," Swamiji said, "don't blame Divine Mother. Leave a little room for *human* error."

A few weeks later, another devotee was feeling discouraged and said to Swamiji, "Perhaps Divine Mother doesn't want us to be here."

"If Divine Mother didn't want this work to happen," Swamiji said, "She would make it *impossible* for us to go on. We could happily go home, then, knowing it was Her will. Instead, Divine Mother makes it *barely* possible. So we can't give up; we have to go on."

Not long afterward, an opportunity came to rent a 45-room house in one of the nicest areas of the city. As soon as Swamiji stepped over the threshold, he said, "This place feels like ours."

It was ten times as large, and ten times as costly, as the place we were currently renting. Swamiji felt Divine Mother wanted us to have it, however. He called a meeting of everyone in the city who might be interested, and in an hour raised the thousands of dollars needed to move in.

It was the turning point. It wasn't easy, but for the next decade, Divine Mother made it barely possible for "Ananda House" to survive as an urban ashram.

Eventually, Divine Mother made it clear that San Francisco was not to be Ananda's permanent urban home. The house was sold and the new owner didn't want to lease it to us anymore.

The timing was perfect, however. The Ananda community in Palo Alto, on the peninsula south of San Francisco, was just getting underway. It soon replaced San Francisco as the center of Ananda's work in the San Francisco Bay Area.

God's Choir

I was part of the choir tour to Italy in May of 2000. Night after night we performed the Oratorio Swamiji has written about the life of Christ to full houses of enthusiastic music fans. In each city, they gave us a standing ovation and then crowded around to talk to the choir members.

The problem was, we were mostly Americans who only spoke English and naturally they were Italians who mostly spoke their own language.

"I want so much to share with them," I said to Swamiji after a few nights of this. "What can I say?"

We were in a restaurant and very carefully Swamiji guided me as I wrote out on a napkin: "*È tutto per Dio.*" Then he taught me how to pronounce the words, which mean, "All is for God." He then suggested I teach it to the other American choir members who might be having the same problem.

After that, I still didn't have a lot of words, but my one little phrase came straight from the heart and communicated everything I wanted to say.

~ From Steve Navisky ~

He Can Stop Me

A young man who called himself a disciple, but who lacked the necessary receptivity, was determined on a course of action that Swamiji thought unwise. When Swamiji hinted that perhaps it was not the best decision, the man responded arrogantly, "If Master doesn't want me to do it, he can stop me."

Later, after the man left, Swamiji said, "Why would Master stop him? The guru lets us do as we please, *if* we so please! If you want him to respond, you have to approach him with openness, devotion, and humility."

Indeed, Master did not stop the man, who soon afterward forsook his spiritual practices.

Nishkam Karma

My husband and I were in charge of setting up a lecture for Swamiji in April 2002 at his alma mater, Brown University. Everything went wrong. People we relied on didn't keep their promises. Promotions didn't go out on time. Even the beautiful spring weather turned suddenly cold and drizzly.

Swamiji had been hoping for a big crowd and I was embarrassed and nervous about letting him down. At breakfast the morning of the event, I warned him about what was to come, so he wouldn't be disappointed.

"*Nishkam karma*," Swamiji said calmly, quoting in Sanskrit from the *Bhagavad Gita*. He was reminding me to be detached, to perform "action without personal desire for the fruits of action." Do your best; then leave the results to God.

We were understaffed, and I had to work right up to the moment when Swamiji began to speak. The effort aggravated a physical condition I have and I was in such pain I couldn't sit up, but had to lie down on a bench in the lobby.

It didn't help that my worst fears were realized. Only a handful of people came. "*Nishkam karma*," I repeated quietly to myself. Finally I felt well enough to sit up for the lecture.

By the time we closed down the hall and joined Swamiji for a late dinner at a nearby restaurant, I was in such pain again I could barely move my arms. I'd had episodes like this before, and they lasted for days.

Swamiji had saved a place for me right next to him. When I sat down, within 30 seconds all the pain was gone. Just like that.

The lecture that night was based on *Hope for a Better World!—The Small Communities Solution*, the book Swamiji had just published. In it he takes on, as he puts it, the "Big Guns" of Western civilization: Plato, Machiavelli, Marx, Darwin, Freud, and others. He shows the reader not to be awed by "intellectual authority," but to reason from one's own experience.

"This is a book for young people," Swamiji said, "idealistic, imaginative. They are the ones who will understand."

His hope (for a better world) was to do a series of lectures on college campuses and start a youth movement toward cooperative communities. Brown University was the trial balloon.

Now Swamiji said, "When I was meditating this afternoon, before we left for the lecture, Divine Mother told me it wasn't going to happen in the way I had hoped. This, evidently, isn't the right time."

On another occasion, Swamiji said, "Many good and beautiful things that are God's will for this world never manifest, for lack of willing human instruments to receive them."

For this reason, Jesus wept for Jerusalem. "O Jerusalem, Jerusalem how often would I have gathered thy children together, as a hen doth gather her brood under her wings, and ye would not!" (Matt. 24:37)

The planning for this lecture had been a comedy of errors. I remembered a time during a lawsuit against Ananda, when *every* decision went against us, no matter how unfair. Our spirits were sagging, but Swamiji buoyed us up when he said, "The law of averages dictates that at least a few things will go in your favor. When *everything* goes against you, you know it is Divine Mother making it happen that way. I simply accept Her will, whatever it is."

Nishkam karma. Do your best, then leave the results to God.

~ From Elizabeth Palmer ~

Truth vs. Fantasy

A woman was betrayed by her closest friend. "I don't want to blame him or live in the past," she said to Swamiji. "I have to adjust to reality as it is now. So when I think of what happened, I tell myself, 'It was just fine. It had to be that way.'"

"No," Swamiji said. "It was not fine. It was very wrong and he should not have done it. You need to adjust to reality. Instead, what you're doing is retreat into a fantasy world. To *overcome* means to face the truth, not run away from it; to see the situation for what it is. Next raise your energy level and consciousness to the point where his behavior can no longer affect how you feel."

Let God Decide

In my secretarial jobs before coming to Ananda, it was my practice not only to type the letters my boss gave me, but also to edit them for clarity, grammar, and flow. I enjoyed having something creative to do, and the people I worked for appreciated my contribution.

In my first secretarial job at Ananda, I continued in the same way without bothering to ask the person I worked for now if this was what he wanted. It turned out it he didn't want it—emphatically not.

I defended my right to make needed improvements to letters that went out from "our" office. When Swamiji heard about the controversy, he did not side with me.

"I wouldn't want my secretary to edit my letters," he said.

"But, Sir, *his* letters need editing," I replied.

Swamiji answered, "Seek to be the least, and God will give you your rightful place."

~ From an Ananda devotee ~

God's Love

"I feel more love from you than I do from my own family," a retreat guest said to Swamiji. "How is that possible? We are meeting for the first time. You don't even know me."

"You are right, I don't know the details of your life the way your family does," Swamiji replied. "My love for you is impersonal. It does not come from knowing you in that way. When I look at you, I see within you the presence of God, Whom I already love. The love you feel from me is the love I feel for Him in you."

Eye to Eye

We were having dinner at Swamiji's house, about six of us, all old friends who had worked closely with Swamiji for years. A married couple in the community had just announced that they were separating. It was sad news, though not unexpected; their relationship had always been difficult.

"A few months ago," I said, "I went shopping with her to buy a shirt for her husband. I found one that looked perfect. 'This would match his eyes,' I said. Her reply astonished me. She said, 'It would? I don't know what color his eyes are.'

"No wonder they are getting divorced!" I concluded.

"They've been married for years, and she doesn't even know the color of his eyes!"

Almost everyone at the table agreed that it was astonishing. Then Swamiji, looking puzzled, said, "I never notice the color of people's eyes. I don't look *at* their eyes, I look at *them*, behind their eyes."

Someone quoted the well-known saying, "The eyes are the window to the soul."

Swamiji continued, "I don't even know what color Seva's eyes are." For years, Seva had been one of his closest friends and co-workers. He saw her nearly every day. Her big brown eyes are almost her defining feature.

Seva happened to be sitting next to him, so Swamiji turned and looked carefully at her face.

"Oh, I see," he said. "They are brown."

He knew her eyes, he would recognize them anywhere, not by their color, but by the goodness and divine aspiration he saw in them. In fact, the first time they met (in this lifetime) in San Franciscio, in 1967, from her eyes Swamiji recognized her as an old friend from the past and knew they would be friends again in this lifetime.

The Sound of Music

As soon as Swamiji began to sing, it was obvious that the cough and sinus infection he had been battling for months had seriously affected his voice. I am a professional musician and my heart went out to him. I play the flute and I know what it is like to try to perform when the body isn't working right.

The song was *Where Has My Love Gone*. It is hauntingly beautiful and quite long. His voice was weak and inconsistent and I projected as much positive energy to him as I could just to help him get through it. With my sensitive ears, I expected to endure rather than to enjoy his performance.

To my astonishment, this turned out to be a truly exquisite performance and a defining moment for me as a musician, because the real secret of Swamiji's musical genius was revealed to me.

Until then, I had made the natural mistake of thinking that when Swamiji sang, the beauty of the music came from the *sound* of his voice. Now, the sound was distorted by his illness, but the music was more beautiful than ever. For the first time I saw it clearly: Music comes from *consciousness*. Swamiji's body was impaired, but his spirit was soaring.

This realization brought to a clear focus something that had puzzled me for years.

I was always something of an anomaly among my classical music colleagues. Before big performances, I would devote comparatively little time to practicing the music itself, and an inordinate amount of time to "warming-up." On my instrument this meant long slow tones, which required deep breathing and concentrated attention to every nuance of sound.

I knew from experience that if I got *myself* in order, the music would come out fine. During the performance I could lose myself in the music in a way that wasn't possible unless I prepared in this way. I understand now that it was my way of meditating.

It had never occurred to me, though, until Swamiji showed me with his performance, that consciousness *is* the music. Sound itself is secondary.

~ From Bhagavati ~

Giving Back

"Where is the bill for filling my propane tank?" Swamiji asked Seva. "It should have come by now."

"I already paid it," Seva said with a small triumphant smile.

"You shouldn't have done that," Swamiji said sternly. "I'm not here to take from Ananda, I'm here to give."

"Most of the propane goes to run the generator to power the typewriter so that you can write books that support Ananda," Seva replied emphatically. "Since you won't accept royalties, at least we can pay for the fuel!" It was obvious she was not going to give in.

"Okay, I'll accept it this time," Swamiji said reluctantly. "However, you must promise next time to bring the bill to me."

In the early years of Ananda, when Seva managed most of Ananda's finances, I witnessed many such friendly tussles between her and Swamiji. She was determined to give him at least a modicum of financial support; he was equally determined not to accept it.

When Swamiji needed money for personal expenses, or more often, for Ananda projects that couldn't be financed in any other way, he would go out and earn it, usually by setting up a lecture tour or a series of classes.

After Swamiji became a disciple at the age of 22, he never again worked for any cause other than to spread Master's teachings. Even right after he was expelled from SRF at the age of 36 and found himself penniless and alone, everything he did to earn money also helped to spread Master's teachings.

The principle, "Where there is dharma, there is victory," governs all aspects of Swamiji's life, including his personal finances. If he feels it is right for him to spend money in a certain way, he'll commit to it, even if he doesn't have the money and has no idea where it will come from.

In 1979, he went on a lecture tour of Europe with barely enough money for expenses and nothing for his return fare. "I wasn't concerned about how I would get home," Swamiji said later. "I concentrated on serving God and left the matter to Him." He didn't even charge for his lectures. Still, all the money he needed easily came to him.

Once for a community fundraising effort, Swamiji pledged $3000 to repair a section of Ananda road. "I didn't have the money, but I knew no one else did either," Swamiji said later. "The work had to be done. 'You'll have to provide it,' I said to Divine Mother when I made the pledge."

A few days later, a man Swamiji hadn't seen for years slipped an envelope under his door. Inside was a note: "My mother died recently and I wanted to give you something from her estate." He included a check for $3000.

When he was a young monk, living on an allowance of $15 a month, Swamiji felt intuitively that he should have a nine-gem bangle. "Even now, I'm not quite sure how it happened, but somehow I got that bangle." Later he sold it to help pay for the land to start Ananda. A few years later, a woman insisted on buying him another bangle.

"At first I was reluctant to accept it," Swamiji said. "I thought there were better uses for the money. Then I realized it was Divine Mother giving it back to me, since I had given up the first one in service to Her."

A wealthy and generous friend phoned Seva one day and told her he was going to give Swamiji $40,000 to use in any way he chose. It was enough to buy a new car, bring in electricity and a phone line to Swamiji's house, and build a much-needed recording studio there. The total cost for all of this was $41,000.

Two weeks later, the car had been purchased and the work was underway but the check still hadn't arrived. No one was concerned. The donor was a man of his word and had given generously before— although never such a large amount.

Finally the check came. When Seva took it out of the envelope, at first she thought there was something wrong with her eyes.

"I made a small mistake," she said to Swamiji. "Just a matter of one zero." The check was for *four* thousand dollars, not *forty* thousand. Somehow Seva had misunderstood.

Swamiji laughed when he heard the news. "We are committed to a line of action," he said. "We can't stop now. I guess Divine Mother wants me to go out and earn the money." And he did.

Even before he was on the path, Swamiji had this same curious mixture of confidence and detachment from money. "When I was 16 years old," Swamiji said, "my father wanted to buy me a tuxedo to wear to the opera and to dinner parties when I grew older. I knew that would never be my lifestyle. 'Don't waste your money,' I told him. 'I'll never earn enough money even to pay income tax.'"

When he was in college, Swamiji said, "I had an allowance of $3 a month, which wasn't much even then. Somehow, though, on that little bit, I was able to treat all my friends to milkshakes. There always seemed to be enough."

Over the years, Swamiji has earned or raised millions of dollars. He has kept nothing for himself; all of it has gone to build Ananda. His father was never able to understand Swamiji's attitude toward money. Once in exasperation he exclaimed to Swamiji, "*You simply must stop giving all your money away!*"

Although Swamiji doesn't like to be in debt, he will borrow money when needed, especially to launch a project or finish one when costs exceed the estimate.

In the summer of 1976, shortly after a forest fire had devastated much of Ananda Village, Swamiji found out that the foundation to his own house was dangerously weak. At any moment, the whole dome might go careening down the hill.

In order not to take energy away from rebuilding the community, Swamiji arranged for an outside contractor to work on his house. The original estimate proved ridiculously low and $30,000 more was needed. The work had to be done, so Swamiji borrowed the money from a friend and paid it back in a matter of months, just as he had promised.

He is so conscientious in financial matters, he jokingly suggested that his epitaph could be, "He paid his debts."

In 1981, Swamiji was visiting friends in Hawaii. The conversation turned to Ananda and Swamiji's relationship to the community. His friends were astonished to hear how much money Swamiji had earned and given to Ananda and how little was given to him in return.

"You are the founder and spiritual director, and you don't even take a salary?" his friend said. "You are treating the members of Ananda like children. They will never mature as devotees unless they also give back to you. It is not fair to *them*."

Swamiji had always been adamant about not taking a salary, and his friend was prepared to argue the point at length. That proved unnecessary, however, for Swamiji saw the wisdom of what he was saying.

"You are right," Swamiji said simply.

When the community leaders heard that Swamiji was willing now to accept a salary, they began to pay him $2500 a month.

Later, Swamiji said, "When I was in college, I took singing lessons. My teacher charged me $5 a week. 'It is not that I need the money,' she said to me, 'but you need to pay it.' It is the same in this case. It is not that I need the money, but the community has reached the point now where it needs to pay it."

Still, whenever larger sums were needed to help Ananda, Swamiji would earn it by teaching outside of the community. For the many classes and services he gave within Ananda, he never accepted payment. Finally, when Swamiji started making plans for yet another lecture tour, David, the Retreat manager, said to him, "Why don't you teach here and let me pay you whatever you would earn by going out?"

"How could you afford it?" Swamiji said, "The Retreat budget is so tight."

At that time, the Retreat was paying well-known teachers from outside Ananda to come and give weekend retreats. "Don't you think it is ridiculous to pay others when we'd much rather have you than anyone else? The only reason we didn't schedule you, is that you were busy writing. If you are available to teach now, teach here." David said. "The money doesn't all have to come out of the Retreat budget. I think community members would be happy to donate for the classes you give, if it means you'll stay here and teach more for them."

"I founded Ananda to give to others, not to take for myself," Swamiji said, the same answer he'd given Seva years before.

"It is only right that we give back to you," David said.

"That is true," Swamiji replied thoughtfully. "For that reason I accept." Then he added, "It mustn't, however, be a requirement that people pay. I don't want anyone to be turned away for lack of money."

Once it was settled, Swamiji admitted that he hadn't really felt inwardly that it was right for him to go away from Ananda, even for a lecture tour, but he was willing because it seemed like the only alternative. He was grateful to Divine Mother for arranging it in a different way.

Patanjali's *Yoga Sutras*—the ancient 'handbook' for yoga practice—describes the *yama*, or spiritual practice, called "non-avarice." (The *yamas* are all written in the negative—*non-violence* being the best-known example.)

Non-avarice is more than just non-attachment to money. "What the spiritual seeker must renounce," Swamiji explains, "is the desire for anything that he does not acquire by merit. The implication is that if he does merit it, he needn't fear that he won't attract it. Even if he must work hard to attract it, he should remain relaxed as to the outcome, leaving the results wholly in God's hands. This is a prescription for peace of mind even during intense activity."

For thirteen years, Swamiji accepted this income from Ananda. Then, in 1994, the Bertolucci lawsuit was filed against him. Among other things, it accused Swamiji of using Ananda for his own financial gain.

When his parents died in 1983, Ananda's work in Europe was just getting underway. Swamiji wanted to be able to spend time there without being a burden on the devotees. Most of the inheritance he received from his parents, Swamiji used to build Crystal Hermitage as a spiritual center for the community. Ten thousand dollars, however, he put into a Swiss bank account—not a numbered account, but one with his name on it. He never made another deposit. Swamiji used the money for his personal expenses in Europe, including buying a pair of Swiss-made hearing aids. A few years later, long before the Bertolucci lawsuit was filed, the account was down to $3,000 and Swamiji closed it.

Bertolucci's attorney, however, claimed that this long-defunct "Swiss bank account" proved that Swamiji was skimming money from Ananda and hiding it in Switzerland.

"Most people assume I must be getting rich off of Ananda," Swamiji said. "It is how they themselves would act in my position. In fact, many people would think I was a fool not to take money from the community."

The court ruled in Swamiji's favor. Still, he felt tainted by the whole process.

"It was right for the community to give me a salary," he said in 1998, after the lawsuit was over, "but I've never felt right about taking it. From now on, I won't accept anything from Ananda. Divine Mother can support me or not support me, by whatever means and to whatever extent She chooses."

His salary was largely symbolic anyway, more for our sake than for his. Swamiji's life and his service to Master have always been sustained by Divine Mother through spontaneous giving from friends and devotees around the world. It is not surprising that those to whom Swamiji has given so much would be inspired to give back to him.

"The quality of non-avarice, developed to perfection," Swamiji explains, "generates a subtle magnetism that enables a person to attract things to himself effortlessly. He is never anxious then, that his needs, whatever they may be, won't be supplied. They *will* be, infallibly."

God's Will

A strange moral dilemma puzzled me for years, even though the problem was purely hypothetical, in that it could only arise if I were a prisoner in a concentration camp! Perhaps because I was born Jewish just after World War II, it seemed important to resolve. Finally I found the right moment to ask Swamiji.

"If I were in a concentration camp, and a guard started beating the person next to me, what should I do?" I said. "Is it right to do nothing? Or should I intervene, even if it costs me my life?"

"What you are really asking," Swamiji said, "is how to know God's will. Maybe you could get the guard to stop. But maybe if you intervene, the guard will retaliate against *all* the prisoners and many people will be hurt or killed. You can't figure it out logically. You need intuition.

"If you want to know God's will in a moment of crisis, you have to *practice when it is easier*. You have to develop in all circumstances of your life the habit of listening for God's will. Then, even in extreme conditions, you will know what to do."

Singing Out of Tune

In the 1980s I got involved in a small singing group within Ananda. It was a time when Swamiji's music had just begun to take hold, and all the "official" groups concentrated exclusively on the music he had written.

This group's stated purpose was to sing everything *but* Swamiji's music. We were all classically trained and our evenings with Mozart, Haydn, Bach and others were musically blissful.

After we'd been meeting for several months, Swamiji invited me over to talk about the group.

"It would be better if you dropped out," he said.

I was astonished. It seemed like a harmless hobby. I pressed Swamiji for an explanation, but he was reluctant to speak.

Finally he said, "It is a matter of attunement." Then he made a few kind but frank remarks about the underlying attitudes of some of the key members. "Musically you may enjoy it, but spiritually I don't think it will help you to be with them."

I didn't fully understand, but I trusted Swamiji. I knew it was important or he wouldn't have taken the trouble to speak to me. The singing was fun, and was hard to give up. But that same week I dropped out.

Within three years, everyone in the group had left Ananda.

~ From an Ananda devotee ~

Consciousness Over Form

I RECOGNIZED YOU

Even though Swamiji was quite near-sighted, he always took his glasses off when he lectured.

"The disadvantage is that beyond the first row I can't recognize faces," he said. His eyes were too dry to wear contact lenses. "But glasses draw the energy outward, and I find it harder to be intuitive when I wear them. Also, consciousness is transmitted through the eyes, and glasses are a barrier."

He suggested we should all lecture without glasses, but most of us couldn't function as well as Swamiji did without being able to see. We wore contact lenses if we could, or perforce ignored his advice. When correcting vision through laser surgery became an option for Swamiji and for many of us, the problem was solved.

At one event, when he still wore glasses but didn't wear them to lecture, Swamiji was speaking in a huge auditorium as part of a group program that included Louise Hay and a few other well-known teachers.

Savitri was standing against the back wall when Louise slipped in and stood beside her. They were acquainted, and Louise whispered, "I have to catch a plane, but I wanted to hear at least a few minutes." She described Swamiji as "the kindest man I have ever met."

About fifteen minutes later, as Louise was walking toward the door, Swamiji stopped his lecture to greet her.

"Hello, Louise. Do you have to leave now?"

"Sorry to walk out on you Swamiji, but I have to catch a plane."

"It was wonderful to be with you, Louise. Have a safe journey." She left and he went back to his lecture.

Later, someone wondered, "He doesn't see very well. How could he be so confident it was her?"

"I didn't have to see her face," Swamiji said. "I recognized her consciousness."

I DIDN'T RECOGNIZE YOU

On another occasion, Swamiji was meeting a friend at a railway station in Europe. It was someone he knew well. The woman was facing a serious spiritual test, however, and her consciousness was under a veil of darkness.

"I watched everyone get off the train, but I didn't see her," Swamiji said later. "I wandered around the station a few moments, wondering if I'd missed her. Then I went into the waiting room. There was only one person there, a woman standing alone. I looked at her uncertainly, then tentatively called to her, naming my friend. She answered me! Her consciousness had changed so much because of the test she'd been going through, that I actually failed to recognize her!"

WHY DON'T I RECOGNIZE YOU?

One evening, a woman whose mind tended to be quite restless, was sitting with Swamiji and a few others in his living room. He knew she was there, but she was behind him, out of his line of sight.

A sense of deep calm descended over the woman, and her mind was more still than she had ever known it to be.

After a few moments, Swamiji said, "Why can't I feel your consciousness?"

"Because it is unusually still," she said, speaking to his back.

He didn't turn to face her, but with his eyes closed, he said to the air in front of him, "Ah, yes. There you are. That is the explanation."

What Comes of Itself

When he arrived in America for a two-month visit from his home in Italy, Swamiji's health was poor and, as the weeks passed, it got worse. Finally, he was so weak he could barely walk. Swamiji was staying at the Crystal Hermitage and Jyotish and Devi, who live nearby, tried to persuade him to go see his doctor, but Swamiji refused.

One of the benefits of being at Ananda Village in America is that his long-time physician and friend, Dr. Peter Van Houten, lives there. Swamiji's medical history is complex and Dr. Peter is the only one who knows the whole case. Swamiji doesn't call the doctor every time he sneezes, but he does accept medical care. His condition seemed serious, so the intensity of his refusal was puzzling.

He didn't have the energy to work, so he invited a few friends over to watch a video after dinner—Jyotish, Devi, me, and a few others. When we arrived, Swamiji was stretched out on the big blue recliner that is "his" chair in the small living room of his apartment at the Hermitage. It was clear from the stillness of his body, the slow way he moved, and how much he labored to breathe, that he was quite unwell. He greeted us happily, however, and started right in talking about which movie to watch.

When I had a chance, I asked, "How are you feeling, Sir?"

"Not well," he replied.

"Have you seen Dr. Peter?" I asked, pretending I didn't know he had already refused.

Swamiji was not fooled. "No!" he said emphatically.

We turned on the video, but it was hard to concentrate. With one ear, I listened to the movie, with the other ear I listened to Swamiji's breathing, afraid that at any moment it might stop. I think everyone in the room was doing the same thing. A couple of times we took a break and put the movie on pause. Each time, Swamiji seemed weaker. When Devi again suggested we call Dr. Peter, Swamiji put what little strength he had into his reply, "Do not call the doctor!"

When the movie was over, none of us wanted to leave Swamiji alone. He looked like an accident or a heart attack waiting to happen. Devi made one last try, but Swamiji was adamant. It was too much for her, and really for all of us. We silently cheered when she went to the kitchen and called Dr. Peter anyway.

For just an instant, Swamiji seemed annoyed. Then, when he saw that Devi had taken the decision out of his hands, he relaxed completely and became almost childlike in his acceptance. A few minutes later, when Dr. Peter arrived, Swamiji was so warm and welcoming, it was hard to believe that just minutes before he had been absolutely set against the doctor coming.

Dr. Peter decided the probable cause was a blood sugar imbalance. The next day, tests confirmed the diagnosis. After a few days of medication, he was 100% better. For the rest of his time in America, Swamiji frequently referred to how unwell he had been and how fortunate he was to have Dr. Peter there to help him.

This was not the first or the last time I have seen Swamiji unwilling to take action when the only thing at stake is his own welfare. "I am here to get out of my ego," Swamiji says, "not to protect it." As long as he was asked to decide, he refused to ask for help. When the decision was taken out of his hands, he acquiesced.

One incident happened years before. This time the issue was not calling the doctor, but calling on Divine Mother for help.

It was 1968 and Ananda was brand new. Swamiji gave all the Sunday Services and classes himself (as well as teaching in the city throughout the week).

One Sunday morning at 9am he was suddenly smitten with a severe kidney stone attack. He was shaking with pain, like a leaf in a storm. Going to the hospital would have meant driving several miles over bumpy, unpaved roads. The journey would have been torturous. Besides, he had a Service to give.

Despite his suffering, Swamiji would not pray for relief. His attitude is, "What comes of itself, let it come." For almost two hours he suffered with intense pain. Women who have experienced both say that a kidney stone attack is more painful than childbirth.

Finally, fifteen minutes before the Sunday Service was scheduled to begin, Swamiji prayed to Divine Mother, "If you want me to give this Service, You'll have to take away this pain." It wasn't a prayer for himself. It was for those who were coming to the Service to hear him.

Instantly, the pain disappeared. Swamiji still had difficulty giving the Service. This time, however, his difficulty in speaking was not because of the pain, but because of the joy.

Should I Give Up?

"The doctors have offered me more chemotherapy," Happy (an Ananda member) said to Swamiji. "They say it will keep me going for at least another few years. Should I take it?" Happy had AIDS and several times had come close to dying. "The treatment could be quite unpleasant. Death doesn't frighten me and maybe it would be better to get on with the process of dying."

"If you die, you'll just have to start over in a new incarnation," Swamiji said to her. "It may take you a long time to get to where you are now—all those years of childhood, then finding your spiritual path and learning Kriya again. If it were I, I would keep trying to live until I couldn't meditate anymore. Or until I felt that the treatments or the body itself was an insurmountable obstacle to spiritual progress. Then I would consider letting it go."

"Swamiji's advice was a great comfort," Happy said later. "It became my criterion for how much treatment to take. As long as I could meditate or at least practice the presence of God I would do everything I could to stay in the body."

Happy lived on for several years more. She was never really well, so it took considerable effort to keep her body going. The will power and understanding she gained was of great spiritual benefit to her, progress she wouldn't have made if she had given up sooner.

Stillness

Swamiji was extremely ill with double pneumonia and it wasn't safe to leave him alone. He had a high fever and his lungs were so compromised I didn't need a stethoscope to tell what was going on—I could hear from across the room. In the intervals between the coughing fits, he gasped for air.

A few of us had spent a long afternoon and half the night with him. He was so weak he could hardly get to the bathroom. Finally, at 2am Swamiji decided he wanted to try to sleep, although he was coughing so much, I didn't see how he'd be able to. Because I am a trained nurse, he suggested I remain nearby while others went home.

If the patient had been anyone but Swamiji, I would have taken him to the hospital. When I suggested it, however, he wasn't interested and I didn't insist.

His illnesses don't always follow a conventional medical model. Many times I have seen him ill and weak, or in such pain that he finds difficulty in walking on his own. Then, minutes later—if duty calls—he'll give a class or a ceremony or a counseling session, sometimes for hours, during which time he shows no hint of weakness. Then, when his duty is done, once again, he is debilitated.

Swamiji has a simple explanation: "Master gives me energy when I need it."

We settled Swamiji in his room. The others left, and I went down to the basement guestroom. There was an intercom; all Swamiji had to do was push a button and no matter how softly he spoke, I would hear him. His cough was so severe I could keep track of it from downstairs. I thought I wouldn't be able to sleep, but I guess I did for a few hours.

About five or six in the morning something woke me. Immediately, I raced upstairs to see if Swamiji needed anything. I assumed he would be in his bedroom since he could scarcely get in or out of bed without help.

I came into the living room, rushing as nurses do, when suddenly I was stopped by a wall of stillness. I felt unable to move. In the presence of that stillness, motion would have been not only an intrusion: it seemed to me impossible. Even the usual humming sound of the refrigerator and the ticking clock seemed drowned out by the silence.

It was dark and at first I couldn't see much. As my eyes adjusted to the dim light, however, I saw that Swamiji was sitting in the living room meditating. He wasn't coughing, he wasn't gasping, in fact, I don't think he was breathing. I had heard about the breathless state of meditation, but this was the first time I had seen it.

Clearly, he didn't need any help from me. I stood for a moment, taking in the wonder of the scene before me, then turned and went back downstairs.

About an hour later, I knew his breathing had returned, for I heard him coughing. The whole pneumonia cycle soon started over again.

~ From Miriam Brown ~

~ 3 ~

DIVINE FRIEND & TEACHER

"I have had two desires in my life.
The first is to find God. The second is
to help others to find Him."

Swami Kriyananda

White Umbrella

We were returning from a visit to the ashram of another spiritual teacher. The size of the crowd and the reverential ceremony surrounding the teacher there far exceeded anything we had at Ananda.

"If you would just let us follow you around with a white umbrella," I said to Swamiji with a smile, "we could really get this show on the road!" In India, as a gesture of respect, the guru is sometimes accompanied by a devotee whose sole responsibility is to shelter him from the sun with an umbrella.

Swamiji knew I was joking, but he answered seriously.

"I have always thought I could do more for people as a simple, unaffected friend than in any other role."

Swamiji wasn't diminishing the importance of his role in our lives; he was explaining how he carries it out. "Master told me I would do more than teach. He said that I would be spiritually responsible for others. Most of you at Ananda have a link with me, and through me you are linked to Master."

But when a devotee puts too much emphasis on Swamiji's role, he said, "I may be the one you come to for guidance, and perhaps for inspiration, but the power is God's and Guru's alone. Don't stop here [meaning himself]. Go all the way to God."

Swamiji does not allow his picture to be placed on the altar in any of the Ananda temples. "Master is an avatar. We all look to him."

Once Swamiji paid a rare visit to a small Ananda center. The devotees there, not knowing any better, had respectfully placed his photo on the altar. When Swamiji saw it he walked over and took it down. "This doesn't belong here," he said quietly.

"There are plenty of teachers. What is needed now are examples of how to be a true *disciple*."

Friend in Need

I had gotten myself into a bad situation. I would have talked to Swamiji right away, but he was in seclusion, and I didn't want to bother him. Someone told him anyway, and Swamiji sent a note asking me to come and see him.

He was in silence, so we communicated at his typewriter. I spoke, and Swamiji typed out his answers. It took some discussion, but eventually I felt resolved. Swamiji walked me to the door.

"Thank you for your help, Sir," I said. "But I am sorry you were told. I didn't want you to break your seclusion because of me."

We had reached the front door by then, but Swamiji insisted we go back to his office so he could answer me.

He smiled at me sweetly, but wrote, "You insult my friendship."

"I'm sorry, Sir, I didn't mean to do that," I said.

"I would be very sorry if you didn't ask for fear of bothering me. It would mean you had lost faith in my friendship. This is what friends are for. And this is what I am for."

From His Own Wallet

Often Swamiji will accept people who are spiritually sincere, but difficult to get along with, giving them a job when no one else in the community will. Usually, contact with Swamiji deepens their attunement and helps smooth out their rough edges.

Aiden* was one such person Swamiji tried to help in this way, putting him in charge of multi-media presentations. I was one of several volunteers working under Aiden.

One day Aiden asked me to pick up a printing project from town. I paid the bill, assuming I would be reimbursed, a common practice at Ananda. When I asked Aiden for the money, though, he laughed at me. He said it was foolish of me to front it and he had no intention of paying me back.

Though the loss of money hurt me financially, the main offense was the attitude behind it. This sort of breach of trust and friendship is unthinkable at Ananda.

The next day, while working with Swamiji on a project, Aiden's name came up. I told Swamiji what had happened.

Immediately he asked, "How much money was it?"

"Four hundred dollars," I said.

Without another word, Swamiji pulled out his checkbook and paid me what I was owed.

Even though Swamiji chose many of the people who worked in that department, he didn't have much involvement in the money aspect of it. It was his own money he was giving me, which he had very little of at that time. I was stunned by the way Swamiji so quickly assumed responsibility, taking the burden onto himself without question. There was no waffling on his part, just a deep adherence to dharma.

Unfortunately, Aiden didn't take advantage of the spiritual opportunity of working with Swamiji. He never developed his attunement, but kept to his worldly ways, and soon left Ananda.

~ From an Ananda devotee ~

A Foolish Mistake

A woman at Ananda made a foolish mistake. Her thoughtless remarks at a public gathering placed Swamiji in a bad light. This caused a misunderstanding with others that took some effort on his part to rectify. Swamiji took it calmly, and fortunately no lasting harm was done. Days later, however, she was still depressed about it.

"What are you moping about?" Swamiji asked her.

"I feel so badly about that stupid mistake," she said.

"What an *egoist!*" Swamiji replied.

She was shocked. "I feel terrible about what happened! I'm not puffed up with pride about it."

"Pride is ego*tism.* An ego*ist*," Swamiji explained, "is someone who concentrates too much on himself—whether in praise or blame.

"Was it so surprising to find that you aren't perfect? Why—days later—are you still brooding about it? An egoist thinks too personally about himself. Be realistic. Everyone makes mistakes. There is nothing special in that. Take it in your stride, learn from your errors, and go on.

"The essence of the spiritual path is *self-forgetfulness*—to break free from the confining little bubble of ego-consciousness."

Private Misery

I was on pilgrimage with a group from Ananda. The inspiration of the event was marred for me by grief over personal difficulties I was facing at the time. One bus ride, I was sitting alone, staring sadly out the window. I tried not to be conspicuous, but others must have sensed the cloud of misery around me. Perhaps not knowing how to console me or thinking I wanted to be left alone, no one sat next to me.

No one, that is, except Swamiji. He took the seat next to mine, pulled out a harmonium, and began to show me some new chords he had worked out for one of Master's chants. I could barely speak, but I knew on a subtle level he was helping me redirect my energy upward rather than let it sink into a quagmire of pain. Just being in his presence lifted the energy in my spine.

"One of the purposes of Ananda," Swamiji has said, "is to show the world examples of true friendship. Cooperation doesn't have to be coerced. It is the natural result of that friendship."

A woman in the community sent Swamiji a note that could have been written by any one of us.

"A friend came to me for spiritual counsel," she wrote to Swamiji. "He was tormented by the fear that God does not love him. I did what I could to reassure him and in the process came to an important realization of my own. I never doubt that God loves me for one simple reason: I have experienced unconditional love from you,

Swamiji, as God's instrument. That has given me unshakeable faith in Him."

"The relationship with God as Friend is in some ways the sweetest," Swamiji writes in his commentary on the *Bhagavad Gita*. "When one…thinks of God as Friend, there steals into the heart that sweet confidence by which one feels, 'But *of course* You love me! I am Yours; You are mine. How could either of us ever turn away from the other? We are one!'"

~ From an Ananda devotee ~

I Will

I was talking with Swamiji and several others about a project that needed to be done. Someone complimented me for putting out a lot of energy and working hard. Self-effacingly I quipped, "I am a *Willingness* Monster." (Referring to Master's exhortation not to give in to the "Un*willingness Monster.*")

Swamiji approved of my attitude, but I think he wanted my self-concept to be entirely positive. Softly, with a sweet smile, he said, "No, you are not a 'Willingness *Monster.*' You are a 'Willingness *Princess.*'"

~ From an Ananda devotee ~

Marilyn

Two days before she died of cancer, Marilyn was lying in bed barely moving or talking. Most of the time she seemed to be asleep.

A dear friend came to say good-bye. She sat very close to Marilyn. There was no one else in the room. A few minutes passed; it seemed Marilyn didn't even know she was there. Then suddenly Marilyn opened her eyes and gazed at her friend.

Slowly and deliberately she said, "Swamiji is so attuned to each one of us."

"He is?" the friend replied. It had not occurred to her that his sensitive awareness was so expanded.

For a moment longer, Marilyn looked at her friend, then closed her eyes and said nothing more.

Hello, Great Souls!

I started as Swamiji's secretary, but soon the job expanded into being his personal assistant and sometimes cook and housekeeper. For several years during the mid-1970s, unless he was out of the country or in seclusion, I spent hours with him almost every day. His schedule varied, and his needs were unpredictable, so I avoided making any plans that might interfere with my service to him. On the rare occasions when other responsibilities took me away, Swamiji accepted it graciously, but I suffered. Serving Swamiji was my first priority.

He paid my salary from his own wallet, but to him I was not an employee. I was a friend, and he saw my service to him as an act of kindness and generosity on my part. Even when he had a specific request, he put it in such a way as to leave me free to accept or reject it. It was as if, at night, he wiped away every expectation, and was genuinely surprised and delighted the next day when I showed up to help him again.

During most of the time I worked for him, he was writing *The Path*. He spent many hours a day at home alone, writing. In the late afternoons, Seva and I, and sometimes a few others, would often come over to see him. By then he had accumulated a stack of edited manuscript pages for me to retype. This was the last book he wrote on a typewriter; after that, he used a computer. He was eager to get the clean copy, and I was eager to do the work. But he never related to me as "the person who comes to retype my manuscript."

"Hello, Great Souls!" he would say when he heard us come in. "Would you like some tea?" Usually the subject of work only came up after the tea had been served.

"I have edited quite a few pages today," he might say. Or, "I've made dozens of changes in the chapter I thought was finished. I think you'll like what I've done."

I knew what he was hinting at, so I asked him, "Would you like me to retype those pages for you, Sir?"

"That would be a great help," he would say. Then he would insist, "First, finish your tea." If I knew he was particularly anxious to see the retyped pages, I could sometimes persuade him, "I don't need any tea. I can go right to work."

A request to cook dinner would follow a similar pattern.

"I got so involved in writing today," he might say. "I haven't had anything to eat since breakfast."

Or, I might be the one to bring it up, since I knew his habits. "Did you have any lunch today, Sir?" If he had to stop and think about it, it meant he hadn't eaten. "You must be hungry, may I fix you dinner?"

"That would be lovely." Sometimes he would add, "Perhaps you and Seva would like to join me?"

Or he might say, "What are your plans for this evening?"

"I don't have any plans. Is there something I can do for you, Sir?"

Only then would he say, "Well, if you aren't busy, there may be something in the refrigerator that could be turned into a dinner. If I don't have to cook, I can do a little more writing."

An Ananda leader once spoke enthusiastically about a way of working with people he had read about in a book. "Whenever you have to point out a shortcoming to someone," he said, "always start by mentioning at least two things he does well."

"That seems *manipulative!*" was Swamiji's only comment. Then he added, "A sensitive person would see right through it."

The respect Swamiji showed us was not a technique to get something *from* us. It didn't matter what role we played in his life, to him we were all "Great Souls," children of God, and that is how he has always related to us.

with Asha

Two of Those Left Behind

On July 28th, 1962, Swamiji was summoned to New York City for a private meeting with Daya Mata and Tara Mata. Effective immediately, they told him, he was expelled from Self-Realization Fellowship.

For the last four years, Swamiji had been living in India, serving SRF. Thousands of devotees looked to him for spiritual guidance. Now Tara and Daya ordered him never again to contact any SRF member.

"From now on," Tara Mata told him forcefully, "we want to forget that you ever lived."

Out of ingrained monastic obedience, and in the hope that by cooperation he could bring about a reconciliation, Swamiji agreed.

To ensure that he never returned to India, an SRF representative reported to the Indian government that Swamiji was a CIA agent and a Christian missionary in disguise. For ten years, the government refused to give Swamiji a visa.

To the Indian devotees, Swamiji simply vanished without explanation, and without so much as a "good-bye."

"Being forced to betray the trust of all those people was, for me, the most painful part of the whole experience," Swamiji said years later. "I couldn't bear to think about it."

Sri N. Keshava was the first mayor of Bangalore after India's independence. He was so well known that for much of his life a sufficient mailing address for him was simply, "Sri N. Keshava, former Mayor of Bangalore."

He was one of many who took initiation into Kriya Yoga from Swamiji. Outwardly Swamiji disappeared from his life, but inwardly Sri Keshava remained faithful and continued to practice Kriya.

In the early 1970s, Sri Keshava's sister moved to Oakland, California. She happened to see an announcement about a "Swami Kriyananda, direct disciple of Paramhansa Yogananda" who had an ashram a few hours away. When her brother came to visit, he was overjoyed to discover Swamiji's whereabouts and made a pilgrimage to Ananda Village.

When he saw Swamiji again for the first time after so many years, he made a full prostration in front of him and bathed Swamiji's feet with his tears. Swamiji was deeply moved by the reunion. He, too, wept—not only for Sri Keshava, but for all those in India whom he'd been forced to leave behind.

When Swamiji was finally able to return to India, there were many similar reunions. Kishan was one such friend from the past.

In 1962, Kishan was sixteen years old and often drove Swamiji around Delhi. Kishan has described himself as "Swamiji's driver," but Swamiji corrects him, saying, "You were (and are) my friend."

"In those years, Swamiji gave weekly discourses in Delhi," Kishan said. "Thousands of people came. He was still a young man, but already it was obvious that he was a great soul. Very few are so devoted to their guru and so in love with the Almighty. We spent as much time with Swamiji as we could.

"In the years since, I have often said to my friends, 'Even then, he was a Christ-like figure. Think what he has become now!'

"Sometimes I used to worry, 'It has been so long since I have seen Swamiji. By now, he will have forgotten all about me.' Then I thought, 'If an ordinary person like me can still remember him, then a great person like Swamiji will still remember me.'

"Finally I saw Swamiji again. And it was true. After all these years, he had never forgotten me."

with D. R. Kaarthikeyan

Help Should be Individual

Ananda is an ashram. We don't advertise to find the most qualified people for the jobs that have to be done. We welcome devotees and find a way for them to serve. We do the best we can with whomever God sends. "People are more important than things," is one of the principles Swamiji has taught us.

One of the gardeners was having difficulty with some of those whom God had sent. Late in the autumn, she said to Swamiji, "We have to get the crops in before the freeze comes, or months of work will turn into compost overnight. There's no margin. People's *souls* may be more important than things, but aren't some things more important than people's *egos?*"

Swamiji laughed. "Yes, of course they are! But look to your own motivation. For you, that is a more important consideration even than the crops. Before you challenge others, discriminate carefully—for your own sake. Be sure you are differentiating between the demands of *your* ego and the well-being of your soul.

"What you say to others, when your own motives are clear, will show respect for them as people. When your own attitude is right, you will say to them, 'This is what *we* must do,' not, 'This is what *you* must do.'

"Circumstances often drive us in directions we'd rather not go. Sometimes we have to be pushed hard to see which way we'll break. How people *respond*, however, must be left to their free will."

A woman was supposed to be working as my assistant, but her moods made her so unreliable it was like not having an assistant at all. I appealed to Swamiji for help.

"She is full of reasons why she can't do the work I give her. What is my responsibility to her?" I asked him.

"She hasn't yet committed to this spiritual path," he said. "It will be a victory for her if she does, but she is still making up her mind. We should help her if we can, but we don't have an obligation to her. If you feel to speak frankly, go ahead. She needs to see this path for what it is."

At first, the woman rose to the challenge. In the end, however, Ananda was more than she'd bargained for and she left. Swamiji said, "For her sake I am sad that she wasn't able to stay."

A few years later I had another assistant with a similar temperament. I sensed, however, that her case was different. Again, I appealed to Swamiji.

"If I speak frankly, I think she'll quit, and will probably leave Ananda," I said to him. "Should I risk it?"

"No," replied Swamiji. "She isn't mature enough to respond in the right way. She isn't ready to meet your needs, or even the needs of the work. Still, you have to accommodate her because she belongs here. She is part of our spiritual family. The work she does is less important than keeping her in this positive environment so she can grow spiritually."

I found a way to work with her, and, as Swamiji predicted, Ananda has been of great help to her spiritually.

I Bless You

A devotee was about to make an important decision, and spoke with Swamiji about it. After the meeting, Swamiji said, "He asked for my *advice*, but what he wanted was my *approval*. I can't approve, because what he plans won't bring him happiness. He *wants* to do the right thing, but he doesn't have the strength to renounce his desires in this matter. If I asked him to do so, it would just put him in an impossible position, and how would that help him?

"I have to be sincere, however, so when he asked me to bless his decision, I said, 'I bless *you*. You always have my blessings.' That didn't mean I blessed his decision! Still, I felt I couldn't speak more plainly at the time. I felt I had to leave it to his own intuition."

Later, the man told his friends, "Swamiji approves of my decision, he gave me his blessing."

When Swamiji heard this, he did nothing to correct the misunderstanding. "I wanted to spare him needless suffering," Swamiji said, "but I see he is going to have to live through it."

For Your Sake

"I don't think I have the spiritual depth to carry through with the job you have given me," a devotee wrote to Swamiji.

"I am not asking you to do this job because it will help others," Swamiji answered. "I am asking you to do it because it will help you develop the qualities and consciousness you want for yourself."

Another devotee, after suffering a painful disappointment, decided to renounce worldly life and become a monk. At that time, however, there was no monastery at Ananda. He decided to create one by putting up a building where the monks could live.

"I told Swamiji I was going to raise money and do this," the man said later. "Swamiji's response was two-fold. First, he went into his wallet and pulled out $50, which he donated to the project. Then he said simply, 'Buildings alone do not create monasteries and communities. They are created by people.'"

Nothing came of the monastery project and a few years later the man got married. "With Swamiji's permission, I kept the bills he gave me," the man said later, "as a reminder of his encouragement and support."

"I don't start from the point of whether or not a project will succeed," Swamiji explained on another occasion. "My starting point is whether or not it will be spiritually beneficial to those involved. If it is, I encourage it, even though I may know in advance it will come to nothing. The mere effort will help people develop the magnetism eventually to succeed, if not in this project then in some other.

"In the same way, even if success is guaranteed, if the project is not spiritually beneficial for those involved, I won't encourage it. Even if it is something Ananda needs, I'll wait for years if necessary, until there are people for whom the job is spiritually right before putting my support behind it.

"And if no one comes, I'll give up the project. To act in any other way would be *using* people, which is contrary to every principle of our path."

You Don't Need It

In my first year at Ananda I also studied Reiki, a form of hands-on healing. It seemed consistent with Master's teaching, and I saw no harm in studying both. With great enthusiasm I told Swamiji how much I was learning in my Reiki classes.

"If it's that good," he said, "then maybe I should learn it, too."

Instantly I responded, "Oh no, Sir. *You* don't need Reiki."

Swamiji made no reply, and there the matter rested. As I got more into Master's teachings, I gradually lost interest in Reiki, especially when I began to see that there are important differences between it and what our Master teaches.

According to Reiki, once you have been initiated and the channel is open, the transfer of healing energy is automatic. Master, however, says the flow of energy depends on concentration and willpower. "The greater the will, the greater the flow of energy," is one of the fundamental principles of his teachings.

The point here is not who is right and who is wrong. The point is: Master is my guru. I began to see that I would never get in tune if I went here, there, and everywhere looking for inspiration. For a disciple, attunement is everything.

I always remembered that conversation with Swamiji, but it wasn't until fifteen years later that I appreciated how sensitively he'd responded to me.

Swamiji wanted me to concentrate on Master's path and not dilute my progress by following a mixture of teachings. But I was so enthusiastic about Reiki, he knew I wouldn't understand if he simply said, "Don't do it." I needed to learn the lesson for myself.

But Swamiji also had to be sincere. So he planted a seed of understanding that would germinate when I was ready to see it.

Instead of going *against* my energy, Swamiji went *with* it, and showed me the logical conclusion of my own way of thinking: If Reiki is so good, then Swamiji should study it too.

I didn't know much about attunement then, but I knew this was an absurd suggestion. What could Swamiji get from Reiki? Master gives him *everything* he needs.

I answered Swamiji instantly, but it took much longer for me to realize that Master will also give *me* everything I need, if I follow the path of discipleship with faith, and whole-hearted commitment, the way Swamiji has done.

~ From Dhyana ~

Time Out

"I felt I was in a certain box at Ananda and I'd never be able to break out of it unless I left, at least for a time," Marcus* said, years later. "Maybe it wasn't true, but that's how it looked to me at the time."

A friend had some land and a few cabins on the coast and Marcus decided to move in with him. He proposed to Swamiji that they could start an Ananda community there.

"Did you *send* Marcus to start a new community?" I asked Swamiji. It hardly seemed like the right time; we could barely keep up with what we were already doing. But I didn't think Marcus would leave without Swamiji's approval.

"Spiritually, it would be better for Marcus to stay here," Swamiji said frankly. "But he feels oppressed at Ananda right now and wants the freedom to do things in his own way. If I oppose him, we could lose him completely and that would be tragic for him.

"He has decided to move to the coast, so let us consider him sent. Better for now just to be his friend and support whatever he feels to do."

Several times a year after that Marcus would meet with Swamiji to talk about the community he was trying to start. Swamiji was full of ideas for how to make it a success. He even gave a weekend retreat there.

But each time, before the discussion started, Swamiji would test the water to see if Marcus would be receptive to a frank suggestion that he drop everything and come back to Ananda. Swamiji was subtle about it, though, and I don't think Marcus ever knew.

Each time, when it was clear Marcus was determined to continue in the direction he was going, there would be a small, almost inaudible sigh from Swamiji as he mentally shifted gears before throwing himself into a creative discussion of how to make the community a success.

It went on like this for ten years.

Marcus did good work and many people were helped. But in the end, the coastal community never did take hold. Confident now that he could define his life any way he chose and Swamiji would still support him, Marcus' rebellious mood waned. He began to long for the happiness he had known at Ananda.

Finally, one day Marcus said to Swamiji, "I want to come back."

"That would be wonderful," Swamiji replied.

Please Come In

The fever was so severe Swamiji was shaking with chills and panting to breathe. In those days, his whole house was the dome that is now just the living room of Crystal Hermitage. His bedroom was a loft a few steps to the left of the front door. Several of us were sitting in the loft on the floor near his bed keeping him company.

When Shivani came in, Swamiji said, "Don't come too close, you might catch what I have."

"If you have it, I *want it*," Shivani said, then walked to his bed and took his hand.

Not long after there was a loud knock on the door. When I opened it, Sidney* was standing on the doorstep, quite agitated. I stepped outside and closed the door behind me, so that our conversation would not disturb Swamiji.

"Please whisper," I said, "Swamiji is very sick."

"I have to see Swamiji," Sidney said in an urgent whisper.

"I am sorry, that is not possible. Swamiji is quite ill," I said. I was his secretary and made the appointments for people to see him.

"But I *have* to see him," he said again.

"Please understand, he is too sick to see anyone," I said.

We were whispering; our voices could not have carried through the closed door. But now Shivani stepped outside, sent by Swamiji.

"Please come in," she said to Sidney. "Swamiji says he'll be right down to see you."

For the next twenty minutes, Swamiji stood in the entry way, clad in pyjamas and bathrobe, talking with Sidney until the problem was resolved and Sidney felt calm enough to go home.

A few minutes into their conversation, I interrupted to say to Swamiji, "Perhaps it would be better if you sat down."

"I'm fine just where I am," he said firmly. His voice was strong, his breathing normal, the chills were gone.

However, as soon as Sidney left, Swamiji went back to the loft, climbed into bed, and immediately resumed his fever. For the rest of the day, he was gasping for breath and his body shook with chills.

A Good Deal

When personal computers became available, because of all the writing he does, Swamiji was one of the first people at Ananda to buy one. When he needed to upgrade his printer, he heard that a woman in the community had one she needed to sell.

Her son, hoping to make her retirement more secure, had invested some of her money in a business that had looked promising. Instead, it went bankrupt. Now she needed money, and on her behalf, the son came to talk to Swamiji about the printer. Swamiji knew the woman had paid $4,500 for it. It was the early days of computing and equipment was quite expensive.

"Because it is for my mother," the son said, "I was hoping to get $3,500 for it, even though it is used. I imagine you'd rather spend only $1,500." Swamiji hadn't said anything about a price. "So why don't we settle for $2,500?" the son suggested, thinking it would be a favorable deal for both sides.

Swamiji didn't have much to spend on this piece of equipment. He knew from experience, however, that if he committed money to a righteous cause, even if he didn't have it, the money would come.

So with a confidence that soon proved justified, Swamiji said, "I don't like that suggestion. She is my mother, too. I will pay you $4,500 for the printer."

The Bus Ride

When Ananda ran a bookstore and café in San Francisco, Vairagi often worked the late shift. Many times all alone, at 11pm, she had to take a city bus back to the ashram. The route went through a rough part of town.

"I want to be a good devotee, and do what is needed," she said to Swamiji. "There is no one else who can work in the store. But when drunks and people on drugs and others who look like criminals get on the bus with me, I feel scared."

"It doesn't sound like the best situation," Swamiji said. "Is there an alternative? Can you drive your own car or take a taxi?"

"A taxi would be too expensive, and I don't have a car."

"Can someone pick you up?"

"Everyone else has his own schedule, Sir. It isn't practical."

"Then you have no choice," Swamiji said. "It is for a good cause, and you've been forced into it. Here is an idea that might help you: As soon as you get on the bus, choose one of the passengers, perhaps someone who frightens you, and pray for him. If that person gets off before you do, then choose someone else. Pray continuously, from the moment you get on, until you get home at night."

"The very next day, I tried it," Vairagi said. "When I started praying, I felt like God and Master had gotten on the bus with me, and I was no longer afraid. In fact, the bus ride home became my favorite part of the day."

Family Duty

"I am grateful to my parents for giving me a good home and treating me with kindness and respect," a devotee told Swamiji. "Beyond that, however, I don't feel much of anything for them. Is there something wrong with me?"

"Sometimes a devotee deliberately incarnates into a family where he doesn't have a deep connection," Swamiji said. "Maybe just one or two qualities are all he has in common with his parents. That way, when he finds his spiritual family, it is not difficult to leave his birth family behind.

"Still, unless your parents try to prevent you from following your spiritual path, you owe it to them to be kind. If they force you to choose, however, between your loyalty to them and your loyalty to God, God comes first."

When Swamiji first came onto the spiritual path, his father showed no respect for the choice Swamiji had made.

"I had to write him a very strong letter," Swamiji said. "I told him, 'I love you as my father. God, however, has been my Father for all eternity. Please don't force me to choose.'

"I don't think he ever understood what I was doing, but after that, he never spoke against it, so we were able to maintain a cordial relationship."

On another occasion, Swamiji said, "The best way to serve your family is to go deep spiritually. Their *egos* may object to your absence from the family nest or your refusal to fall in with their plans for your life, but their *souls* will rejoice because your spiritual progress also blesses them."

Swamiji once suggested a course of action to a young man that would have set his life in an entirely new direction spiritually. The man demurred.

"If I did that," he said, "my mother would be so disappointed."

"To find God," Swamiji replied, "we must all be prepared, if necessary, to disappoint our mothers."

Past Lives

Nothing else but karma carried over from past lives could explain the intense antagonism I felt for a woman in the community and the equally intense antagonism she felt toward me.

One night I had a vivid dream of a previous life in which she had inflicted great suffering on people I loved. When I told Swamiji about it he said, "I am inclined to believe your dream is true."

I didn't tell her myself, but somehow the woman heard about my dream and Swamiji's comment. To even the score, she consulted a psychic who obliged her by describing an incarnation in which I had treated her in an equally brutal manner.

When Swamiji heard about this he asked us to meet with him together. He saw that instead of using our past life memories to *overcome* karma, we were heading down the slippery slope of further karmic entanglement, using the events of the past to *justify* wrong attitudes in the present.

"This is a very old spiritual family," he said to us. "We've been together for so many lifetimes, we have been all things to one another—friends and enemies. It is not important what you did in past lives, what matters is who you are now. 'The past lives of all men,' Sri Yukteswar said, 'are dark with many shames.'

"Whatever you did you have paid for it with suffering. Why dwell there? 'Everything in future will improve,' Sri Yukteswar also said, 'if you make a spiritual effort now.'

"Self-evidently you have learned from your mistakes. In this incarnation and for many lives before now, neither of you would be capable of such terrible actions. You are both sincere devotees. Concentrate on that aspect of one another's character. Forget the past and relate to life as it is now."

The anger and mistrust between us was deep-seated and it took years of persistent effort to break the hypnosis of the past and "relate to life as it is now." Eventually we succeeded.

Without Swamiji's timely intervention, though, the negative karma might have continued not only in this life, but for incarnations to come. Because of his clear advice, we were never able to justify our wrong attitudes, but always saw them as delusions to be overcome.

~ From an Ananda devotee ~

Subtitle

My first real difference of opinion with Swamiji came not long after he put me in charge of Crystal Clarity Publishers. He suggested a subtitle for his book, *Awaken to Superconsciousness*, that I thought did nothing to clarify what the book was about. I told him I didn't like it, and explained why. But he wasn't open to my reasoning.

I cared about the subtitle, but most of all I didn't want to be at loggerheads with him. So I took two questions into meditation: "What is the right subtitle?" and, "How do I get along with Swamiji?"

I got no answer to the second question, but I did get a perfect subtitle. When I told it to Swamiji, he accepted it immediately. It was as different as night and day from the previous conversation. Which answered my second question.

"No!"—even with a good explanation—is not an adequate response. I have to *give* to the process, not just block the energy he has in motion. Blocked energy stops creativity.

Even if my ideas are not very good, I have found that if my attitude is right, Swamiji is always receptive. At least he'll give my ideas a fair hearing.

The subtitle: *How to Use Meditation for Inner Peace, Intuitive Guidance, and Greater Awareness.*

~ From Sean Meshorer ~

The Importance of One

At a very important public program, Swamiji gave over to someone else a portion of the time allotted for him to speak.

"Others advised me not to do it," Swamiji said. "'People have come a long distance and it is you they want to hear,' was their reasoning. In addition, the man was not a particularly good speaker.

"But I saw how much it meant to *him* to have an opportunity to address the crowd. I let him speak because I wanted to help him and I wanted to set the example that sometimes it is right to inconvenience everyone for the sake of one."

Helping a Schoolmate

As a child, Donald's [Swamiji's] health was precarious. "I was thin as a pencil and always coming down with something unusual," he says. When he was nine, living with his parents in Rumania, Donald nearly died of colitis. The doctor recommended that he be sent to Switzerland where, he said, the mountain air would make him healthy. Unfortunately, it didn't work as well as had been hoped. Donald spent many weeks ill in bed.

Usually, now, what he had was a kidney infection, which was sometimes quite severe. Donald was more than once confined to his bed for three days at a time on a diet of zwiebach (dry bread) and vichy water. This lack of food, plus the infection, left him so weak he could barely stand.

A schoolmate coveted some object Donald owned. Seeing his weakened condition, this boy assumed the thing could be his for the taking. He went into Donald's room, boldly snatched the coveted item, and ran away.

Much to his surprise, Donald jumped out of bed and ran after him, catching him on the landing. He snatched the article back then staggered back upstairs to bed.

"I don't even remember what the item was," Swamiji says now. "If the boy had asked for it, I would probably have given it to him. But I couldn't accept his taking advantage of me when I was weak and vulnerable, because it wasn't good for *him* to commit such an injustice, or to think he could mistreat others and get away with it."

How to Answer Letters

For several years in the 1970s I worked as Swamiji's secretary. He was often in seclusion, writing *The Path*. He had no phone, and e-mail didn't exist then. He lived two miles back on a dirt road, and his only mailing address was the community's. I would bring him his letters late every afternoon. Community members respected his privacy, and visitors didn't know how to find him. If you wanted to see Swamiji, usually you had to go through me.

It wasn't an easy position for me. I was very protective of his privacy, which was more important to me than fulfilling other people's needs. Swamiji expressed disapproval of this attitude.

"You have to relate to people in the way I myself would relate to them," he insisted. "Sometimes, of course, you must tell them, 'No, what you want isn't possible.' But you must never make people feel that my *convenience* is more important to me than their *welfare*. It is not. I am here to *serve*. If circumstances dictate the need to disappoint them, make it clear that you, too, are disappointed in not being able to give them what they want."

Swamiji read every letter that came to him. When he had a letter in his hand, he wouldn't relate to anything else until he'd finished reading it. Usually he concentrated so deeply he wasn't even *aware* of anything going on around him.

Sometimes he dictated an answer, or gave me key points on what to say. He explained to me how to tune in to his consciousness and write letters the way he would. The longer I worked for him, the more he was able to rely on me to know what to say. Still, he carefully read each letter before signing it. If it wasn't right, he asked me to do it again, sometimes more than once. Here are the guidelines he gave me.

"First ask yourself, 'What kind of person wrote this letter?' Use your intuition to tune into the 'feelings of the heart' that prompted the writing.

"As much as possible, write back in the same mood—business-like, devotional, joyful, in need of sympathy—whatever it might be. Answer their questions if you can, but (more importantly) respond to the underlying energy of their letters. That is what makes people happy to hear from you.

"Always tell the truth. Be simple and real with people. Keep in mind, however, the difference between truth and mere 'facts.' If you know something is going to work out, you may not want to list all the obstacles that have to be overcome before it does. Emphasize the positive. Think about how the person will feel who receives the letter.

"Don't praise excessively, if that isn't what's warranted. Be supportive, be kind, but say exactly what you mean. Truth has power and is more comforting than platitudes."

A man sent Swamiji a collection of poems he had written. On Swamiji's behalf I wrote, "Thank you for sending your beautiful poetry."

When Swamiji read that, he said, "It wasn't bad poetry, it was nice. But it wasn't *beautiful*. What will you say when someone sends *beautiful* poetry, now that you have used up that word on poetry that is merely *nice?*"

"Think creatively and lovingly of the person you are writing to. Then ask God to help you answer in exactly the way that is needed."

True Teaching Is Individual

When I came into the living room of Swamiji's house, Deirdre* was sitting next to him on the couch, sobbing uncontrollably. Swamiji said nothing, just looked at her kindly, and occasionally patted her hand to comfort her.

He explained to me briefly about a crisis in Deirdre's personal life that he was trying to help her through. After a few moments, she gained control of herself.

"Thank you for being so understanding," Deirdre said to him, as she stood up to leave.

I myself had come to Swamiji with troubles of my own. He had given me a difficult writing project, and after days of effort I still hadn't accomplished anything. My confidence was at a low ebb. When I tried to explain to Swamiji how I felt, all I, too, could do was sob. As I sat there crying, I thought of how sweetly Swamiji treated Deirdre. I'd often seen him console people in that way, and many times in the past he had also consoled me.

Today, however, what he did was get up from the couch where we were sitting, walk over to the bureau and open the drawer in which he stored his depleted flashlight batteries. Carefully he began sorting through them, applying to each one a voltage meter to see which ones still had life left in them.

I was shocked. Why would he attend to his batteries, instead of tending to my needs? His apparent indifference was so startling, I stopped crying. "I guess I'll go home now," I said tentatively, still hoping to get some kind of response from him.

"Good-bye," he replied casually.

On another occasion, when Swamiji was advising us on how to counsel others, he said, "Usually you should show sympathy, but there are times when sympathy is not helpful. If someone is already feeling weak and defeated, your sympathy, instead of strengthening his will, may only reinforce the idea in his mind that the problem is too big for him to solve."

Apparently, Swamiji considered such to be the case this time. And he was right. I left his house determined to prove I could stand on my own two feet. Going straight home, I "attacked" the project again, and finished it!

A few days later, at a community satsang, Swamiji announced, "Asha faced an important test this week, and I am pleased to say she passed it. If she hadn't, it would have been a major setback for her in this incarnation. There was nothing I could do to help her; she had to do it herself."

Afterwards, I said, "Why didn't you tell me how much was at stake?"

"Because I didn't think it would help you to know," he said. That was good enough for me. His method worked, and that was all that mattered.

A Strong Desire

For many months, a woman tried to resist a desire that Swamiji had encouraged her to overcome. Finally she said to him, "I have to be honest with you, Sir, I have not been following your advice. The desire is too strong. I am not proud of my failure, but I don't want to hide it from you, either." She expected that Swamiji would exhort her to try harder.

Instead, to her surprise, he said simply, "So much for theory, now let's deal with reality." He went on to suggest she follow the very desire he had warned her against, but to maintain while doing so an attitude of non-attachment. Giving in to the desire meant making a major change in her way of life.

Later, on the eve of the change, she asked him, "Is what I am about to do a good or a bad thing for me spiritually?"

"In itself, it is neither good nor bad," Swamiji answered. "It is merely a thing. How it turns out for *you* depends on how you relate to it, whether with pride and ego, or with humility and devotion."

Swamiji is a practical man. He had hoped she could overcome the karma without living through it. But when that proved impossible, he didn't insist on a level of perfection she couldn't meet. That would have made her feel like a spiritual failure, which would have been far worse for her in the long run than following the desire itself.

Swamiji's initial reluctance, however, alerted her to the pitfalls. Because he was willing to adjust his expectations to meet her reality, she remained open to him. With his continuing support, she was able to work with the karma and was not derailed by it, but remained strong on the spiritual path.

Saving Face

When it came out that Jeremiah* was using his position as a leader to gain power and privilege for himself, several people angrily confronted him about it. Instead of bravely admitting his faults, Jeremiah insisted, against all reason, that he had done nothing wrong.

Swamiji was out of the country when the situation came to a head. By the time he returned, there was nothing he could do to salvage it.

"What they did," Swamiji said, referring to those who instigated the angry confrontation, "was like going after a gnat with a baseball bat. Jeremiah is a proud man. He needed a way to extricate himself and still save face. Instead, they humiliated him. It left Jeremiah no recourse except to deny, even to himself, that he had done anything wrong."

Swamiji did what he could, but it was too late. The only way Jeremiah could save face now was to leave Ananda altogether, blaming the community for all that had gone wrong, rather than accepting blame himself.

"It hurt me to lose him," Swamiji said. "He had his weaknesses, but he was a good man."

Marriage Counseling

I was with my husband at a party at Crystal Hermitage. Swamiji came over to where we were standing, greeted my husband, asked about some of the things he was doing, then stood and chatted with him for a few minutes longer. He didn't, however, say a single word to me; he didn't even glance in my direction. When he finished the conversation with my husband, Swamiji turned his back on me completely and started talking to someone else as if I didn't even exist.

Usually Swamiji is warm and gracious, not only to me, but to everyone. I was deeply hurt and tried to think what I might have done to displease him, but I couldn't think of anything. Fortunately, that was the only time Swamiji treated me this way.

Not long afterwards, I had an argument with my husband. It was nothing important, just a difference of opinion. I was so annoyed, however, that he wouldn't go along with me, I turned my back and refused to speak to him. This was not the first time I had frozen him out in this way.

This time, however, when I turned my back on my husband, I remembered Swamiji turning his back on me. Suddenly it was obvious why Swamiji had done that. He picked that behavior right out of me! My husband is far too kind ever to respond in such a hurtful way. Swamiji had to show me what it felt like.

Immediately I turned to my husband and said, "Dearest, please forgive me. I'll never treat you that way again."

~ From an Ananda devotee ~

A Matter of Dharma

The department Jessie* was running was located at Ananda Village in California. Swamiji was living thousands of miles away in Assisi, Italy. Jessie often talked on the phone to Swamiji about what he was doing, but he misled Swamiji and withheld key information. So it was months before Swamiji understood from others what was really going on.

Jessie was energetic, creative, and dedicated, but he gave too much importance to his own ambitions. He had long wanted a position of influence. Swamiji knew Jessie's shortcomings, but nonetheless felt he deserved a chance.

Unfortunately, the little influence he had went to Jessie's head. Gradually the department drifted off course. It was becoming just a vehicle for Jessie's pet projects, no longer serving the needs of Ananda. He didn't use money rightly. It wasn't fair to those who worked in the department to have their dedicated efforts so misdirected.

"I would rather lose all of Ananda," Swamiji said, "than do something that is contrary to dharma."

Just hours after he found out what was going on, Swamiji called Jessie and told him to close down the whole department that very day. This was no small disappointment to Swamiji. He had spent years and a great deal of money developing that aspect of Ananda.

As for Jessie, Swamiji's only desire was to help him.

"We need to talk face-to-face. Why don't you come to Italy for awhile? I'll pay for half your ticket and Ananda will pay for the rest," Swamiji told Jessie in that same conversation.

"A leader has to be willing to do whatever is necessary to help people," Swamiji explained later. "Certainly I was disappointed in how Jessie had behaved, but the point now was to lift him out of that, not drive him further down. Sternness would not have helped; kindness might. It was as simple as that."

Sometimes, however, even Swamiji's best efforts do not succeed.

"I didn't bring you here to scold you," Swamiji reassured Jessie when he arrived in Italy, "I brought you here to help you."

Still, Swamiji couldn't go along with all the things Jessie wanted. When he expressed an opinion different from what Jessie declared to be true, Jessie decided Swamiji was no longer his friend. Later he described his trip to Italy as having been "called on the carpet." Jessie stayed only a week. Then he left Italy and, soon after, left Ananda.

Flexibility

It had been about a year since *Ananda Publications* became *Crystal Clarity Publishers*. I was in charge of this aspect of our work, and had had to do a lot of work to change our public identity. Finally, our new name had begun to take hold.

I was talking to Swamiji about some other aspect of the business, when suddenly he said, "I got a note today suggesting a name that might be even better than *Crystal Clarity Publishers.*"

I responded instantly with intense, emotional opposition to the mere suggestion, explaining from every angle I could think of why changing our name again was a *terrible* idea.

Then, in the midst of this tirade, I looked into Swamiji's eyes. I realized all at once that I'd been completely off-center. I saw no judgment in those eyes, just calmness and peace. His eyes were like a clear mirror. Suddenly I felt like a person acting in a surrealistic movie: I saw myself as a huge, flapping mouth!

Thoughts which, a moment before, had seemed so important to express, now seemed foolish. I simply dropped the subject. Swamiji never mentioned it again.

He had no commitment to changing the name. He had just brought up that person's comment as an interesting fact. But he was also testing my flexibility, and allowing me to see my own attachment to the status quo. He then helped me to find my own center in calmness again.

"A skier standing at the top of a hill," Swamiji explained on another occasion, "may not be able to see all the way to the bottom. To stay on course and not fall, he has to be able to turn at a moment's notice. We must learn to move through life like a skier going downhill, committed to our general direction, but able to adjust specific decisions in a moment as the need arises."

~ From Padma ~

Kriya Friends

A friend had major surgery. Afterwards, Swamiji went to the hospital to see her.

"I feel so foggy and ill," she told him. "I can't do my Kriyas." The Kriya technique is the heart of our meditation practice.

"Don't worry," he said reassuringly. "I'll do Kriya for you."

A few days later, she was well enough to go through the motions of doing Kriya, "But it is like sucking on a straw in an empty glass."

"Don't do it now. Your energy is needed elsewhere," Swamiji said. "Ask one of your friends to do Kriya for you."

Once when Swamiji was recovering from surgery, a devotee nurse kept watch by his bed. Seeing her meditate he said, "I can't do Kriya right now. Would you be kind enough to do my Kriyas for me?"

On his birthday, Swamiji was deeply touched by a gift he received from a man in the community. "As a birthday present, Swamiji, I will give you three hours of my meditation and Kriya practice."

A Reason To Be Happy

Circumstances brought me into daily contact with a woman I simply couldn't get along with. Everything about her irritated me. Nothing in the present explained the intensity of my negative feelings. It had to be unresolved karma from the past.

Finally, circumstances changed. Where before we had met almost daily, now we met only occasionally. Absence made my heart grow fonder. Viewing her from a distance, I came to appreciate her many fine qualities. Respect, and then affection, grew in my heart. When we found ourselves traveling together, I felt so kindly toward her I invited her to share my accommodations.

After only one day, however, I became as irritated and upset with her as ever. I thought I had grown in love and forgiveness; in fact, it was just a karmic intermission. Tearfully, I explained to Swamiji how disappointed I was with myself.

"I understand why you feel that way," Swamiji said. "But here's another way to look at it. You thought the karma was over, when in fact it was just under the surface, waiting to re-emerge. If this hadn't happened, the karma might have gone on for more incarnations, since you weren't putting out the energy needed to overcome it. Now you know and can get to work on it. This is a reason to be happy, not to weep."

As Master said: Conditions and circumstances are always neutral. It is one's *attitude* that makes them seem happy or sad.

~ From an Ananda devotee ~

Spunk

At first, the meditation group leader worked in cooperation with me. I visited that city several times a year and was the group's main connection to the rest of Ananda. Then I found out he had established the group as a separate corporation, using Ananda's name and most of our bylaws. The only difference was he, not Swamiji, was Spiritual Director for life.

I tried to explain to him that it was hardly fair to use Ananda's name and reputation to attract people, then offer them something quite different, that is, himself rather than Swamiji as the spiritual authority. My reasoning, however, did not persuade him.

Ananda was just beginning to expand beyond the borders of the Village and none of us quite knew how to handle this, so Swamiji stepped in.

He invited the man to come for a visit to the Village and to come to his house for lunch. I was included in the luncheon and it was a very pleasant afternoon. The two men discussed a wide range of topics and only at the end touched into the reason why Swamiji had called him there.

"You are doing good work," Swamiji told the man. "But since you have put yourself in charge, instead of me, perhaps you should also come up with your own name."

That's all Swamiji said, but it was enough. The man went home and changed the name of the corporation.

After the man left, Swamiji said to me, "No one with spunk will wait to be told what to do. It wasn't right that he declared himself Spiritual Director, but at least he has energy and initiative. I prefer a man like that to one who won't lift a finger without first getting permission from the head office."

Time Is Passing

After he moved to India in 2003, Swamiji began to correct those who were close to him more frankly and directly than he had in the past, sometimes with little regard for their personal feelings.

"I don't mean to hurt you," Swamiji said to a close co-worker after reprimanding him sharply in front of others on an important spiritual issue. "I expect my friends to understand that I can't be as patient as I used to be. I don't know how much time I have left.

"I used to be able to tell someone just a little bit of what I wanted him to know, then give him ten years to grow into it before saying more. Now I don't have ten years, and I want to help you all as much as I can."

Swamiji's Love

When I got myself into trouble before, Swamiji sent me a simple message: "Tell her she is making a mistake." If he hadn't said that, I might have found a way to rationalize my actions. Instead, I was never able fully to commit to the course I'd chosen. I didn't understand *why* it was a mistake, but I couldn't forget that Swamiji thought it was. As I thrashed about in the ocean of delusion, his words kept me tethered to Master. And when I was ready, they were the lifeline that brought me safely back to shore.

Now I was in trouble again. *Much* worse than anything I had done before. This time my actions jeopardized not only my own well being, they threatened disaster for many others as well. Swamiji was out of the country so we talked on the phone.

Before and after the call, I was almost paralyzed with grief and shame. While talking to him, though, to my astonishment, all my emotion subsided. I was absolutely calm and not the least defensive. Everything he said I knew was true and I agreed with him.

He scolded and scolded and told me how disappointed he was in me. He would pause for a moment then scold again. At least it felt to me like a scolding, although in fact, I think he was just talking in plain terms about the consequences of what I was doing.

In the middle of it all, suddenly his energy changed completely. So gently, so sweetly, he said, "You know, of course, my love is always with you."

"Yes," I said, "I know that."

Then he went back to scolding me.

I promised to do better, but it was a long time before I was able to keep that promise. He knew I was floundering and sent another message: "Tell her to sing Master's chant, *Polestar of My Life*."

Over and over I sang that chant until it was blazoned on my soul.

> *I have made Thee Polestar of my life.*
> *Though my sea is dark*
> *And my stars are gone,*
> *Still I see the path,*
> *Through Thy mercy.*

When I finally saw Swamiji again in person, my life was more on track. However, I was so ashamed of what I had done, I couldn't bring myself to greet him. When he saw me standing as far away from him as possible, he came right over to me. Immediately he told me that Master was pleased that I was working things out now in the right way.

I had always been afraid to open myself to Swamiji's guidance for fear he would ask me to do something I wouldn't be able to do. Behind that fear was the thought that if I disappointed him, he would never love me again.

I have suffered intensely over the wrong things I have done. Even though my suffering has transformed me spiritually, I cannot sincerely say, "I am glad it happened this way." Too many other people were hurt.

There is one reason, though, why I *am* glad. Now I know the pure, unconditional nature of Swamiji's love.

~ From an Ananda devotee ~

The Importance of Harmony

Whenever he visited Lugano, Switzerland, Swamiji would have a treatment he called a pedicure, but it had nothing in common with getting your nails painted. It was an hour spent removing calluses and soothing the cracked skin that often afflicted him.

When a group of us were vacationing with him in Taormina, Sicily, a friend and I both had conventional pedicures at a beauty shop there. My friend knew that Swamiji enjoyed his "pedicure" in Lugano and wanted him to have one here, too. When she presented the idea to Swamiji, I tried to explain to her that this was nothing like what he was used to, but she insisted on making an appointment anyway.

The shop was some distance from the hotel and up two long flights of steep stairs. It was a strain for Swamiji to make the trek. When we arrived it was immediately obvious the treatment wasn't anything he wanted and he left without taking it.

On our way back to the hotel, for a few minutes I was walking alone with Swamiji. He asked me rather insistently, "You knew I wouldn't want that pedicure. Why did you let her make the appointment?"

"I tried to tell her but she wouldn't listen. If I had insisted, it would have created disharmony and made her wrong in front of you. I didn't want to do that."

Swamiji relaxed completely. "Of course," he said, "you did the right thing."

During a period of particularly strenuous work in one of our colonies, people were becoming a little impatient with one another. One person angrily confronted another with a list of his shortcomings.

When Swamiji heard about it, he called everyone together. To be fair to both sides, he said, "Perhaps he needed to have his faults pointed out to him, but it should not have been done in an angry way." Then he went to the real purpose of the meeting. "If you do nothing else that I have asked of you, please at least do this: Be kind to each other." The meeting lasted a total of two minutes. Swamiji had called them together just to say that.

"I am not concerned about the details of how things are done," Swamiji has often told us. "My only concern is that they be done with the right energy. Right energy, above all, means with harmony. This world is nothing but energy, ruled by magnetism. If the magnetism is wrong, even if you are successful in the short-run, in the end things will not turn out right. If the magnetism is good, especially if you work together in harmony, even if it takes longer because you have to take into consideration the feelings of others, in the end you will have a glorious success. That is the secret of Ananda."

A Wealthy Woman

One of the wealthiest women in the United States became interested in Ananda. She came to several of Swamiji's lectures, asked to see him for private counseling, and was so impressed, she invited him to stay in her house during one of his tours.

"I am so lonely," she confided to Swamiji. "Because of my money, I never know who is a true friend and who is just trying to get something from me."

"What a curse money can be," Swamiji said to some of us later, "especially when you've grown up with it as she did. Her parents often warned her, 'Don't trust anyone outside the family. They are just after your money.' I would like to help her, but I don't know if I can."

Swamiji paused a moment, then went on, "One evening, when I was visiting at her home, I deliberately brought up a subject I knew she felt strongly about: women's rights.

"Of course I think women should be treated fairly; that is self-evident, and she knew that is what I believe. But I don't agree with much of the 'women's movement.' There is too much ego in it. I deliberately spoke about the subject in a way that challenged her to meet my way of thinking.

"Because she is rich, most people cater to her. I wanted her to know that I wouldn't do that, that she could always trust me to be sincere with her.

"Instead she decided, because my point of view differed from hers on a subject so dear to her heart, that she didn't want me to stay in her home anymore. She soon lost interest in our teachings altogether.

"I knew I was taking a risk. But there are many things about Master's teachings that she wouldn't be able to understand right away, anyway. She would have had to expand her mind to accept them. I didn't think it was fair to draw her into Ananda without letting her know what she was getting into. Better for her to find out sooner than later.

"But I felt sad about it for her sake. She is a good woman and I believe we could have helped her if she had been open to it. I would not cater to her, however, merely because of her wealth. To me, she was the same as every other devotee."

Service Is Joy

When I first came to Ananda, I thought the only thing a devotee needed to work on was the depth and quantity of his meditation. I was surprised at the emphasis placed on serving others. "Service is joy," Swamiji often said. Frankly, I thought he said that to give those who couldn't meditate something else to do.

I took a break between medical school and my internship to spend a year at Ananda Village. During that time, I worked hard on my meditation. A beginner in Kriya Yoga does 14 repetitions, twice a day. The recommended maximum is 108. I quickly worked up to the maximum.

Just before I left to start my internship, I spoke with Swamiji. I was shocked when he said, "During the next year, keep your practice to 36 Kriyas twice a day."

The internship turned out to be far tougher than I expected. Two interns quit early and for the rest of the year we were short-staffed. I worked 80-100 hours per week. Toward the end, I was so sleep-deprived, whenever I sat down, or even stopped moving, I would immediately fall asleep.

When the year ended and I moved out of my apartment, I noticed a dark spot on the wall next to where I sat to meditate. I realized it was where my head rested when I sat to meditate but instead slumped over and fell asleep. In that whole year, I don't think I meditated longer than 15 minutes at a time. It was humbling. Thank God

Swamiji had encouraged me to diminish my Kriya practice before the year began.

During the internship, I was so stressed and exhausted, when I took care of patients, I did a lot of praying. "Dear God, please don't let me hurt this person. You have to help me." Often, then, the right treatment or diagnosis would come to me. At the end of my internship, even though I was hardly meditating, I felt closer to God than I ever had before.

When I returned to Ananda, I felt I needed to start over from scratch with my meditation. I was doing 14 Kriyas a day and not going very deep. So I was astonished when Swamiji said to me, "I think you should do 108 Kriyas twice a day, starting now."

It took me a while to understand his advice. Gradually I began to see that success in meditation isn't just a matter of calculating the hours. You also have to have the right attitude. Before the internship, I didn't understand the importance of balancing meditation with service. It wouldn't have worked just to tell me. Swamiji had to guide me to learn the lesson through my own experience.

~ From Peter Van Houten, M.D. ~

Let Him Take It

The money belonged to Ananda, but the man had access to it. It was more than $10,000, a lot of money by any measure, but especially in the early years of Ananda when every dollar had to do the work of ten!

The temptation proved too great, and the man wrote a letter explaining why he needed the money and why he felt justified in taking it. He was an old friend, so it was up to Swamiji to decide what to do.

"If he takes the money," Swamiji said, "don't interfere, just let him have it. There is no point in trying to explain to him why he shouldn't. He has it all worked out in his own mind and he wouldn't understand.

"Maybe later he'll see what he has done and return it to us. But whatever happens, I refuse to let money get in the way of my friendship with him. Many people choose money over friendship. I place friendship higher than money.

"This whole world is consciousness. If our consciousness is right, everything else will follow. We don't have to be concerned. Where there is dharma, there is victory. If the money is meant to be ours, it will find its way to us by some other route."

Martha or Mary

I had many responsibilities in our community in Assisi, Italy. When Swamiji invited me to accompany him on the tour of the American choir through northern Italy, I said yes, but I was concerned about my work. I decided I would accompany him only for two cities, then go back to the community and take care of my duties.

When Swamiji heard about my plan, twice he asked me not to leave. Twice I insisted I had to go. "I have so much work to do," I explained.

Then a friend took me aside and told me about something similar that had happened to him. In his case, it was a lecture tour. He was traveling with Swamiji, but instead of going to hear Swamiji speak, he stayed in his hotel room and worked.

Afterwards, Swamiji asked him, "Where were you?"

"In my room, working," the man answered.

"We do not have many opportunities to be together," Swamiji told him gently. "You should be where I am."

This made a deep impression on me and I decided to stay with the tour.

I was still new on the path. Swamiji was living right in Assisi with us and I thought it would always be that way. I think Swamiji intuitively knew how little time we had. Now he lives in India and I rarely see him.

Swamiji is my spiritual father. The time I have spent with him is the cornerstone of my spiritual life. That choir tour happened years ago, but the experiences I had with Swamiji are as clear in my mind as if they had happened yesterday. And I can't remember any of the "important work" that almost took me away from him.

Just before Swamiji left for India, I said to him, "Please bless my spiritual practices."

Sweetly, almost with surprise, he replied, "Oh, but I always do!"

Later, when a group of us went to India to see him, I said, "Swamiji, I miss you so much. What can I do?"

"I also miss all of you," he said.

After a moment, he went on. "Even though the demands of Master's work keep us separate outwardly," he said, "ours is a divine friendship. In meditation I feel you near."

I knew he was speaking not only to me and those of us sitting in front of him, but to devotees around the world who carry Swamiji in their heart as I do.

"With God's love," he said, "I love you all."

~ From Premi ~

In His Hands

Spiritually, I have been fortunate. I came to Ananda at an early age and have never wavered in my commitment and devotion to this path.

For many years, however, my personal life was tumultuous—two divorces, cancer, and years of crippling self-doubt. Through all that long difficult time, Swamiji's patience with me has been nothing less than heroic.

Dozens of times he counseled me for substantially the same reasons, offering the same advice, couched in different words, according to the context at the time. "God loves you. Don't give up. Keep offering your devotion to Him. You can do it. I know you can."

There was no one dramatic moment when my life changed completely. Swamiji's influence has been like water on a stone. At first imperceptible, then gradually, over time, carving into the rough surface of my ego a smooth receptacle for God's love.

My story will not be written in large letters across the pages of history. Mine has been a humble life. In his poem *Samadhi*, Master offers divine reassurance to devotees like me: "The sparrow, each grain of sand, fall not without My sight."

I am like the sparrow. Many times I have fallen. Each time, God has noticed, and through Swamiji's love, lifted me up again.

~ From Nalini ~

From This Sleep

It was mid-afternoon and I had just arrived in Europe from America. Dinner with Swamiji and other friends was set for a few hours later, so I went to my room to rest and freshen up. When evening came, however, and I was supposed to be ready to go out, I was sound asleep in a chair. I had sat down for "just a moment," but jet lag overcame me and now I was dead to the world.

When I didn't show up as scheduled, Swamiji came to find me. Seeing me sound asleep, he began gently stroking my cheek with one finger, his touch as light as a feather. There are many ways to wake a person, but I can't imagine one more considerate than the way Swamiji chose. Ever since then, when the occasion arises, I awaken people this way. I will never forget the feeling of gradually being drawn back to this world by that gentle gesture.

In itself, it was a trivial event, but it affected me deeply. It seemed to epitomize years of friendship and loving guidance from Swamiji— calm acceptance of our weaknesses, willingness to work with us as we are, a remarkable sensitivity to the needs of the moment, and the patient application of kindness and respect in all circumstances.

My life with Swamiji is rich with profound incidents. Yet one of my most precious memories is how he took such care in waking up a friend when nothing more was at stake than going out to dinner.

"Omnipresence," Swamiji said, "encompasses not only the infinite, but also the infinitesimal."

~ From an Ananda devotee ~

Waiting

In 2003, when Swamiji returned to India to resume the work SRF had forced him to abandon four decades earlier, one of the first people to come to see him was a man who had known Swamiji from that earlier time.

"I was twelve years old, in 1961, when my father took Kriya Initiation from you," the man said. "I wanted to take Kriya, too, but you told me, 'You are too young. You will have to wait.'"

"I remember," Swamiji said.

"I have had many other opportunities since then to receive Kriya, but you told me to wait. So I waited, even though I didn't know if you would ever come back."

Softly Swamiji replied, "All these years, I, too, have been waiting for you."

~ 4 ~

FROM JOY
I CAME

"My clearest early memories all relate
to a special kind of happiness, one that seemed
to have little to do with the things around me,
that at best only reflected them."

Swami Kriyananda

The Same Moment

As a child, Donald [Swamiji] often went into superconsciousness. "At night, while lying in bed," Swamiji wrote later, "I would see myself absorbed in a radiant inner light, and my consciousness would expand beyond the limits of the body." It was so natural Donald thought everyone went to sleep this way.

A serious illness at the age of nine, then the challenge of finding his place in the world again, undermined Donald's easy acceptance of this superconscious state.

"It didn't relate to the world I was growing up in and had decided I must relate to. I began thinking of that light and expansion as something strange, and pushed it away," Swamiji wrote in his autobiography. "But I always remembered it."

After he became a disciple and learned to meditate, Swamiji said, "In meditation, I entered that same state I had experienced as a child. It was as if all the intervening years had ceased to exist. Then and now was the same moment. That reality is eternal. In superconsciousness, time doesn't exist."

Like Royalty

When I met Don [Swamiji] we were both about fifteen years old. Our fathers worked together and the families became friends. I have always been very religious. As a child I thought of myself as "Beloved by God." Even then, Don had a strong spiritual presence and his mother, Gertrude, was like a saint. I felt immediately drawn to both of them.

Gertrude had a gentleness about her, and radiated warmth and concern for others. I was just a child, but she was so respectful whenever she talked to me, asking questions about my family and friends. The way she listened to my answers, I felt everything about me mattered to her.

She had perfect manners and a certain graceful elegance in everything she did. I remember a formal dinner party with servants bringing each of the courses. No one paid any attention to the servers, except Gertrude. Whenever a plate was put in front of her she would turn and look into the eyes of the person who brought it and thank him for it. It was a small thing but it showed her character.

She was a natural aristocrat in the best sense of the word. Cultured, refined, not at all snobbish. I loved to be anywhere with Gertrude. When she and Don were together, their spiritual connection was like an aura around them. I remember on a ski trip seeing them walking together. It was as if they were in a world of their own.

The house they lived in, though not ostentatious, was Spanish in style and reminded me of a castle. It fit them. The whole family was like royalty. And Don was the young prince, proper and reserved. Not aloof, just quiet and serious. He had a bit of an English accent, which added to the impression that he wasn't like the rest of us young people.

His brother Bob, who was closest to him in age, was completely different. He was a bit of a rapscallion, a high school hero, out-going, handsome. He exuded glamour like a movie star.

To Bob, I talked about dances and who was going out with whom. With Don, it was always serious subjects, never anything superficial. I remember a school picnic where we spent hours together, discussing every deep subject we could think of.

I never got to know his father Ray the way I did his mother. But he was always gracious, kind, and appreciative. My father thought the world of him and even gave my older sister the middle name "Ray."

Gertrude and Ray had a real love affair. You could feel it between them and in the atmosphere of their home.

When Don became a monk at SRF, Gertrude was sympathetic with this unusual choice. She didn't understand the details, but she felt his sincerity and the depth of his commitment, and respected his ardor.

Ray was not spiritually inclined. For him, Don's choice was incomprehensible. He seemed almost to rebel against it. I remember him shaking his head in bewilderment.

One day, I happened to be visiting the family when Don was home as well, soon after his rather startling life change. I asked him, "What are you seeking?" I wanted to know how it felt to leave everything behind and take up an entirely new way of life.

"I am seeking Truth," Don said. Later he explained to me, "Truth is not a set of facts. Truth is whatever helps me find joy, understanding, and inspiration in life."

For years I have contemplated his answer.

~ From Mary Gibson Friedlander ~

with his mother

His Parents' Last Year

When Swamiji's father became too ill for his mother to care for him alone, Swamiji asked me if I would move in with them. No one in the family was free to help and they were reluctant to have a complete stranger in the house.

I had visited several times with Swamiji and occasionally did housework for them, so they were willing to accept my help.

After years of being in an ashram I wasn't eager to live in an ordinary way again, but I told Swamiji, "For your sake, I would be willing to do it."

I lived with Ray and Gertrude Walters for eighteen months. Ray died at the end of the first year, Gertrude died six months later.

When I moved in, Ray was already greatly debilitated. I never got to know him the way I got to know her. He was losing his sight and his hearing, and was so weak that when he sat down, he needed help to get up. Once or twice he fell and we had to call a neighbor to lift him to his feet again. It was not an easy year for either of them.

Nonetheless, Gertrude was always gracious and dignified. She treated me as if I were a guest in her home, not an employee. This was what Swamiji had wanted, as, with his responsibilities at Ananda, he couldn't devote as much time personally to their help as he would have liked.

Once I happened to mention a certain kind of wine that I had liked years ago when I lived in Germany. She ordered a whole case for me, even the right year. I was touched by her thoughtfulness, although I had long since stopped drinking alcoholic beverages.

They had an unusually close relationship, harmonious, and respectful. Gertrude was a gentle person, and it was not her nature to shout. But now she had to yell to make herself heard, and even then Ray would often misunderstand.

It must have been terrible for her. But she didn't let her frustration show. Swamiji said he never knew his parents to have a single argument or even to exchange unkind words.

Taking care of them took all my time. I seldom saw my Ananda friends and missed all the Ananda activities. At times I felt depressed and lonely.

Gertrude was very private. She didn't like to bring feelings out into the open. But she had the ability to tune into people. Whenever my spirits dipped, she sensed it and would take me out to lunch or on some outing to lift my mood. She was very telepathic and we often communicated, even about mundane matters, without either of us saying a word.

Sometimes when I was alone in my room I felt an extraordinary connection with her. I think those were the times when she was praying for me.

Gertrude read the Bible every day, and spent time meditating and praying. Once I suggested we meditate together, but she declined. To her it was a private matter, not something to be shared.

She had healing power. Once she fell and got a big black eye. For a day she wore dark glasses so no one could see it. "I don't want anyone to feel sorry for me," she explained. "I am not looking in the mirror. I am not thinking of it as a black eye. I think of it as being well." It healed remarkably quickly and after a day or two she was able to take the glasses off.

Over the course of the year, Ray gradually became weaker and weaker. Finally the doctor said, "There is nothing more we can do for you." Ray decided to stop taking his medications. Gertrude couldn't bear the thought of losing him. But even more, she didn't want him to suffer. She didn't protest, but accepted his decision bravely.

I knew the end was near, but I didn't realize how little time was left. One evening I went out for a few hours. While I was away, Gertrude tried to change the sheets on Ray's bed, but couldn't finish the job alone. He was too weak to roll over and she was too weak to move him. She became anxious about the half-finished bed and called and asked me to come home right away.

Ray looked a little frightened. He didn't believe in heaven and wasn't sure what was going to happen next. But he remained calm and kind as always. As I finished changing his bed he said, "Someday you'll be a great help to someone." It was his way of saying, "Thank you for all you have done."

Sometime during that night, Ray passed away. Early the next morning Gertrude knocked at my door. "I don't think he is breathing anymore," she said calmly. I went back to the bedroom with her and saw that he was dead.

Later, I learned that Swamiji was praying that his father pass that night. It was the evening of *Shivaratri*, an all-night Indian festival dedicated to Lord Shiva, the Great Renunciate. It is an auspicious time to die.

"Right after he passed away, I felt my father's spirit the way he was when I was a child," Swamiji said. "Dynamic, adventurous, full of enthusiasm. The last years in that aging body were not easy for him. He was glad to be free."

The first person Gertrude called was her youngest son Dick. Then we called Swamiji.

A few weeks later, Swamiji invited his mother to come and live with him at Ananda. It is hilly there, and at that time there were no paved roads. Gertrude said, "I wouldn't be able to take walks." Swamiji wanted her with him so he could help her spiritually, but I think it was just too late for her to make such a change.

Gertrude lived five months after Ray died. She was always beautiful. Now she was luminous. I was prepared to stay with her for years more if necessary. Whatever God wanted, I was ready now to accept.

One weekend during that time, we went to Ananda Village for a wedding. After the ceremony she stood outside with Swamiji and greeted the guests. They were such a regal pair, like the King and the Queen Mother.

Afterwards, at the reception, Gertrude was standing alone gazing out the window. It was obvious she was thinking about Ray.

Sensing her mood, a woman asked, "How long were you married?"

"Sixty years."

"That's a long time!"

"No, it wasn't," Gertrude said softly.

Two months later, I left her alone for a weekend. On Saturday night I called and she seemed fine. But when I arrived home Sunday evening, the house was locked, the alarm system was turned on, and when I rang the bell there was no response.

Fortunately, I knew how to get into the house without setting off the alarm. I found her unconscious on the floor. A nurse friend came over. We called Swamiji, then called an ambulance.

I think Swamiji knew she would never regain consciousness. He didn't come to the hospital, but stayed at Ananda and prayed for her. "I can help her just as much from here," he said. Two days later, she died.

Right afterwards, Swamiji gave a funeral service at Ananda Village. He was so moved he could barely speak when he described her deep devotion to God, her spiritual freedom, and the love they shared. "I feel her spirit clinging very close to me," he said afterwards.

A few days later, there was a funeral at the Episcopal Church Gertrude regularly attended. Years earlier Swamiji had written a piano sonata dedicated to her. He called it *The Divine Romance.* At her funeral he played it for her. In the middle of the music, many of us felt a great power descend over the church.

Speaking of that moment, Swamiji said later, "When the service started, Mother was still holding on to me. But in the middle of the service I felt her soul leave and go into the light."

~ From Vairagi ~

~ 5 ~

FIRST
IMPRESSIONS

"Even one moment

in the company of a saint

can be your raft

over the ocean of delusion."

from a Sanskrit chant, *Anandam*

Love Song

"If you want to know me," Swamiji has said, "listen to my music." That's how I first "met" Swamiji—alone in my car singing one of his songs. I lived in Portland, Oregon, and had just started going to the Ananda center there. The choir director asked me to sing a solo for an upcoming performance of the Oratorio.

I am embarrassed to admit that my attitude toward Swamiji's music then was a little condescending. "How charming," I thought, "that the founder is also a composer." I liked his music, but I have been studying music since I was six years old and, compared to what I was used to, his music seemed too simple to take seriously.

I was a member of the Portland Symphony Orchestra. Sometimes the life of a professional musician is not all that rosy. On this particular day, I had spent hours in a cramped orchestra pit playing music I didn't like under a mediocre conductor, surrounded by musicians as unhappy as I. Driving home that night, my spirits were about as low as they have ever been. The Ananda concert was coming soon and I thought I might as well practice my solo.

The song was *This is My Son*. I'd never heard it, but I could tell from the score it was easy to learn. I am a cellist, but singing has always been a happy sideline for me. Keeping one eye on the road, I glanced over the music and then ran through the song a couple of times. I was about to sing it for a third time when I realized I had better pull off the road.

Not only had the song banished my sour mood, my consciousness was now so expanded it wasn't safe for me to drive. I was astonished. How could such a simple song change my consciousness completely? It was the beginning of a new musical career for me, a career devoted almost entirely to Swamiji's music.

Not long after, I had a chance to play cello for an Oratorio performance in which Swamiji sang. Afterwards, there was a standing ovation and Swamiji was called to the front to accept a huge bouquet of flowers.

I have seen many great musicians accept accolades from an appreciative audience, but I have never seen anyone respond as he did. It was more than humility. It was a complete absence of ego.

"This is not my music," Swamiji often says. "It is God's music. It is given to me. I hear it and then I write it down."

Listening to Swamiji sing was a musical experience like none I'd ever had before. Yes, he has a beautiful voice, but the beauty is more than the sound. When he sings there is an actual transfer of consciousness. Seeing him before the audience now I realized that what Swamiji transmitted was pure love.

That understanding completely changed the way I perform. I still work on the technical aspects of playing. What I've learned from Swamiji has helped me with that, too. Naturally I play better when I still my thoughts, relax and center my energy, and concentrate more deeply on the music and the inspiration behind it.

Above all, however, what I focus on now is the consciousness with which I play. It is all about love. Love for the music and love for those who come to listen—God's love flowing through me.

I am not a world-class cellist, but sometimes now people respond to me as if I were, especially when I play Swamiji's music. I understand now that to be a musician is to be an instrument, like my cello. In the divine performance of life, I play my cello and God plays me.

~ From David Eby ~

Philosophy Major

As a philosophy major at Stanford University, and an atheist, it was a point of honor with me to be filled with questions no one could answer. It was an intellectual game I enjoyed playing. I was as left-brained as a person could be.

I got into yoga as bodywork and ended up taking the Yoga Training Course at Ananda Village. I really "vibed" with the whole place, but it was just an interlude. When the course was over, I went back to Stanford to finish my degree.

But life didn't go on as expected. I became jittery and depressed, overwhelmed by existential anxiety. I wanted to believe there was something more than the suddenly meaningless life I was living. But with all those carefully cultivated, unanswered questions, I could not.

Then I read Swamiji's book, *Crises in Modern Thought*, now called, *Out of the Labyrinth: For Those Who Want to Believe, But Can't*. (That subtitle described me perfectly.)

Skeptic though I was, I had to concede he made some good points. I was impressed that he was willing to grapple with the very things I was studying in school, like Jean-Paul Sartre, and whether or not we are descended from the apes. He didn't just brush these things off with vague statements like, "It is but it isn't. And then again, it is."

I went on the internet and found out that J. Donald Walters, aka Swami Kriyananda, had attended Haverford College and Brown

University. It was immensely important to me that he was educated in the same way I was.

But instead of calming my anxiety, *Crises* unleashed a cavalcade of further questions. I couldn't take another step forward until I had the answers. I wrote Swamiji a letter filled with questions—handwritten, not impersonally typed.

Soon after, I had a break from school and went to Ananda for two weeks. Swamiji hadn't yet answered my letter. There was some major event, with a big lunch in the dining room. Afterwards, Swamiji was sitting all alone. This was my chance. I introduced myself and asked if I could sit down.

"I read your letter," he said. "It was fascinating."

Seize the moment. "Can I ask you a question?"

"Go ahead," he said.

I started down the long list I had in my head.

"Ramakrishna claims that he saw visions of Krishna and Kali. How can the universe be structured so that an entity like Krishna, that doesn't exist anymore, or an entity like Kali, that never existed, can manifest as a vision? Is it real or merely mythical?"

This seemed like a good place to start. It was typical of what I had written him.

Without any hesitation, he answered. "Krishna and Kali are just a collection of qualities," he said, "like you or me. Those qualities exist in the cosmos. If you meditate on cosmic vibration with enough energy and concentration, you can pull those qualities out of the universe into that form."

I asked him a second question, more complex than the first, and with the same easy grace he answered it. When it was time for the third one, it was over. I knew he could answer any question I asked. But now I didn't need to hear the answers. It was enough to know they were there.

I thanked him and said good-bye. He responded, "I hope you come back again."

From that point on, I've never had another moment of existential doubt.

And Swamiji's hope for me was fulfilled. I did come back. Ever since I graduated from Stanford, Ananda Village has been my home.

~ From Sean Meshorer ~

Grace Under Pressure

I had been at Ananda only a few months, and was helping out in the Retreat kitchen, chopping vegetables. Usually we listened to chants, but this time we had the radio on because Swamiji was being interviewed on a Sacramento station.

The interviewer was quite unpleasant. So rude and aggressive! I began to feel quite upset. Then I realized: Swamiji is not upset. No matter how the interviewer treated him, Swamiji responded in the same thoughtful, kind, and gracious manner.

And gradually, the whole tone of the interview changed. By the end, the radio man was completely won over. Now he was cordial and respectful! If I hadn't heard the whole show, I wouldn't have believed it was the same person.

It won me, too. I was new at Ananda, and still making up my mind. Swamiji's kindness and grace under pressure made a deep impression on me. "That's the kind of person I want to be." Soon after, I made the decision to commit my life to this path.

~ From an Ananda devotee ~

Light or Dark

When I met Swamiji for the first time, I didn't know anything about him or Master. I hadn't even read *Autobiography of a Yogi*. I had been practicing Hatha Yoga for a couple of years at the Yoga Institute in Houston, Texas where I lived. Swamiji was giving a free lecture there and I was intrigued by the idea of meeting a real swami.

I arrived late and the only seats left were in the front row, which suited me fine. I wanted to be close. Swamiji was on a nation-wide tour and about a dozen people were traveling with him. The program started with a few songs by the *Gandharvas,* as the Ananda singers were called then.

The visual impression they made was a little disconcerting. Everyone I knew who was into yoga had a kind of hip, city vibe. The *Gandharvas* didn't have any of that. They looked like what they were: devotees from a rural ashram. When I closed my eyes, though, and listened, I forgot all of that. The music was sublime.

The first visual impression I got of Swamiji was also unusual. With his beard and long hair, and orange, Indian style clothes, he didn't look like anyone I had ever seen before. When he began to speak, I closed my eyes so I could concentrate better. Instantly I was catapulted into a deep place within myself where I'd never been before. I felt I was drinking from the depths of Swamiji's peace.

His voice echoed and re-echoed within me, as if my insides were a huge empty cavern. Gradually, though, his consciousness began to fill my inner emptiness, and the echoing subsided. Once or twice I opened my eyes, but quickly shut them again. Nothing outside was as interesting as what was going on within me.

Eventually, the program came to an end. I felt like I was coming back from another world. It shocked me to see that people were leaving the hall.

"Where are you going?" I wanted to shout out to them. "Didn't you hear what he said? This man has the answers! He knows the truth!"

Then, for just a moment, I doubted. "I guess it's over," I thought. And I, too, stood up and started to leave. But when I turned toward the exit door, my body felt sluggish, and I could hardly move. And the exit door turned into a huge black hole that was sucking people out of the room!

I turned back and faced Swamiji, who was still on the stage, talking to a few people gathered around him. This direction, I saw nothing but bright light, and my body felt relaxed and free.

Once again, I turned toward the exit door. "Don't go there!" my inner voice cried. That was enough for me. I turned toward the light and never looked at the door again.

Swamiji gave programs all weekend and I spent every minute I could with him. By the time it was over I was moving into a newly formed Ananda ashram in Houston, even though I barely knew what an ashram was. Six months later I was living at Ananda Village.

That first experience with Swamiji was like hooking into a spiritual 'tractor beam' which has guided my life ever since.

~ From Krishna Das ~

Arizona 1963

I was raised Pentecostal, went to the Assembly of God Church, Bible School…the whole package. By the time I was 19 or 20 years old, I'd already been working a few years and I decided I'd had enough of that. I wanted to go to a Bible school in Texas and become a Pentecostal minister.

But instead, I started fooling around and ended up married with a couple of kids. My mother-in-law was living with us, too. No hope of going to school, I had to work.

In 1963, we were living in California and decided to make a trip to Albuquerque, New Mexico. I put the family in the car, including my mother-in-law, and we stopped off in Los Angeles to pick up her sister.

Right away things started going bad. Those two women were screaming and disagreeing with each other about every little thing. My mother-in-law had some serious mental problems and her sister was a nut. Even before we got out of Los Angeles, they nearly came to blows.

My two kids were just babies, and they started screaming and crying. My wife broke out in hives. And that's the way it went, for hundreds of miles.

I prayed to God every way I could think of to *"Heal the darkness in this car!"* But nothing happened. If anything, it got worse. Just before we stopped for the night, my mother-in-law started yelling at me for not pulling into a boarded-up gas station when she said she wanted to stop. She just wouldn't listen when I told her it was nothing but an empty building.

Finally, we got to the old motel in Williams, Arizona, where we were going to stay. The couple that owned it used what they earned to help the local Indians. I wanted to see what they were up to and give my money to a good cause.

The woman greeted us, suggested we freshen up and come right to the dining room where she had dinner ready for us. When we sat down to eat there was no one there but my family and the couple who owned the place.

Then in walked this guy I'd never seen before and the whole room filled with light. It was amazing.

The woman introduced us. She said his name was Kriyananda. Turned out he had been in seclusion south of there, in Sedona, for three months, and was just coming out of seclusion.

He started talking to me about spiritual things. My wife, kids, mother-in-law and her sister, just went on with their dinner as if he wasn't there. But to me, his voice *thundered*. And every word he said, I knew it was true.

He spoke to me only for a short time, ate a little bit, then left to go to his room. Even though my family paid no attention to him, I noticed they were unusually quiet. Later, when we were saying goodnight outside our rooms, my mother-in-law and her sister, who had been fighting every minute of the trip, suddenly embraced.

From then on, we traveled in perfect peace.

I was a good Christian, and according to the Pentecostals, yogis like him were going to Hell. But all my prayers brought nothing. Kriyananda *produced*.

It blew me away. And started me on a Search. I knew I was not going to become a Pentecostal minister.

I went back to California and studied Religious Science. I became a minister for them and had a Religious Science church in Reno, Nevada for twenty-five years. A couple of times Kriyananda came over the mountains from where he lived and spoke to us.

Just those few minutes with him in 1963 had changed the whole course of my life.

~ From Warren Chester ~

Wind of Words

It was Christmas Day and I was in India with Swamiji. He was giving a satsang in the living room of our ashram. It was five steps up from the outside and another steep flight of stairs once you got in the door. Swamiji wasn't feeling well and, by the time he reached the satsang room, he was panting for breath and so worn out, he virtually collapsed into his chair.

I was nineteen years old and Swamiji was almost eighty. Seeing him sitting there, I couldn't help but think of him as a frail old man needing to be taken care of by someone young and strong like me.

Early on in the satsang, Swamiji started talking about how Master had inspired him to start communities. "It was at a garden party in Beverly Hills," Swamiji said, "in July 1949. I want to tell you what he said in the way he said it." The speech begins, "This day marks the birth of a new era. My spoken words are registered in the ether, in the Spirit of God, and they shall move the West." Master goes on to speak of "thousands of youths" going "North, South, East, and West to cover the earth with little colonies."

I had read the words in Swamiji's autobiography. I remembered it as an inspiring speech but nothing prepared me for what happened next. Swamiji's voice when he spoke Master's words had the force of a hurricane! It was so strong, I found I was gripping the edge of the couch, as if the power of his voice might actually knock me off my seat. Forget the idea that Swamiji is a frail old man! There is so much more to Swamiji than meets the eye!

~ From Peter Kretzmann ~

Golden Aura

The first time I heard Swami Kriyananda speak was at a lecture in San Francisco. I was meditating with another group at the time, but some friends who had been to one of his lectures told me to go and hear him.

I asked them, "What did he talk about?" They couldn't specifically remember, they just knew it had been a great talk.

I went to the lecture and took a seat toward the back of the hall. A couple of people made announcements and then Swamiji came out. When he started to speak, a golden aura began to fill the room. It looked like the angel hair you sometimes see on Christmas trees, only instead of white, this was a beautiful golden color. I watched as it wound itself around the hall until everyone was enveloped in it.

I paid close attention to everything Swamiji said and afterwards I was able to discuss the points of his lecture. But I could see why my friends forgot all the details. The most important thing was not what Swamiji said. It was being in that golden aura. I have not had an experience like that before or since.

About six years later, I went to India for the first time as part of a pilgrimage organized by Ananda. By then I was a disciple of Master and living in an Ananda community. We went to Master's childhood home at 4 Garpar Road in Kolkata (Calcutta).

As I sat there feeling the vibration, it dawned on me that I recognized the vibration because I had experienced it before. I went back in memory trying to figure out how I could recognize something in a place I'd never been, in a country I'd never visited. Then it came to me. It was the same as the feeling I'd had the first time I heard Swamiji speak.

Swamiji has often said, "I pray only to be a channel for Master." My experience says his prayer has been answered.

~ From Rick Bonin ~

From Commune to Community

A group of us lived together on a farm in Southern Illinois. We had all read *Autobiography of a Yogi* and aspired to be a spiritual community along the lines of Ananda. Our hearts were in the right place, but we were all new on the path. What we ended up with was kind of a combination ashram and hippie commune.

A couple in the group wanted to get married. They invited Swamiji to come and perform the ceremony. He had a lecture tour on the East Coast and kindly agreed to stop by on his way back to California. The bride wanted to have the wedding in the Catholic Church, so it was a joint ceremony, presided over by both Swamiji and the priest.

Most of us at the farm had never met Swamiji. We were thrilled that he was coming to visit. Looking back on it now, however, I am embarrassed to see that we had no real idea of who he was or how to show him proper respect.

To begin with, we let him pay all his own travel expenses. We arranged for him to speak at a local college, but they didn't pay him anything. We didn't even give him an honorarium for performing the wedding.

The man who picked him up at the airport arrived late, and then, on the hundred-mile ride back to the farm, drove like a maniac. Twice Swamiji had to cry out, "STOP!" in a loud and powerful voice to avert serious accidents. At least when it was time to return to the airport at the end of the visit, we arranged for Swamiji to fly.

We did give Swamiji the best room in the house, but we all lived pretty simply so it wasn't much—a bedroom in the attic. One of the hippies hanging around the farm kept referring to him as "The Old Man." Swamiji wasn't old, just older than the rest of us.

At the wedding, one of the guests was a typical narrow-minded Midwesterner who didn't want to have anything to do with this "swami from California." When Swamiji greeted him, the man turned his face away and made no reply. For a moment Swamiji stood perfectly still, waiting to see if the man would reconsider. When it was clear he was not going to, a look of compassion came over Swamiji's face. There was no judgment from Swamiji. I don't think he even registered the snub as an insult. I had never seen anyone return sweetness for rudeness the way Swamiji did.

A reporter challenged him, "What is a spiritual teacher like you doing in a place like this?" Rustic is a kindly way to describe the way we lived.

Swamiji said simply, "These are my friends. I have come to visit them."

I was so curious about Swamiji that I watched him carefully all weekend. I was impressed by the calm and dignified way he responded to every situation, no matter how odd or inappropriate. He never showed even a hint of impatience or displeasure.

He was so considerate right up to the last few minutes of his visit. When it was time for him to leave, we gathered outside to say good-bye. Everyone was there but my husband.

"No need to wait for him," I said. "You have to get on your way."

"I can't leave without saying good-bye to him," Swamiji replied. "I'll wait until he comes."

The community was split about our future and we appealed to Swamiji for help. "How can we make what we are doing better?" we asked him. Some felt things were fine as they were, others felt changes were needed to make us a more spiritual community.

"Why don't you just come and live at Ananda?" Swamiji replied. This was not the answer we expected. "You could always come back here later," he added. He made no effort to persuade us, just issued the invitation and let us make up our own minds.

Four of us did move to Ananda and found there the spiritual life we longed for. I see now what Swamiji must also have known—that we could never have created it on our own.

~ From Hassi ~

The Jeweler in Goa

The jeweler and the tailor shared the same small shop, a common arrangement in Goa, India. Both were energetic young men, avid salesmen, eager to make a success of their modest enterprises. A friend had to make a brief visit to the tailor and Swamiji went along. He sat down near the jewelry case and began chatting with the jeweler.

Swamiji mentioned that he lives in New Delhi, is a disciple of Paramhansa Yogananda, and has a daily television show. Beyond those few facts, however, their conversation was mundane: the weather, the state of the economy—that kind of thing. The jeweler pulled a few of his favorite pieces out of the case to show Swamiji. Swamiji showed him the gems in his astrological bangle. The whole visit lasted less than ten minutes.

A few days later, the friend returned to the shop. The jeweler said, "Who is that man? I think he is the most spiritual person I have ever met! Many people, including swamis, come into this shop. Most are puffed up with their own importance. But he related to me simply as a friend. I just talked to him of ordinary things, but never have I met someone so wise, so kind, so humble. You see me. I am just a worldly man. I do not meditate. I smoke cigarettes. I have many desires. But I feel blessed to have been with such a man even for a few minutes."

Like Steel

I was introduced to Swamiji by my wife, who was already a dedicated devotee. Naturally she hoped I would be as enthusiastic about him as she was. She is American, but I'm from Australia. "Down under" we don't much like authority figures and I was more than a little skeptical.

Swamiji was giving a talk in Sacramento. She persuaded me to go hear him and somehow got me to sit with her right in the front row, although I would much rather have been in the back of the room.

In the middle of his lecture, Swamiji started talking about his own physical strength. Maybe it was because I was pretty macho then, young and strong, and he was responding to what was important to me.

"When I was younger," he said, "I could stand on one leg with the other leg extended straight out in front of me and do a one-legged deep knee bend all the way to the floor, ten times in a row. I stopped at ten, not because I couldn't do more, but because that seemed like enough.

"About the only exercise I get now is pushing a pencil, but because of Master's Energization Exercises, I am still as strong as ever."

Then he looked right at me and said, "Would you like to feel the strength of my muscle?" He lifted his arm and flexed his bicep.

I am very shy. I didn't even like sitting in the front row, what to speak to going up on stage in front of everyone. There was no choice, however, so I went up and put my hand on his bicep.

What a shock! I've never felt anything so hard. There was no give at all. I know it sounds like a cliché, but his muscle felt like a piece of *steel*.

Even more impressive, though, was the *power* I felt flowing out of him—and into me. Just touching Swamiji's arm put me into an altered state of consciousness. I could hardly speak or walk. I mumbled something like, "Yes, that's quite a muscle," as I staggered back to my seat.

Swamiji went on with his lecture but I hardly heard a word he said. I was in a daze, completely overcome by what I had experienced. My wife was right: Swamiji is no ordinary man. And whatever it was that made him so different, I was determined to learn more about it.

~ From Karuna ~

Fashion Sense

The first time I saw Swamiji he was dressed like the United Nations. He had on loafers, dark dress socks, an orange *dhoti* (which looks like a skirt), an Indian style shirt, an overcoat, and a French beret.

Before he said a word, I thought, "I like this man. He is completely himself."

~ From Jaya ~

Indigo Aura

"Would you like me to take a picture of your aura?" Swamiji had just walked into a metaphysical bookstore on the Gold Coast of Australia when the owner asked him this question.

"Sure—why not?" Swamiji said.

She took the picture with a special "aura" camera, then went behind a screen to develop it while Swamiji and his companions looked around the store.

Suddenly they heard the owner exclaiming from behind the screen, "My God! I can't believe it! I've never seen anything like it!" She came out holding the photograph, walked directly to Swamiji and reverently genuflected before him.

"I've taken hundreds of pictures, perhaps thousands of them, and I've never seen anything like this," she said. "Usually the picture shows a mixture of colors, through which the person is clearly visible. Look at yours." She held out the photograph. From edge to edge it was covered with indigo blue. The color was deep, and Swamiji's face and upper body were only dimly visible.

When Swamiji returned from Australia, he brought the picture with him. Of the hundreds of photos taken of him over the years, this is certainly one of the most unusual.

Miraculous Encounter

I was living in the Ananda community in Palo Alto when the Bertolucci lawsuit against Swamiji and Ananda went to trial. The court was just a few miles away, so Swamiji stayed in our community for many weeks. I had seen him from a distance but had never met him face to face.

Right in the middle of the trial, there was an earthquake near Assisi, Italy. The epicenter was in a town called Foligno, not far from Ananda's retreat. Ananda suffered only minor damage to a few buildings, but in some of the nearby towns, the damage was severe.

Even though he had more than enough troubles of his own, Swamiji launched a campaign he called *Hope and Homes for Italy*. To raise money, he decided to give a benefit concert.

I came almost an hour early so I could have a seat right in front. Swamiji was still rehearsing and everyone was running around a little frantically to get things ready in time. In the midst of all the confusion, Swamiji remained completely calm and centered.

After the concert, I was determined to introduce myself to him, even though he was surrounded by a large crowd of people. I didn't have quite enough courage to stand in front of him, so I stood behind his back. I didn't say anything, just stood silently staring at the back of his head. Suddenly he turned around, took my hand, and looked deep into my eyes.

I said something like, "I've been waiting so long to meet you."

"It is my pleasure to meet you," Swamiji replied. Then he asked my name. It wasn't much of an exchange, but I felt as if our souls had connected. All night I dreamed that Swamiji was talking to me.

The trial was such a heavy experience. I wanted to do something to help Swamiji. In an art therapy class I had made a sort of mandala of myself when I was feeling depressed and alone. I was a small black blob in the center with lots of color and light all around me. I thought it might make Swamiji feel better. so I sent it to him along with a note thanking him for founding Ananda and making it possible for me to live in such a wonderful community.

A week or so later, two friends, who are not part of Ananda, came to visit me. We were standing on the sidewalk in front of the community, about to go for a ride in my friend's new red convertible. I looked across the street and there was Swamiji. I felt my whole being leap across the street in joyful greeting.

Swamiji came over and thanked me for the mandala. I introduced him to my friends and with great attention he shook hands with each one and carefully asked their names. When I explained we were about to go for a ride, he said "Nice car!" as if he had nothing more important on his mind than a new red convertible. Trials, earthquakes—in that moment, none of it seemed to matter. In my dreams that night again he came and talked to me.

There was nothing apparently miraculous about these encounters. In fact, what made them so extraordinary to me was the apparent ordinariness of them. Swamiji is simply the kindest, most open-hearted, loving, and *humble* person I have ever met. Master made a beautiful comment that I have always remembered. "Humility," he said, "is the greatest miracle." In this sense, Swamiji himself is a walking miracle.

~ From Judy Morningstar ~

Walls Came Tumbling Down

Every summer on the campus of the University of California at Davis, they hold an event called the Whole Earth Fair. In the early '70s it was the American equivalent of the *Kumbha Mela*, a gathering of spiritual tribes and teachers. Ananda had a booth and Swamiji was there, talking to whoever happened to come by. I was just getting involved with Ananda and had never had a personal conversation with him, so I came over to the booth and sat down.

He had just finished writing *The Road Ahead*, about Master's predictions of upcoming cataclysms—natural disasters, economic collapse, social upheaval. Not a pretty picture. Swamiji had been thinking a lot about the economic future of the globe and that's mostly what we talked about.

It wasn't a deep conversation—the price of gold, world trade, the stock market—but it was interesting. I was impressed by how easy and natural it was to talk with Swamiji, how charming he was in an understated way, not ostentatious about his position or his knowledge, just open, available, and totally human.

After about fifteen minutes, the conversation wound down, and I went on my way. About a minute later I felt like an earthquake was going on inside of me. I wandered out to a nearby parking lot and for the next hour sat on a concrete curb thinking about what was happening to me.

It wasn't unpleasant, just dynamic and unexpected. Swamiji and I had been talking about global cataclysms, now I was experiencing one of my own. I felt as if my carefully constructed inner edifice—the very substance of what I called myself—was breaking into pieces. Instead of the neat, seamless reality I was used to, all I had now was a pile of bricks, waiting to be put together in a new way.

Until then, my experience of the path had been entirely mental—just philosophy and ideas. Now, fifteen minutes with Swamiji had catapulted me into the middle of real spiritual transformation. It felt entirely right. I knew Swamiji was the one who would show me the way to God.

~ From Sudarshan~

Rarely Seen

I was walking around a New Age fair called the Whole Life Expo, enjoying the wide variety of booths and people. A psychic from a nearby booth called out to me to come over and talk to her.

She pointed down the aisle and asked, "Who is that man? The one with the white hair wearing the white jacket?" I looked where she was indicating, and saw the back of a familiar figure as he walked down the aisle.

I smiled, "That's Swami Kriyananda, from Ananda Village. He's here to give a talk."

She leaned over toward me and said in a voice filled with reverence, "I have never seen an aura anything like that before. That soul is very rare on this earth. He lives only to do God's will."

~ From Karen G. ~

Folded Hand

I was too shy to introduce myself to Swamiji, so even though I had been a guest at the Ananda retreat for several months, I had never actually spoken to him.

One afternoon he held an open house at Crystal Hermitage. I parked my car in the community so I could walk the one-mile trail through the woods to the Hermitage. I was carrying a shawl and when I came in, I set it down on an empty chair.

A few hours later when the event was over, I went to get it. To my dismay, I found that Swamiji was now sitting on the chair—and on my shawl. I was so nervous, I just tugged at the corner of it and said timidly, "Excuse me, Sir, this is mine." These were the first words I ever spoke to Swamiji.

Fortunately, someone decided this was a good time to introduce me. Swamiji took my hand, looked straight into my eyes and said, "I am so glad to meet you and I am so happy you are here." Then he stood up, so I could get my shawl.

I retraced my steps through the woods, and twenty minutes later arrived at my car. When I started to reach into my pocket to get the keys, I became aware of how deeply moved I was by meeting Swamiji. For the entire walk, in fact, from the moment Swamiji let go of my hand, I had been holding the hand he touched folded against my heart.

~ From Lalita ~

The Divine Romance

I had never met Swamiji or read any of his books, but I had read *Autobiography of a Yogi*, and it had awakened within me a burning soul question: "Is Paramhansa Yogananda my guru?" I felt profoundly drawn to Yogananda, but I wanted to be absolutely sure. I thought if I could be with Swamiji, someone who actually knew him, the answer would be clear.

When I found out that Swamiji was going to give a program in Chicago, Illinois, there was no question that I would make the 1000-mile round-trip from my home in Arkansas to see him. When I arrived at the lecture hall, everyone else was sitting in chairs, but I sat cross-legged on the floor right in front of him.

Swamiji gave a talk on yoga, meditation, and the spiritual life. When he finished, I thought, "That was an excellent talk," and I was grateful to have heard it. I hadn't, however, received an answer to my question. Naively, I thought I had given God every opportunity to answer me. Perhaps I just had to accept, "Maybe Yogananda is not my guru."

After the lecture, there was going to be a musical program by the Ananda Singers who were traveling with Swamiji. Before they started, however, there was some whispered conversation between Swamiji and one of the women from Ananda. Apparently he wanted something that had been left in the motorhome, which was parked several blocks away. Finally, Swamiji said in an insistent whisper, "Please go get it," and she quickly left the room.

While we waited for her to return, the singers filled in, clearly stretching their program beyond the usual. Finally she came back with a milk crate full of sheet music that Swamiji leafed through until he found what he was looking for. There was a baby grand piano in the room. Swamiji sat down and began to play a sonata he had written called *The Divine Romance*.

What I had not been able to understand through words, I now effortlessly understood through music. The vibration was anciently familiar and I was bathed in wave after wave of devotional bliss. With it came the certainty: "Yogananda is my guru—past, present, and for all time to come."

In the years since then I have seen how sensitively Swamiji responds to the inner, intuitive promptings he receives from Master. Many times in the course of a lecture, for example, I have seen that Swamiji is answering the unspoken questions that I, or others in the audience, have. It is not that he "scans" the audience looking for questions. Rather, he feels our needs as a flow of grace being drawn out of him. He has learned to follow that grace without having to know more.

Maybe that evening in Chicago I was not the only one who needed to hear him play *The Divine Romance*. All I can say is that it set the direction for the rest of my life.

After I moved to Ananda Village, I found out that Swamiji had also written lyrics for the sonata that perfectly expressed what I felt in my heart that night when I first heard it played.

Listen! Listen!
Whispering within your soul:
Hints of laughter, hints of joy;
Sweet songs of sadness,
Of quenchless yearning
For the Light,
For My love,
Your true home.
Long your heart has played the dancer.
Long you've toyed with merest shadows
Of the treasures left behind you,
Deep in your soul.
Long you've plumbed the dark for answers.
Long you've begged from beggars' empty hands
Gifts of life they too were seeking:
Gifts none could share.
Friend, how long will you wander?
Friend, as long will you seek your home
In a land where all are strangers,
Love locks her door.
Leave to the weak his craven life!
To the coward leave his dreaming!
Oh my saint, wake-up!
Reclaim the light.
Seek the truth behind all seeming.
Turn, turn, turn within:

In silence of soul, in cave of love
Find My abode.
Listen! Listen!
Whispering within your soul:
Hints of laughter,
Hints of joy;
Sweet songs of sadness,
Of quenchless yearning
For the Light,
For My love,
Your true home.

~ From Mary Kretzmann ~

217

Vision Quest

I took a guided retreat in the wilderness that included a "Vision Quest," a time of solitude and introspection for the purpose of receiving higher guidance. I was entirely alone, although one of the guides was nearby, and if I had needed help, I could have signaled him.

For three days I sat on a hillside in the middle of a circle of stones I had laid out around me, took very little food and no water. Somewhere in the middle of it, the face of a man I'd never seen before appeared in front of me.

"Listen to your heart," he said. It may not seem like very original advice, but at the time it hit me like a bolt of lightning and completely rearranged my life.

"Who are you?" I asked.

"Swami Kriyananda," he replied.

I had no idea who he was. Later, when I saw a picture of Swamiji, I recognized him immediately as the man who had appeared in my vision.

~ From Stephanie Steyer ~

Source of Light

My sister gave me a copy of *The Path*. She saw Swamiji speak somewhere and thought I would be interested. It was several months before I finally started reading it. I had no background in these teachings but from the first page it was like the Fourth of July inside of me—pure celebration. I had been to a number of churches in my life, seeking something that made sense to me, but nothing did. Nothing touched me on a deep level until I read this book. At night I would go to sleep thinking about what I had read. When I closed my eyes, I would see flashing lights, like fireworks.

My husband was fiercely opposed to my interest in Ananda. He called it the "pinko, communist, brainwashing cult." It was four years before I was able to get away from him to come to Ananda for a visit.

It was Winter Renewal Week and Swamiji was giving the first class. I had never seen him before, or heard him speak, and I eagerly took a seat on the aisle near the front of the room. The Ananda singers did a few songs. When they finished and started toward their seats, energy began rising up my spine. All I could see was light. I felt like the top of my head had opened up and my consciousness was expanding out to infinity.

I heard a man's voice, which I immediately knew to be Swamiji's, even though I had never heard him speak. "That was lovely," he said, complimenting the singers.

I opened my eyes and saw that Swamiji was coming down the aisle just a few rows behind me. My consciousness was expanding, I realized, because of his approaching aura. Great joy filled my heart and I felt one in the Spirit with him.

That sealed it for me. I had to face extraordinary opposition from my family, but nothing could deter me. It took time for the karma to run its course, but eventually I was freed to make Ananda my home.

This experience with Swamiji happened twenty years ago. It made such an impression on my consciousness, though, that even now, when I close my eyes, I can replay every part of it.

~ From Marcella ~

Equal in God

I was at the library looking through the section of spiritual books when I first saw *Autobiography of a Yogi*. I felt a connection to Master's picture on the cover so I picked up the book and held it in my hand for a moment. But instead of checking it out, I put it back on the shelf. Next, I picked up Swamiji's book, *The Path*. When I saw his picture, I knew I had to take this book home.

Reading *The Path* made a deep impression on me, but I was just coming out of a decade of drug and alcohol addiction and was still in the throes of a serious eating disorder. The timing wasn't right and it was ten years before I actually met Swamiji.

By the time I was introduced to him in Assisi, Italy, I really wanted what Ananda had to offer. Even though I had been clean and sober for a number of years, I still identified myself as an addict and the eating disorder had me in its grip. I was filled with shame.

I desperately wanted to show Swamiji that I was a spiritual person so that he would want me to live at Ananda, but I was terrified that he would see right through me. And he did, but not in the way I feared.

It wasn't anything he said, it was just the way he looked at me. It was more than just the complete absence of judgment. It was hope—hope for a future that was free from the addictions that had made my life a living hell. Swamiji could see what I was up against, and wordlessly communicated to me that my present condition was just temporary. The spiritual freedom he had, I could have, too. In fact, *would* have. It was my destiny as much as his.

Meeting Swamiji was the turning point. It gave me the courage to move to Ananda, and not long after, to give up the eating disorder.

The first time Swamiji came to visit the community where I was living, I somehow ended up being part of a small gathering with him in the living room of the house where he was staying. I was the only newcomer. Everyone else there had been at Ananda for at least a decade. I wondered how I ever got to be in that room.

When Swamiji began to speak, he included me in the conversation in the most natural way, as if I, too, was one of his oldest friends, and as much a part of Ananda as anyone else. He asked my point of view, and listened respectfully to my answers. It wasn't that he made me feel special. In some ways, it was just the opposite. He made me feel equal. I felt anyone could have been there and he would have treated that person, too, in the same respectful way.

A couple of years later, I was having a hard time. The "honeymoon" was over. Now I had to face life, day after day, without any of the addictive "props" I had used for so long. It was my birthday and I felt so lonely, I didn't know how I would be able to go on.

Swamiji happened to be visiting again and had bought a little present for me. When he handed me the present, he looked into my eyes and said, "Never forget where your home is." When he said "home," I knew he meant more than the place called Ananda. He meant, "Home is Master. Home is God."

It was another turning point. I've had hard days since then, but never again have I fallen so low.

~ From an Ananda devotee ~

Love Is a Magician

I was well on my way to accepting Master as my guru, but I had never met Swamiji and I had a hard time seeing how he fit into the picture of my spiritual life.

I am a music teacher and a professional musician. I play the flute, but music isn't something I *do*. Music is what I *am*. So it is no surprise that Swamiji entered my heart through his music.

I had picked up a free tape from a basket in the lobby of the Ananda Mandir where I went to classes and services. It was called *The Spirit of Ananda in Music.*

I had an art project to do, so I put the tape on as background. It was chants, Ananda Singers, choir pieces, and several selections of Swamiji singing solo. I enjoyed the melodies and the vibration, even though my trained musician ears picked out every missed note and flawed intonation. I carried on listening in this way, half-enjoying, half-criticizing, all the way through a few of Swamiji's solos at the end of the tape.

Then he started to sing *Love is a Magician:*

> *Love is all I know:*
> *Sunrays on the snow*
> *Of a winter long*
> *In darkness, without song.*
> *Oh, my heart's afire,*
> *Burning all desire.*
> *Only you remain, and life again!*

He sang with exquisite beauty, but I hardly noticed. My musician ears had disappeared, overwhelmed by my devotee heart. And that heart had been pierced by something so profound I knew it was irrevocable. As the words unfolded, I began to cry, then to sob.

Too long I did stray,
Flung lifetimes away,
Imagined you did not care.
I know now your smile,
Was mine all the while;
I listened, and love was there.
I can't breathe for love.
All the stars above call to me:
"Come home,
Life's waves all end in foam!"
Only love can heal
All the pain I feel.
What a fool was I to turn away!

When the song began, Swamiji was irrelevant to my spiritual life. By the time the song ended, Swamiji had a permanent home in the center of my heart.

~ From Bhagavati ~

IN SERVICE

TO

HIS GURU

"You have a great work to do."

Paramhansa Yogananda
to his disciple, Swami Kriyananda

Will I Find God?

In August 1948, Master experienced a great *samadhi* [experience of cosmic consciousness] during which Divine Mother spoke both *to* him and *through* him. A striking feature of that samadhi were these words She addressed to Master:

"In the beginning, I sent you a few bad ones to test your love for Me. But now I am sending you angels, and whoever smites them, I will smite!"

Just over a month later, September 12, 1948, Swamiji arrived.

Toward the end of their first meeting, Master said to him, "I give you my unconditional love."

"Have I been a yogi in other lives?" Swamiji asked his guru.

"Many times," Master replied.

Swamiji's name then was Donald Walters. For reasons he never explained, Master always called him "Walter."

During the all-day Christmas meditation in 1949, Master said, "Walter, you must try *hard*, for God will bless you very much."

"Your work," Master told him, "is lecturing, writing, and editing."

"Sir," Swamiji inquired, "haven't you yourself already written everything that is needed?"

Master looked a little shocked. "Don't say that!" he exclaimed, "*Much* more is needed."

When Master lamented the number of ministers who had fallen because of ego, Swamiji said, "Sir, that's why I don't want to be a minister!"

Master replied with deep seriousness: "You will *never* fall due to ego!"

To a young monk at Mount Washington, Master said, "You must mix more with Walter. You don't know what you have in him."

Master once said to Swamiji with deep earnestness, "Apart from St. Lynn [Master's spiritual successor, also known as Rajarsi Janakananda], every man has disappointed me. And you *MUSTN'T* disappoint me!"

Master had good men disciples. Swamiji understood him, therefore, to be referring to the role Master wanted him to play in spreading his teachings, and not specifically to his life as a devotee.

"Your life is one of intense activity, and meditation," Master told Swamiji.

"Though I tried always to make meditation my primary focus," Swamiji said years later, "I couldn't help noticing that Master placed activity first in this sequence."

Master once told Swamiji, "God won't come to you until the end of life. Death itself is the final sacrifice you'll have to make."

On several occasions, Master said to Swamiji, "You have a great work to do."

After Master's passing, Rajarsi Jankananda repeated the same words, "Master has a great work to do through you, Walter." Then he added, "And he will give you the strength to do it."

Swamiji once asked Master, "Will I find God in this life?"

"Yes," Master replied. "But don't think about it." After a pause, Master continued, "After many lifetimes, everything has balanced out now."

Near the end of his life, Master said to Swamiji, "You have pleased me very much. I want you to know that."

with Paramhansa Yogananda

Cousins meet Yogananda

Two of Swamiji's cousins met Master and saw Swamiji interacting with him. The encounters were brief; neither became a disciple. But these cousins are notable because there are few reliable eyewitness accounts of that relationship. When his *gurubhais* [fellow disciples] ostracized him years after Master's passing, the memories held of Swamiji by others became tainted by their prejudice.

Marjorie Brunhoff Lutz told me she had visited her cousin Don [Swamiji] at Mt. Washington in 1948, just before she started college.

"I went with my father (my mother was no longer alive) to see him. This was not long after Don had moved there. No one in the family understood what he was doing. We all thought he must have joined some weird cult and wanted to make sure he was all right.

"I remember there was a beautiful building set on a hill in the middle of a lovely garden. I saw this man in long robes. I knew immediately he was from India. I don't know how I knew, no one told me, I just knew. Of course, it was Yogananda. Everything there was so serene, especially Yogananda himself. He had lovely, soft eyes. I remember those eyes.

"Don was very pleased to be able to introduce us to him. We didn't really talk with him, just exchanged a few words, like 'How do you do?' and 'It's a pleasure to meet you.'

"What I remember is how warm and loving Yogananda was toward Don. It made a big impression on me. It was a father-son relationship. I can't explain it in any other way."

Bet Brunhoff Hover, Marjorie's older sister, met Yogananda around the end of 1950. In *The Path,* Swamiji describes the meeting.

"I introduced Bet to Master as he was leaving one afternoon for a drive. From his remarks later on it was clear that she had made an excellent impression on him.

"'Would she make a good yogi, Master?'

"'Oh *yes.*'"

About Yogananda, Bet told me, "I was thrilled to meet him. He really impressed me. He had a good presence and a wonderful aura. You could really feel it. He seemed to be such a loving person.

"And it was obvious he thought the world of Don. Don was the 'apple of his eye.'"

I asked Bet if there was anything specific that Master did that showed his high regard for Swamiji.

"No, nothing specific," Bet said. "He did praise Don, but that was only part of it. It was the overall impression I remember." Then she said again, "It was obvious that Don was the 'apple of his eye.'"

Meditate on Greatness

"Writing this book [*The Path*] should have taken me ten years, but I worked on it with great intensity, and finished it in three," Swamiji said. "Of course, that doesn't count all the years I spent collecting the stories and meditating on them.

"I didn't dare write a single episode of Master's life until I had meditated on it and was sure I had understood, as far as I was able, what it meant. Sometimes it took years. In order to explain them to others, I had to go deeply into every facet. It was a growing experience for me; no one could learn as much from this book as I have, myself.

"Then I had to decide how many of those levels of meaning I would explain and how much I would leave to the reader to meditate on and grow in the experience, as I have. Meditating on greatness is a way of achieving greatness oneself."

Creativity

Jody* wanted to leave Ananda, at least for a time, so he could concentrate on writing and recording an album of his own songs. People at Ananda are free to come and go as they please, but Jody didn't want to make such an important decision without first getting Swamiji's advice.

"Spiritually," Swamiji said, "it would be better for you to stay here and continue to sing the music I have written. Later you can write songs of your own."

This was not the answer Jody was looking for. "I love your music," he said. "But you know how it is to be an artist. Sometimes you just have to express *yourself*."

"No," Swamiji replied, rather sternly, "I *don't* know how it is. Nothing I have done has been to express *myself*. If I never wrote another word or note, it wouldn't matter to me."

Swamiji went on to explain what does motivate his prodigious creative output—he has written scores of books, composed hundreds of pieces of music, taken thousands of photographs, and even done a few paintings.

"I am not an *artist*," Swamiji said. "I am a *disciple*. As a disciple, I am *driven* by the thought of all that is needed to fulfill Master's mission. Everywhere there is such hunger for it. When it comes to serving Master's work, I feel like I am sitting on top of a volcano of creativity. It would take more energy to suppress that creative urge than simply to let it keep on erupting."

To Jody, he said, "Right now, the songs you write are imitative. If you can get more in tune spiritually, then you will be able to create music that is truly original. Attunement will come to you more easily here in the community, where you have the support of like-minded friends, than if you go out on your own."

"To be original," Swamiji explained on another occasion, "doesn't mean doing something that has never been done before. It means to come from one's own point of *origin*, which is to say, God within, one's higher self. Creativity is simply the expression of the inspiration you feel inside."

Later, Swamiji said to a few of us, "It is a bit awkward, having to recommend 'my' music. I am not impressed with myself as a composer. I am, however, very impressed by the compositions that have come through me. They express the vibration of this path and for that reason can help people spiritually.

"So many artistic people," Swamiji explained, "go about it in the wrong way when they think 'I am going to create a *poem*, or a *song*, or a *painting*.' I think first of the *consciousness* I want to express. When I have that clearly in mind, then I ask God to help me express it through whatever medium I am using.

"I don't feel I have done anything. God has done it through me. The 'secret' behind my creativity is the power of the Guru. I can't tell where I end and Master begins."

Swamiji made a slide show composed entirely of photographs he had taken of people from many countries, cultures, ages, and states of consciousness. He called it *Different Worlds*. For the sound track, he wanted a melody that would express the entire human condition: joy, sorrow, aspiration, fulfillment—everything.

"I had a very clear idea of what I wanted, but I began to think it was impossible to put all that into one melody. 'Before I give up,' I thought, 'let me give it one more try.' I sat down at the piano and prayed, 'God, give me a melody.' Then I watched as my hands played the notes.

"A friend happened to be nearby and heard what I was playing. 'That is the perfect melody for *Different Worlds*,' she exclaimed. And it was.

"When I visited the Holy Land [Israel] in 1985, the inspiration I felt was complete in itself. I didn't need to express it outwardly. When melodies came to me, though, that expressed the consciousness of that experience, I saw that the music could be a bridge between Master's teachings and the Christian churches.

"I had to work hard to take what I felt inside and make it into the *Oratorio*, but I was happy to do it for the sake of Master's mission."

Swamiji got into photography because pictures were needed and no one else at that time was photographing Ananda in the way he thought it should be done. Several years later, when others also began to take fine pictures, Swamiji put down his camera and hasn't picked it up since.

He created a few paintings, too, when they were needed and he couldn't find an artist who could express the inspiration he felt. The painting of the spiritual eye, for example, was for a booklet of Master's *Prayer for the Disciples*, which Swamiji printed as a Christmas gift for the monks when he was still in SRF.

"I had my heart set on including an uplifting painting as a frontispiece. A member of the Hollywood Church had a daughter living in Germany who had done some beautifully sensitive paintings, almost astral in quality. I asked the member if she could ask her daughter to do the frontispiece and she agreed.

"At the beginning of December, I received several paintings from her. They were entirely unsuitable—angels playing violins, that sort of thing. Another member of the congregation was an artist for Walt Disney and I asked him to make a sketch. It, too, fell far short of what I wanted.

"I sat in meditation and asked Master for an inspiration, thinking I could then convey it to the Disney artist. Immediately the inspiration came to make a painting of the spiritual eye. I thought it would help the artist if I made a graphic illustration of it, so I bought some watercolors and brushes.

"I meditated as I worked. I made mistakes, but gradually the painting as it is now emerged. In the end, every 'mistake' proved a necessary part of building up the proper texture for the final result.

"I wanted a sense of surge, like a wave, carrying one up to the spiritual eye. First, the way I painted it, the 'waves' were just blackish curves. That didn't work, so with a fine brush I painted innumerable white lines all sweeping upward and inward toward the spiritual eye. They proved too brilliant, so I covered them over with a fine blue wash. All those different layers gave it a deeper dimension."

At the base of the spiritual eye, Swamiji painted a figure seen from the back, which was Master reaching upward toward the light. "Master's arms," Swamiji said, "I deliberately curved in such a way as to complement the wave effect and the round spiritual eye, and his hair line was drawn to complement those other lines.

"I had planned to make the painting just to give the artist an idea of what I wanted. It came out so well, however, I didn't need another artist after all."

Over the years, the painting has been used in many different ways, including on the cover of Swamiji's autobiography.

"The other paintings I've done all happened in the same way. I couldn't find a professional artist to express the inspiration I felt, so I did it myself. No doubt, my paintings are 'primitives.' They please me and seem also to touch others, though, because of the feeling they generate."

"Too often on the spiritual path," Swamiji explained on another occasion, "devotees are afraid to be creative because they think creativity itself leads to ego. This is not true. When the ego is offered into the divine, then creative work becomes an expression of God. Then it helps you spiritually.

"In fact, in order to grow, you have to express yourself in this way—creatively, as an instrument of the divine.

"People can look at what I have done in two ways," Swamiji explained. "They can point to my accomplishments and say, 'My, isn't he talented!' Or they can try to understand *how* I have done it. Then they can take the inspiration *they* feel inside and express it creatively. This is what I have done, and what I hope others will also be inspired to do."

The melody for one of the most beloved songs in the Ananda repertoire, *O Master*, was not written by Swamiji, but by a woman in the community named Mukti. She also wrote lyrics. The chorus is hers, but the verses Swamiji rewrote to be clearer and more poetic. When Mukti heard Swamiji's version, she was delighted. "Yes!" she said. "That is exactly what I was trying to say!"

"Mukti took the inspiration she felt from my songs," Swamiji said, "and used it to tune into her own creativity, to express the divine in her way. She succeeded beautifully. I can hardly listen to that song without weeping."

"What we are trying to do," Swamiji once said to me, "is revamp a whole culture, to show how Master's teachings, creatively applied, can change the entire pattern of our society. I am just one person, and there is only so much I can accomplish by myself. If I can start a *movement*, however, and many people begin to act creatively from inner inspiration, as I have, then a *great* work can be done."

His Year of Rest

Since he became a disciple, it is a rare day that Swamiji does not engage in creative or serviceful work. Even in his busy life, however, 1995 stands out. "My Year of Rest," Swamiji jokingly calls it.

The stage was set a few months earlier in the autumn of 1994. The Time-Warner Company had published one of Swamiji's books and then sent him on a ten-city tour to promote it. For years, his heart had been giving him trouble, and the strain of the tour proved to be the last straw. By the time he reached the tenth city, his heart was racing at 160 beats a minute and refused to slow down. He had to cancel a few of the final engagements and return to Ananda Village.

His cardiologist issued a stern warning: "Your heart requires urgent surgery. The longer you wait, the greater the chances that you'll simply die suddenly, during the night."

The operation was set for December 18th. Between the doctor's warning and the time of the surgery, Swamiji received a legal summons. An ex-Ananda member named Annemarie Bertolucci had filed a lawsuit claiming that Ananda was a cult and that Swamiji an abusive cult leader. The media picked up the story right away, and for the next several years, as the lawsuit made its way through the court system, Ananda and Swamiji received a great deal of negative publicity.

Just before surgery, Swamiji found out that if he didn't immediately finish editing the Preface to his latest book, *Expansive Marriage*, it couldn't be printed in time for its scheduled launch. He had already entered the hospital, so Swamiji spent the day before the operation lying in bed working on the Preface.

The open-heart surgery took four hours. The doctor did a bypass, inserted a pacemaker, and replaced one of Swamiji's heart valves with an artificial one. Afterwards, Swamiji often referred to the operation as his "valve job." That evening, the surgeon told Swamiji "You *must absolutely* take a year off, now, from all work and all stressful activity."

Unfortunately, Swamiji still hadn't quite finished the Preface. So the next day, using his willpower to drive the lingering fog of anesthesia from his brain, he finished editing it.

"As things begin, so they continue" is a rule of life Swamiji has often quoted. It certainly proved true for that year. Circumstances, and Swamiji's own life-long commitment to honoring his word, combined to make 1995 one of the busiest and most stressful years of Swamiji's life.

Another publisher, Workman, had for the last two years put out calendars based on Swamiji's *Secrets* books. Each book in the *Secrets* series contains a month of aphorisms on a particular subject, like happiness or peace of mind. Swamiji had agreed to give Workman sayings for one more calendar. He had hoped to have enough *Secrets*, but it turned out there weren't enough. It was too late to cancel the contract. Swamiji had already spent the $11,000 advance royalties on equipment for the recording studio at Ananda and was in no position to refund the money.

Fortunately, he had another book, *Do it Now!,* not yet published, which had 365 sayings, one for each day of the year. He'd written that whole book in one day a few months earlier, concerned that if he stretched it out over a longer period he would forget what he had written and repeat himself.

Now Swamiji carefully edited some of the sayings and wrote new ones to replace those he considered weak. The deadline was the end of January and he got the calendar to Workman just in time. Swamiji felt it was best to finish *Do It Now!* while he was in the flow rather than starting over again later. So the month of February he spent polishing that book.

When he was done, Swamiji felt the sayings could be of such benefit to people, he didn't want to wait for the usual print and purchase cycle to get it into the hands of readers. Instead, at his own expense, he printed 5000 copies and gave them away free. By this time, the Bertolucci lawsuit had become a full-blown personal attack on Swamiji's integrity as a spiritual leader. *Do It Now!* was one way for Swamiji to counter all that negativity with positive energy of his own.

Before the surgery had been scheduled, Swamiji had committed himself to a lecture tour of Southern California in March. Many people had put time, energy, and money into setting up the tour and Swamiji felt it wouldn't be fair to them to cancel it. Besides, with all the negative publicity, this was not the time to hide at home. The best antidote was for Swamiji to speak openly in public so that people could meet him and make up their own minds.

By April, all this work began to take a toll on Swamiji's weakened body and he went to Hawaii for a few weeks of rest. He had promised Time-Warner another book by the end of June. The agreed upon title was *Meditation for Starters*. Swamiji was confident, after all his years of teaching, that he could turn the book out in a few weeks. While he was in Hawaii, however, he received notice from the publisher that they wanted to change the title to *Superconsciousness*.

A book on superconsciousness was quite different from a meditation book for beginners. Swamiji felt it would take at least a year to write, and, ideally, two years. Time-Warner informed him, however, that they expected him to honor his contract and complete the book by the end of June. He had a little more than two months to write it.

And two weeks of that time had already been committed to giving lectures in Chicago and Denver, also promised before the operation. Again, people were counting on him and Swamiji didn't feel he could cancel. Nor could he cancel the book contract. He had already spent the $75,000 advance royalties on equipment for the recording studio and there was no way to pay it back.

At the end of April, Swamiji returned to Ananda Village to begin what looked to him like a Herculean labor to write the book in time. In May he received a letter from Derek Bell, the noted Irish harpist, offering to record an album of Swamiji's music. This was an offer Swamiji couldn't refuse. Derek Bell was a member of the multiple Grammy-award winning group, *The Chieftains*, and a world-renowned musician in his own right. To have an album by Derek Bell would help put Swamiji's music on the map.

The problem was, Swamiji didn't have any specifically Celtic melodies for Derek to record—he'd have to write them. *The Chieftains* toured almost continuously, so Derek had only a small window of time in the summer in which he could come to Ananda to make the album. At the moment, however, with the looming deadline for the book, Swamiji had to put the music project on the back-burner. Perhaps some of his existing melodies would do? He asked a friend to review the music he had already written and see what he could come up with.

Apart from the lecture tour, Swamiji spent May and June writing the book *Superconsciousness*. In order to understand the subject, he said later, he had to be in a superconscious state himself. He shut off his phone, accepted no mail, and fairly poured himself into the writing. With divine grace he finished the book on June 29th and got it to Time-Warner by the deadline of June 30th.

Three days later, he was scheduled to leave for a two-week visit to the Ananda communities in Portland and Seattle where he was to give a series of lectures and classes, another promise made before the operation. Now that the book was done, he turned his attention to Derek's request. Unfortunately only two of his songs—*Desdemona's Song* and *Invocation to Woodland Devas*—seemed right for the album.

"I was already in a superconscious state," Swamiji said later, "from writing the book." With that expanded awareness, in the next two days, Swamiji was able to write the seventeen additional melodies needed for the album they had decided to call *Mystic Harp*. This left one day relatively free to pack for the tour.

After the tour, Swamiji had a few days to polish the melodies and write lyrics for a number of them before Derek Bell arrived to do the recording. A few days after the recording was finished, Swamiji left for San Francisco to meet an entirely different kind of demand on his time—the beginning of what were to amount to 80 hours of deposition in the Bertolucci lawsuit.

The opposing lawyer was so openly hostile to Swamiji, that at one point he shouted in anger at an Ananda member, "You can tell your Mr. Walters [Swamiji] that I am going to *destroy* him!" (As a deliberate insult, the lawyer refused to address Swamiji by his spiritual name and title.) The lawyer was a long-time member of SRF. The Bertolucci lawsuit itself was only an extension of SRF's ongoing effort—through the courts and by other means—to take away from Swamiji his right as a disciple to serve his guru.

The hours of deposition were filled with innuendos, outright insults, mockery, and sneers. Swamiji took it all calmly, but to protect his still precarious health, a doctor remained in the room with him to monitor the condition of his heart. Some days the deposition had to be terminated early to allow Swamiji's body time to recover.

Meanwhile, the Ananda community in Italy was building a new temple. A large fundraising event in which Swamiji was the guest of honor was key to their success. Once again, Swamiji felt committed. Midway through the deposition process, Swamiji took a break and went to Italy. After the event, he and a few friends went to India in the hope that the spiritual atmosphere of that country would rejuvenate him. Instead, almost immediately, Swamiji came down with walking pneumonia and had to return to Italy early in order to recover enough to go back to San Francisco to complete those eighty hours of deposition.

In Italy, yet another demand was placed in front of him. Some years earlier, Swamiji had written a three-volume, stanza-by-stanza comparison of parallel passages in the Bible and the *Bhagavad Gita*. He called it *Rays of the Same Light*. The purpose was twofold: as a study in itself and also as weekly readings for the Ananda Sunday worship services.

The farther Swamiji had proceeded into the year, however, the longer the "readings" had become. He had known for some time that he needed to write two separate books: a shorter one for Sunday readings and a longer one for study.

"Asha felt particularly burdened by those long readings," Swamiji said later. "She gives most of the Sunday Services in the Ananda colony in Palo Alto where she and her husband David are in charge. She had been happy to get a reprieve when we switched for awhile from *Rays of the Same Light* to reading from the newly published commentary, *The Rubaiyat of Omar Khayyam Explained.*"

Now that 'reprieve' was coming to an end. "I could almost see the teardrops on the fax she sent me," Swamiji joked later, "pleading for an alternative to those long readings."

Swamiji decided it was time to write the shorter commentary, which he called *Rays of the One Light*. "I finished the first reading just in time to fax it to Asha for the first Sunday Service after the *Rubaiyat* was done," Swamiji said.

By the end of the year the book was finished.

In December, Swamiji returned to San Francisco and completed the remaining forty hours of depositions. Thus ended his "Year of Rest."

A guest once said to Swamiji, "This may be a hard question for you to answer. Do you serve man or do you serve God?"

"It's not at all hard to answer," Swamiji replied. "I serve God. If I felt God wanted me to, I could walk away from everything. When we die, we leave it all behind anyway. Only God is real. One reason I am able to accomplish so much is because I feel inwardly free."

Two Paragraphs

The book, *The Essence of Self-Realization: The Wisdom of Paramhansa Yogananda*, is composed entirely of Master's words as Swamiji recorded them during the years he lived with his guru. The book is dedicated, "With love and humility to all his [Master's] disciples."

It was published in 1990, more than 25 years after Swamiji had been expelled from SRF. In all that time, the SRF leaders had never softened in their condemnation of him. Still, Swamiji hoped that SRF members and its leaders would be inspired by this book, and that inspiration would soften their attitude, perhaps even leading to a reconciliation.

I couldn't understand why Swamiji was so determined to bring the two organizations together. Three times since Ananda was founded, he had offered to give it to SRF. Daya Mata, the SRF president, refused even to consider the possibility. Once Swamiji even suggested to Daya that all Kriya Initiations at Ananda should be given by monks from SRF. I was profoundly relieved when Daya Mata unequivocally rejected that proposal.

"Why do you keep reaching out to SRF when you know you will only be insulted and rebuffed?" I asked Swamiji. "They don't respect you and we don't need them."

"It doesn't matter how they treat me," Swamiji replied. "I am not thinking of the *present*. I am thinking of Master's mission for centuries to come. Look at all the blood that has been spilled because of the split in Christianity, and that didn't happen until hundreds of years after

Christ died. If a schism develops in the first generation of Master's work, just think how the antagonism will grow over time. I owe it to Master to do what I can to keep that from happening."

Whatever he did, Swamiji always took into account how it might affect SRF. For years, he focused Ananda on those aspects of Master's work that SRF was not serving, such as spiritual communities. Gradually, however, he began to feel that Master no longer wanted him to "stoop over," as Swamiji put it, so that SRF would appear taller. Still, Swamiji moved slowly and carefully.

Master had spelled his name "Paramhansa." A few years after Master died, however, some Sanskrit scholars in India convinced Daya Mata that the proper way to spell it was with the extra "a" in the middle: "Param*a*hansa." Swamiji, who was still part of SRF at that time, spoke strongly against changing it. His argument was simple common sense.

"First of all," he said, "not all the scholars agree. Many feel 'Paramhansa' is equally correct. In any case, why look to the scholars? Master is our Guru. Besides, he is Indian. He knew what he was doing. It is a transliteration, and the pronunciation is more accurate without that 'a'."

Swamiji was overruled and SRF began spelling it the way those scholars had recommended. And after Swamiji was expelled, out of respect for SRF, he continued to spell it the way they did.

When it came time to publish *Essence*, however, Swamiji felt he had to be true to what Master had done. He wrote a simple "Editorial

Note" for the beginning of the book explaining what appeared to be the "new" spelling, "Paramhansa."

In the Editorial Note, Swamiji explains the origin of the word and its importance as the highest spiritual title in the Hindu tradition, conferred only on those who have attained Self-realization. He speaks of the differing points of view among the scholars about how to write it and his decision to go with the spelling that most closely resembles the way the word is pronounced.

And that is where the note ends. Since SRF had long since obliterated all traces of Master's original spelling, even altering his signature by copying an "a" from elsewhere in the word and inserting it between the "m" and the "h", the reader will naturally draw the conclusion that it is *Swamiji* who is going against Master's way of doing things.

In fact, when Swamiji first wrote the Editorial Note, it had two additional paragraphs explaining that SRF had changed the spelling after Master died and that Swamiji was restoring it.

As is his habit when writing a book, Swamiji shared his work-in-progress with his secretary and a few other friends.

When his secretary read the Editorial Note with the paragraphs about SRF, he spoke frankly to Swamiji. "This is a beautiful book of universal teachings," he said, "and now it begins with a squabble between disciples. People won't understand and it may cause them to lose faith in Master. 'He can't be much of a spiritual teacher,' they'll think, 'if his followers can't even get along.'"

"You are right," Swamiji said. He picked up a pen and deleted the offending paragraphs. Of course, without that explanation, the blame falls on Swamiji. To him, however, that was preferable to the risk of hurting the faith of any devotee who might otherwise be inspired to read the book.

In 1990, the same year that *Essence* was published, SRF filed a massive lawsuit against Swamiji and Ananda. Swamiji knew the lawsuit was coming. Six months earlier, while he was still writing *Essence*, he had received a threatening letter from their lawyers. Still, he chose to delete those paragraphs for the sake of the devotees.

As the years passed, and the lawsuit went on and on—it took twelve years to resolve—it became obvious from the way SRF was conducting the lawsuit, that the organization and its leaders had drifted far from the path of dharma Master had set for them.

Finally, in the hope of helping SRF to see itself more clearly and embrace the path of dharma once again, Swamiji felt inwardly guided by Master to speak more frankly about SRF than he had ever done before.

"It hurts me to do so," he said, "more than you will ever know. I know those people," meaning Daya Mata and the other leaders of SRF, "in a way no one else at Ananda does. I know their hearts and their devotion to Master. I would do anything to help them, if they would only let me."

He went on to say, "I see now, though, that it had to be this way. Master was behind it from the start. Ananda has its own mission. It is Master's will that the two organizations work separately."

Thinking of the centuries, though, Swamiji has done what he can to ensure future harmony. In two paragraphs of the document he called *The Last Will, Testament, and Spiritual Legacy of Swami Kriyananda*, he wrote:

> "Regardless of anyone's treatment of us, we must work steadfastly for universal spiritual harmony and unity. Schism, even if forced upon us, must never be initiated by Ananda itself, nor recognized as desirable. Ananda must work for the well-being of all, and never give greater importance to its own perceived well-being and prosperity in any circumstance in which these ends must be obtained at the cost of the needs and well-being of anyone else.

> "Self-Realization Fellowship (SRF) must always be considered part of Ananda's broader spiritual family. If at any time the occasion should arise that might permit the two organizations to work cooperatively, Ananda ought to make every reasonable effort to do so. For SRF is the organization founded by our Guru, and must be given full respect, for his sake. Although certain Ananda members have expressed a feeling (admittedly with some reason) of resentment over the treatment I myself have received from them, my earnest request is that they, too, behave always kindly and respectfully toward SRF, regardless of any provocation from them—as indeed I myself have always tried to behave. Our attitude toward them should be one of forgiveness and love. I ask this not out of ordinary human consideration, but out of love for our mutual Guru, who came on earth to inspire people with divine love, and not to infuse in them a spirit of sectarian rivalry."

Retraction

It was Spiritual Renewal Week and Swamiji was giving the morning class. He started talking about a subtle point: how people who are highly advanced spiritually can still have serious flaws in their character.

"Think of light shining through a stained glass window," he said. "When the light is dim, the colors all look gray and you can't see the flaws in the glass. When the sun shines brightly, the colors are revealed, but so also is every flaw. So it is on the spiritual path. As a devotee advances, his energy increases and everything about him becomes more apparent—both his strengths and his weaknesses."

To illustrate the point, Swamiji began to talk about one of his brother disciples. "He was advanced spiritually, and very close to Master. But he could also be jealous and petty in ways you wouldn't expect in such an advanced soul." Swamiji didn't say this in a judgmental way, he just stated it as a fact.

It was an interesting point, and when Swamiji suddenly went silent, at first we thought he was just giving us time to absorb what he had said. Swamiji was completely still, his head slightly turned, as if listening to something none of us could hear.

Finally, Swamiji resumed speaking. In a quiet, serious tone of voice he said, "When I speak, I try to be a channel for Master. He is not pleased with me for saying those things about my brother disciple.

Please consider them unsaid." Then Swamiji described that disciple again, this time speaking only of his many fine spiritual qualities.

It was striking to see how subtle Swamiji is in his attunement to Master. And how unconcerned he was about embarrassing himself in front of us by admitting his error. The only thing that matters to Swamiji is that he please Master.

Ah, Moon of My Delight

In January 1950, when Master went into seclusion at his desert retreat to complete his commentary on the *Bhagavad Gita*, Swamiji went with him.

"I prayed to Divine Mother and asked Her whom I should take with me to help with the editing," Master told Swamiji. "Your face appeared. That's why I am taking you."

For a few days, Master had Swamiji sit with him while he dictated the commentary. After that, he instructed Swamiji to work on his own at the monks' retreat a few miles away, going through years of old SRF magazines and clipping out all the articles of commentary by Master on the *Bhagavad Gita* and the *Rubaiyat of Omar Khayyam*. (Most people think of the *Rubaiyat* as a love poem. In fact, it is a deep mystical scripture.) While Master finished dictating the rest of the *Gita* commentary, Swamiji's job was to begin editing the articles. Master wanted him to do not only the *Gita*, but also the *Rubiayat*, and then the Bible.

For several months, mostly in solitude, Swamiji worked on the assignment Master had given him. He never got to the Bible, however, the *Gita* and the *Rubaiyat* took all of his time.

Master had asked Swamiji to help him, but he had given final responsibility for the editing to another disciple. That disciple wasn't interested in the work Swamiji had done. In fact, when she saw all the pages of corrected articles, she simply threw them away. Swamiji was just a young monk, twenty-three years old, and she had been editing Master's writings for years.

She proceeded at a snail's pace, however. When she passed away in 1970, twenty years after Master finished his *Gita* commentaries, none of them had been published. Her successor was equally slow, and forty years after Master's passing, SRF had still not published any of the commentaries except as articles in the SRF magazines.

Swamiji, by now a mature disciple and a proven writer and editor, naturally wanted to carry out the commission Master had given him so many years before, especially since SRF had done nothing.

The whole of the *Rubaiyat* commentary had been published in the SRF magazines before Master died. Swamiji had all the articles, but SRF held the copyright, or so he thought.

Several times over the years, SRF had threatened to sue Swamiji for violations, as they saw it, of their copyrighted materials, but they had never followed through. If he edited and published Master's *Rubaiyat*, however, Swamiji knew SRF would take him to court and his book might never see the light of day.

When SRF expelled Swamiji in 1962, they assumed he would not be able to accomplish anything on his own—that they would be able, as Tara said at the time, "to forget that you ever lived." Instead, Swamiji founded Ananda, wrote books and music, and gained a world-wide reputation as a foremost disciple of Master. SRF considers itself to be the sole authorized channel for the dissemination of Master's teachings. Swamiji's prominence as a disciple outside of SRF has been a great problem for them.

The dispute is theological: Does Master express only through SRF or can he also come through individual disciples, with or without organizational sanction? Swamiji feels this issue is not just between himself and SRF, but is of concern to all devotees of Master. He speaks openly and frankly about it and has encouraged SRF to do the same. For years, SRF has engaged in a whisper campaign to discredit Swamiji as a disciple, but has refused every invitation from him to engage in open debate.

Finally, in 1990, in an effort to settle the issue once and for all, SRF filed a massive lawsuit against Swamiji and Ananda. They asked the court to grant them exclusive rights to Master and his teachings. Religious monopoly is prohibited by American law, so SRF built their case around copyrights, trademarks, and publicity rights to the "name, image, and likeness of a deceased personality."

SRF's claims were so broad that, if they had won, Ananda would have been prohibited from any public use of Master's name or photograph—prevented, in fact, from describing what we offer as Master's teachings, or ourselves as his disciples. A few months into the case, the judge told SRF, "It seems to me you are trying to put Ananda out of business." In America, if you don't defend yourself against a lawsuit, you lose by default. There was no choice but to fight.

The dispute did not belong in a secular court, but some secular laws did apply. Even religious works can be copyrighted and trade-marked. A member of Ananda had openly violated SRF copyrights by distributing to Ananda members copies of hundreds of pages from old, out-of-print SRF magazines that contained Master's commentary on the Bible and the *Bhagavad Gita*. SRF had not published this material in any other form and it was the only way we could have access to it.

Ananda's attorney, Jon Parsons, is a good friend of the community, but was not a member or a disciple. Working on this case for twelve years, though, did turn him into a believer. It was Jon who received the inspiration to defend against the charge of copyright *violation* by challenging the *validity* of SRF's copyrights.

"The idea just appeared in my mind," Jon said later. "It came from Master, that's the only way I can explain it."

Excited by the idea, and by the way it had come to him, Jon plunged into the research and soon discovered that SRF had failed to renew the copyrights on most of Master's original writings. And much of what they had renewed was fraudulently done. SRF owned its later edited versions, but the *original* writings, the only thing we cared about, were in the public domain.

Within a few years, the judge had ruled decisively in Ananda's favor on this and every other significant issue in the case. Through repeated appeals, deliberate delays, and satellite litigation intended to destroy Swamiji's reputation, SRF extended the case for almost a decade longer. SRF is a wealthy organization and easily spent $50 million on their lawsuit against Ananda. Ananda is not wealthy, and being forced to spend $12 million in our defense drove us right to the edge of bankruptcy. But in the end, Ananda survived, and SRF was defeated.

Despite the extraordinary expense and the accumulation of several million dollars of debt, the "Lawsuit Years" (1990-2002) were the most creative and expansive in Ananda's history.

"The more you tell *un*truths about us," Swamiji wrote to Daya Mata in 1982, "the more you set up a karmic condition in which the truth *must* come out." The lawsuit proved to be a "karmic boomerang" for SRF. Their intention was to close the door to every expression of Master's teaching except their own. Instead, as a direct result of the lawsuit they filed, the door was opened wide. The court declared: No one can own the Master. Master belongs to the world.

As soon as the court ruled that the commentary on the *Rubaiyat* was in the public domain, Swamiji began to work on editing the magazine articles into a book. He made no secret of what he was doing, and SRF soon got wind of it. After delaying for forty years, SRF now announced that it, too, would publish Master's commentary on the *Rubaiyat*, just a few months earlier than Swamiji's book was scheduled to come out.

Swamiji stated frankly that he was editing the commentaries, as Master had asked him to do. SRF made no mention of editing, but gave the impression that their book would be Master's untouched words. In fact, a disciple in SRF had been working on the editing for years. That was one of the reasons publication had been delayed for so long.

SRF's claim could not go unchallenged. Otherwise, the SRF book would be Master's commentary, and Swamiji's would only be his own. Swamiji wrote a letter to the entire Ananda mailing list, answering the obvious question: Why do a Master's words need editing?

"People often confuse wisdom with intellectual learning," Swamiji wrote, "or with the pleasure some deep thinkers find in making clearly reasoned explanations. True wisdom, however, is intuitive; it is an arrow that goes straight to its mark, while the intellect lumbers with labored breathing far behind.

"Master was a sage of intuitive wisdom who disciplined his mind, out of compassion for people of slower understanding, to accept the plodding processes of 'common sense,' and to trudge the twisting byways of ordinary human reasoning. His consciousness soared more naturally, however, in skies of divine ecstasy.

"His preferred way of expressing himself was to touch lightly on a point, inviting others to meet him on his own level. It was to us, his disciples, usually, that he left the task of expanding on, or explaining, the truths he presented in condensed form in his writings."

Swamiji has also explained, "When the creative flow is powerful," as it was when Master was dictating or writing his commentaries, "one cannot give primary attention to perfecting the outward mode of expression. I can understand very well why great masters rarely phrase their words with the care demanded by a careful and elegant stylist. It is for their disciples, to 'pick up the pieces.' Indeed, as my Guru himself indicated to me, this would be the way I myself would grow spiritually."

Compared to the superconscious awareness needed to intuit the meaning of the scripture as Master did, Swamiji humorously described the subsequent editing process as "rather like plumbing: fitting words, phrases, and sentences together in such a way as to make the ideas flow smoothly" so the reader can more easily grasp the Master's intention.

Swamiji's letter soon found its way into the hands of many SRF members, and *they* began to challenge SRF's claim. Eventually, SRF was forced to make a virtue of necessity, and began to tout their editor as the only one authorized by Master. Swamiji was content then to let the public read both versions and decide for themselves.

Master's commentary was written in the same poetic spirit as the *Rubaiyat* itself and Swamiji was careful to preserve not only the meaning, but also the beauty of the way Master expressed it. The resulting book is exquisite. Swamiji decided to make an audio recording of it.

Years earlier, a melody for the quatrains themselves had come to Swamiji in a dream. For the audio book, Swamiji sang each quatrain, accompanied by a tamboura, then read the commentary. It was too complicated for the recording engineers at Ananda, so Swamiji arranged to record at a professional studio in the Bay Area.

Hour after hour, Swamiji stood at the microphone in that rented studio, singing each quatrain, then reading Master's extraordinary commentary. The *Rubaiyat* is no mere tribute to human love. Master showed it to be a divine scripture of the highest order.

Two and half days later, and more than forty years after Master had first asked him to edit the book, Swamiji began reading the commentary on the next to the last quatrain:

> *Ah, Moon of my Delight who knowst no wane,*
> *The Moon of Heav'n is rising once again:*
> *How oft hereafter rising shall she look*
> *Through this same Garden after me—in vain!*

His voice quavered a little, but the commentary was short and he made it through. Then he sang the last quatrain:

> *And when Thyself with shining Foot shall pass*
> *Among the Guests Star-scatter'd on the Grass,*
> *And in thy joyous Errand reach the Spot*
> *Where I made one—turn down an empty Glass!*

When he started reading the commentary, his voice quavered as before, but this time, his feelings were more than he could master. Swamiji started over several times, but to no avail. Tears were rolling down his cheeks. He stood at the microphone sobbing with joy.

"So beautiful," he murmured through his tears. "It is so beautiful. Such a joy to have finished such a great work."

After some minutes, he was able to read again. The emotional overtones in his voice, however, were so great, we knew he would have to do it all over again. It was too much of a contrast to the rest of the book. It was so moving, however, to hear him read in this way, no one dared to interrupt.

When he finished, there was complete silence in the studio. Finally Swamiji asked, "Shall I read that again?" Several people nodded, "Yes." No one wanted to break that sacred silence.

"All of it?" Swamiji asked, meaning everything he'd read since he began to cry. Again we nodded.

Later he said, "No one can imagine the energy it took to do this." He meant not only writing the commentary itself, but all the years of holding fast to what Master had told him to do, in the face of unrelenting persecution from his fellow disciples.

"I couldn't contain my joy," he said. "It wasn't just the fact of having finished this book. It was the joy of being part of such a great, great work."

Special Thanks

Over the years I have had different roles at Ananda. First I was in the financial department. Then I took over the publishing. Now my husband and I lead the Ananda colony and church in Seattle, Washington.

I'm still involved in publishing, though. I coordinate the foreign rights. Swamiji's books are published in 100 different countries and in some 28 languages, so it is almost a half-time job. Foreign rights is the key to spreading the teachings around the world, so Swamiji has always been pleased to see the growth in this aspect of the work.

Many times he has expressed his gratitude to me for all that has been accomplished. But he has never thanked me for doing any one project or any specific thing. What Swamiji says is, "Thank you for *helping.*"

This is the essence of karma yoga: We are all serving—and in that sense helping—God. There is nothing personal about it—not his role, not mine. We are just smoothing the way for *what is trying to happen.*

Often, when a decision has to be made, Swamiji will put it just that way: *"What is trying to happen?"* It is not a question of what "Swamiji wants," or what any of us *want.* This is a divine work. We are all God's instruments.

A few months after he moved to India in 2003, Swamiji came down with a nearly fatal case of pneumonia. He was barely breathing, and had to be rushed to the hospital in the middle of the night. Ever since he had arrived in India his health had been deteriorating.

"Even when I was a young man," Swamiji said, "I found the climate in India difficult. At this age, it may kill me."

Swamiji invited Dharmadas and Nirmala to come from Ananda Village to be leaders of the work in India. Now, a few months after coming to live in a country they had never even visited before, they faced the real possibility that Swamiji's health was not up to the challenge. If he had to leave India, or if the climate killed him, then it would be up to them to make the work happen.

Fortunately, Swamiji recovered. Gradually, his overall health improved, and he didn't have to leave India. But on the day he was checking out of the hospital, after the pneumonia, the future seemed uncertain.

Swamiji was resting on the bed. He asked Nirmala and Dharmadas to come sit on the bed with him. Holding their right hands in both of his, he looked deeply into their eyes.

"This work does not belong to me," he said. "It does not belong to you. This work belongs to Babaji and to Master. It is *their* will we must follow, not our own. If we do that, you'll see that this work will develop beautifully, in ways we can't even imagine now."

This was a dramatic expression of what Swamiji has been saying to me all these years. This is a divine work and it is our privilege to be helping.

~ From Padma ~

March 7, 2004

March 7th is Master's Mahasamadhi, the anniversary of the day of his passing in 1952. *Mahasamadhi* is a great yogi's final conscious exit from this world. A few days before, Swamiji fell and broke a rib. He was still convalescing after a bad case of pneumonia. Now he also had pain from the rib. The pain was so intense at times that he could hardly breathe. This was the first Mahasamadhi since Ananda had begun its work in India, however, and it had to be celebrated. At least, Swamiji decided, he could put in a brief appearance.

Swamiji lived on the top floor of the ashram. To spare him from having to go up and down the stairs, the celebration was held on the roof terrace just outside his door. Two minutes before the satsang was to start, Swamiji said, "I don't know if I can do this." When the hour struck, though, he asked for help getting up from his chair, then, leaning heavily on the arm of a friend, he walked slowly out onto the terrace.

About sixty people were gathered there. As one body they rose to greet him, many coming forward to touch his feet as he moved toward his seat on the dais.

A few hours before, it had been nothing but a bare marble terrace. Now it was an open-air temple, with plants, flowers, candles, pictures of the Masters, and a beautifully decorated chair for Swamiji. Out there under the stars in the balmy night air, it was like being in an astral heaven.

"Please accept my apologies," Swamiji said. "I'm only going to speak for a few minutes." Then, for an hour and fifteen minutes, he talked about Master and his work in India.

Swamiji passed quickly over the events of March 7, 1952, when he had witnessed Master's passing from this world. He wasn't concerned about the past. What he wanted was for us to understand the *living* presence of Master *now*.

A few minutes after Swamiji began to speak, the full moon began to rise behind him. First it peeked over his shoulder, then it glowed behind his head, then it was a shining circle of white light high above him. It was as if Master had come to bless his disciple.

In *The Path*, Swamiji describes how, on July 29, 1949, Master gave a speech at a garden party in Beverly Hills in which he exhorted his listeners to go "North, South, East, and West" to spread the message of Self-realization "everywhere."

In the same spirit, with the same fervor, Swamiji now urged us to give ourselves to the same cause of Self-realization and build a work for Master in India.

In 1949, Master said, "My spoken words are registered in the ether, in the Spirit of God, and they shall move the West."

On March 7, 2004, Swamiji made no such proclamation. Yet to those present it seemed his spoken words were also "registered in the ether, in the Spirit of God," and they will move the *East*.

No Turning Back

"When I was in India forty years ago," Swamiji said, "I traveled around the country and lectured in many cities. Even then, it wasn't easy. At my age now, it would be impossible. How will I be able to reach people?" This was his concern when he left for India in November 2003 to start a work there.

Once he arrived, the solution was obvious. There are several national television stations entirely devoted to religious and spiritual programs. (There was no television when he lived in India forty-five years earlier.) After Swamiji gave a few public lectures in New Delhi, one of those stations offered him a daily half-hour program at a very reasonable rate, about $2000 a month.

To test the water, Swamiji raised enough money from Europe and America to put a show on the air for a few months. He called it *The Way of Awakening* and based it on his book, *Conversations with Yogananda*. He opened every show with a chant and ended it with a song. The songs were recorded in advance, but the chants Swamiji did live each time. He did the show in English. Swamiji speaks some Hindi and Bengali, but English was a better choice. It is so widely spoken in India that it is almost the national language.

After he'd filmed a few shows, one of the cameramen said to Swamiji, "This is the most spiritual program we have ever recorded." Another member of the crew didn't know much English, but he got the vibration, especially from the music. And during the breaks,

Swamiji spoke to him in Hindi. When Swamiji chanted, this man would listen with his eyes closed, often with tears running down his cheeks.

Once the shows began to air, there was an immediate, positive response. People from all over India started calling the ashram. When he went out, strangers began coming up to Swamiji and saying, "I saw you on television." With his American face and orange robes he wasn't hard to recognize. Many were deeply moved to meet him and reverently touched his feet.

Once the concept had proved itself, Swamiji decided to use donations from America to put the show on *two* stations every day, morning and evening at prime times. It would be seen all over India, in many neighboring countries, and, by satellite, even in the United States.

"The most ambitious lecture tour could only reach a few thousand people," Swamiji said. "Through television, I can speak to millions without leaving home.

"If I have 365 shows," Swamiji said, "they can run for years without seeming repetitious." He set aside the month of November to record 235 more—ten shows a day, five days (fifty shows) a week. It was an ambitious schedule, but one of the reasons Swamiji has been able to accomplish so much is that he gives full attention to one project at a time.

The living room of Swamiji's house became a television studio. The furniture was moved out; lights and cameras brought in. The set was a simple, comfortable chair placed on an oriental rug. Next to it was a small table with a picture of Master, a bouquet of flowers, and a copy of *Conversations*. For each show, Swamiji would read an excerpt and comment on it.

Behind Swamiji, as if viewed through a window, was a large picture of the garden at Crystal Hermitage. Around that were a few plants, soft curtains, and a carved Indian screen. Off to one side was a much larger picture of Master that the camera could zoom in on from time to time.

A complicated series of lights and baffles illuminated the set from all angles. Three big cameras were put in place, one directly in front of Swamiji and one on each side. Spectators could sit behind the cameras in chairs and couches against the walls. Having people in the room, listening, helped create a more dynamic atmosphere for Swamiji. Sometimes there were only a handful of spectators, sometimes twenty or more came, comprising a mix of ashram residents, Indian devotees, and visitors from Europe and America.

Swamiji set strict conditions, and repeated them whenever some-one new came in. "You are welcome," he said, "but you must *turn off your cell phone*." (Everyone in India, it seems, carries a "mobile." Phones ring constantly in public places.) "No coughing, no sneez-ing, and no laughing." People found this last one the hardest to follow—Swamiji's humor is irresistible.

He made up a schedule of which excerpt to read and which song would go with it. The songs are all different lengths, so he figured out in advance how long his talk would have to be to accommodate that song. A kitchen timer was set up in front of him, just off camera, so he would know exactly how long he had to speak. Each talk ended promptly on time, and was somewhat less than twenty minutes long.

"How do you know what to say?" someone asked Swamiji. "Usually you tune into the audience, but here you don't have an audience, just a few spectators and a camera."

"When I look into the camera," Swamiji said, "I feel the consciousness of those who will see the program. It's to them I speak. Master tells me what to say."

Conversations with Yogananda is based on notes Swamiji made of his guru's words during the three-and-a-half years Swamiji lived with him. In 365 programs, he reads and comments on almost the entire book. The result is a complete description of Master—his life, his mission, what it was like to live with him, what it means to be his disciple. Swamiji made these shows to build the work in India, but in the process he created a spiritual legacy for the ages.

"In India, I don't have to convince people that these teachings are true," Swamiji said, "or to persuade them of basic concepts like reincarnation, or the need for a guru. It is already part of their culture. I can go deeply into my subject, very quickly."

When he lectures in the West, Swamiji refers to his guru by name, "Paramhansa Yogananda" to a general audience, "Master," when speaking to devotees. In India, he says, "my Guru," like a child talking about his mother.

Before he came to India, Swamiji tended to hold himself in. He rarely revealed the tenderness of his heart and the depth of his own devotion. Now, in India, his eyes often fill with tears and his voice breaks when he speaks of God's love and the grace of "my Guru."

"Of all the countries in the world," Swamiji says, "India feels to me most like home. In America I can share a little of who I am, in Italy I can share more, in India, I can give without reservation."

Swamiji should have added one more instruction for his spectators: "No sobbing." Many times the depth of his feeling touched such a responsive chord in my own heart I could barely see him through my tears.

Between each show, Swamiji would pause for five or ten minutes. Sometimes he stood up, though he seldom left the room. It was very hot in the recording studio, especially for Swamiji, who had to sit in front of the lights. The air conditioner was noisy and had to be turned off when the cameras were on. The moment the recording was over, someone would rush to turn the lights off and the air conditioner on. During the breaks there was always a lot of activity around the perimeter of the room, too, because that was the only time people could go in or out.

Sometimes the technicians had to adjust the equipment, or Swamiji would ask for a cup of tea, in which case the pause would be longer. Usually Swamiji chatted with the spectators until the recording was about to start again. Then he became quiet and concentrated as he reviewed the excerpt and confirmed the title of the song for the next program.

He spoke to the camera directly in front of him. At one point the director said it would be more interesting it he varied the routine and spoke sometimes to the cameras on either side. Swamiji tried it for one show.

Afterwards he said to the director, "I am sure you are right, but I'm very sorry, I can't do it. If I have to think 'Now look to the left, now to the right' I can't keep the same level of inspiration. I am speaking to an audience, not to a camera."

Electricity in India does not always flow steadily. To compensate for intermittent outages, the house had intermediary panels, batteries, and a generator. Still, the wiring was delicate and the crew had to be careful not to blow out the whole system. Several times an outlet would begin to smoke.

Often the recording had to stop because of something to do with the electricity. Swamiji was trying to keep to a strict schedule of seven shows in the morning and three in the afternoon. But if it was interrupted for reasons beyond his control, he accepted it calmly and without complaint.

Once the whole city lost electricity for an entire day. By the end of the morning session, the batteries were depleted. The generator could recharge them, but not while the cameras were running. They had to stop for several hours.

"Call me when you are ready to start again," Swamiji said as he went off to his room.

"It isn't *difficult* for me to do this," Swamiji said. "I mean, it is not hard for me to speak. But it does take a lot of *energy*, and that is what makes it a challenge. And whenever I do something that could help many people, Satan tries to stop me." Often the attempt to stop him is done through his body's weakness.

Since coming to India in 2003, Swamiji had already done much *tapasya*, and his physical reserves were low. In just one year Swamiji had experienced bronchitis, pneumonia, dehydration, a broken rib, several incidents of congestive heart failure, and numerous falls.

Many days, Swamiji's body rebelled against the effort that would be needed to work that day. Yet he had a schedule to follow. Everyone involved tried his best to help him, but the burden was on Swamiji to summon up the strength to carry on. His word is his bond, even to himself. Once he sets his will to something, there is no turning back.

In similar situations in the past, my human heart has quailed and I have urged Swamiji to seek an easier way. Often he has scolded me for my lack of courage. On one notable occasion years earlier, I wanted him to rest, even though he made it quite clear that he intended to go on working. I kept insisting, until finally, with great force, he said to me, "Get thee behind me, Satan!"

I was horrified! "Am I fighting on the wrong side?" I asked.

"Yes!" he said emphatically, "and I *don't* appreciate it."

He needed me to support his resolution, not to give him reasons for abandoning it. By affirming his weakness, I was in effect trying to undermine his will.

Somewhere toward the end of the second week of recording, I fixed breakfast for Swamiji, a bowl of cereal and a glass of juice. It was only a few minutes till the make-up artist came, so I left him alone to eat. When I came back to clear the dishes, the food was untouched. He had his elbows on the table and his head in his hands.

"I couldn't eat," he said. "I don't have enough energy to lift the spoon."

My heart overcame my judgment, and I said to him, "You don't have to do this."

Swamiji said nothing, but I knew I had made a mistake. I was not being a true friend. Somehow Swamiji got himself into the studio. As soon as the camera was turned on, it was if the weakness had never been.

"*I* don't have the strength to do this," Swamiji said later, "But Master does. He always gives me the energy I need."

As the day progressed, the more energy Swamiji put out, the stronger he became. The last shows were among the most dynamic of the whole month. When he exhorted his audience to have the courage to give everything to God, his words rang with the power of his own experience. It was hard to believe that very morning Swamiji hadn't enough energy to lift a spoon.

On many days, Swamiji had to fight the same battle. Satan didn't give up easily. During the last week of recording, Swamiji telephoned Jyotish and Devi in America. He confided to them, "I don't know if I can finish."

Devi said later she was tempted to encourage him to rest, but inner wisdom silenced her. For a moment, neither she nor Jyotish said anything. Then Jyotish responded.

"You have set your will to this," he said. "You *have* to do it."

Again, there was silence. Finally, Swamiji spoke, although he was so moved, he could barely get the words out.

"Thank you, Jyotish," he said. "Everyone tells me to rest. They mean well, but *I can't rest.* I *have* to do this. You understand. That is just what I needed to hear."

Swamiji finished recording the whole year of programs, and they have become, as he knew they would, the cornerstone of Master's work in India. On December 1, 2004, when it was all done, he sent the following note to many of his friends:

> Dear Everybody:
>
> This is an emotional moment for me. I have just finished recording the last of 365 TV programs. I feel I have done a major work for Master, and I am conscious of his happiness in my heart.
>
> There were quite a few days when I didn't think I could carry on. This last day was especially difficult for me—maybe it was my relief at being near the end. But people couldn't see what it cost me; it looked easy. Last July (or thereabouts) when I first decided to do the remaining 235 programs in November, I just didn't dare contemplate the challenge of it: ten programs a day, five days a week, back to back for a whole month and a day.
>
> Last week, to make up for the five extra shows on the last day, I did 13 in one day, and 12 the next. I had many people urging me all month to go slower, but I felt that if I let up I wouldn't be able to come back and finish the whole job.

As Jyotish said, I'll reach more people through these programs than the sum of all the people I've ever spoken to and written for in my whole life.

I felt like weeping at the end, for sheer gratitude at having finished this job for Master. I didn't weep, but, as I said, I feel deeply moved. Quite possibly 200 million people, and even more, will view this program, not only all over India, but also in over 100 other countries.

Jai Guru!

Love,

swami

with Jyotish

Choir of Angels

After a beautiful concert by an Ananda choir, Swamiji said to one of the singers, "You looked like angels. You sounded like angels. That is because you *are* angels."

"If we are," the singer replied, "it is because of you and all you have done to bring out our angelic qualities."

"Well, if you want to put it that way," Swamiji said, "you have to trace it to the true source, which is not me. It is Master."

Last Task

In the fall of 2005, editing Master's commentary on the *Bhagavad Gita* was one of the few unfinished tasks in Swamiji's life as a disciple. It was an assignment given to him by Master more than 50 years before.

Even when Master was still dictating the commentary at his desert retreat in 1950, he had Swamiji editing the portion that had already appeared as articles in the SRF magazine. When the dictation was done, Master had Swamiji work side-by-side with him, every day for two months, helping to edit the newly completed manuscript.

"A new scripture has been born," Master declared ecstatically the day Swamiji arrived to help him. "Millions will find God through this work. Not just thousands—*millions!* I have seen it. I know."

Master wanted the book to be published immediately—before the end of the year. The senior disciple in charge of editing didn't feel the work could be done that quickly. Even two years later, in 1952, when Master passed away, the book still hadn't come out. All sense of urgency died with Master and more than four decades passed before SRF finally published it.

The book was a deep disappointment to Swamiji. "What Master wrote was beautiful, fluent, and easy to understand. SRF has edited it into a scholarly work, difficult to read and hard to understand. Master said, 'Millions will find God through this book.' I don't see how that could happen if this is the only version."

Swamiji prayed to Master for a solution. The *Rubiayat* commentary had been published in the SRF magazine *before* Master died, and was true to his original manuscript. Most of the *Gita* commentary, however, had come out in the magazine *after* Master's passing, and had been highly edited before it saw the light of day.

"If only I had a copy of the original manuscript," Swamiji said. But years passed, and nothing came of that prayer. All the copies were in the hands of SRF, locked in a vault where only a few people had access to them.

Finally Swamiji said, "It could easily take me ten years to write this book. I can't wait any longer."

SRF's version was comprehensive—over 1000 pages of small print in two volumes. Swamiji decided to write a shorter version, *The Essence of the Bhagavad Gita* he would call it, based on the manuscript he had read 50 years earlier, and still vividly remembered.

But for two weeks, Swamiji was hardly able to write a word. "Mostly I just sat and stared at my computer," he said. Finally, on Friday, October 7, 2005, suddenly, "It came." In just a few minutes, he wrote six pages. "I saw it would not be the short book I had imagined, it would be a full commentary."

Swamiji lives in India, just outside New Delhi in a town called Gurgaon, in a house he shares with six others—the leaders of our work in India, plus a secretary, housekeeper, and a nurse, Miriam, who looks after his sometimes-precarious health. Swamiji's office is the only room on the top story of the house, two flights up from ground level.

"As soon as he was done with those first pages," Miriam said, "he brought them downstairs, looking for someone to read them. It was a joy that needed to be shared. Fortunately, several of us were around. It was a thrilling moment."

For the next eight weeks, Swamiji wrote steadily, ten pages a day. Except for some pre-existing engagements, and a daily walk around the block, Swamiji scarcely left the house.

"After being with Krishna in the Infinite," he said. "Why would I want to go gallivanting around on this mud-ball of a planet?"

But he was hardly in seclusion: in those eight weeks he had to play host to more than thirty visitors. Most were key leaders or members of Ananda from America and Europe. In the midst of the writing, he also had to give energy to them.

"Thirty years ago, when I wrote *The Path*," Swamiji said, "I had to stay in strict seclusion in order to hold onto the thread of inspiration. Now I found I could switch back and forth between the different realities. In fact, it was a help to have friends there to read what I had written. It helped keep me grounded in the realities of those who would benefit from what I was writing."

Miriam describes what it was like during those weeks. "Often we would go to bed late, and by early the next morning, there would be ten more pages in the living room for us to read. Swamiji had been up most of the night writing."

"I have to write whenever it comes," Swamiji explained. "This isn't thinking in the ordinary way, it is inspiration. If I don't respond to the inspiration, why would Master talk to me again?"

Even though the book was coming quickly, at first Swamiji was anxious about it. He stated frankly, "I am scared to death of the responsibility." But as the days passed, and the words kept flowing, the anxiety evaporated.

"Inspiration comes to those who are humble about their own achievements and reverential toward the achievements of God," Swamiji said on another occasion.

"The book is being given to me," he said. "Nothing I have ever written has flowed so easily. I pray, and the words are there."

In addition to the commentary, Swamiji also rewrote Master's literal translation of the *Gita* itself, to make it more poetic. Chapter 11 includes a long poem, Arjuna's divine vision of Krishna.

"Usually you can't just sit at a typewriter and write poetry. But I did," Swamiji said. "Master gave it to me."

When he finished Chapter 13, "I went to bed knowing something more was needed," Swamiji said, "but I didn't know what it should be. That night I dreamt the perfect story about a saint and a man called Naresh. When I finished writing it out the next day, I could see that the 'punch line' was missing. Just then, it was given to me. I typed it out as it came to me. The whole *Gita* was like writing music. This is not my book. It is Master's."

Miriam said later, "The night of the day Swamiji started writing, he was so blissful. I was alone with him, attending to various medical duties. He started talking about leaving his body. This isn't the first time he's mentioned it. His body suffers a great deal, and he is 'tired of being tired,' as he puts it. But this was different. It wasn't prompted by how he feels physically.

"He was moved by the thought of finishing his work here and being drawn upward into Master. When he gets into a certain blissful state, his face glows with a beautiful peachy color, a paler version of the orange of his robe. Now that peachy light was everywhere.

"He was talking to me but he kept looking toward the ceiling and to a certain spot by the door. I wondered if he was seeing a vision that wasn't there for my eyes.

"He spoke with such sweet yearning of the day when this life would be done. Until now, he said, he really hadn't been able to think of leaving, because there remained this last, great, unfinished task. Now that the *Gita* was underway, he could think about the time when it would be done. He seemed to be eagerly anticipating a kind of 'divine vacation' with Master.

"But he was also quick to say how happy he is to let his body be used in whatever way God wants to use it, especially to burn up karma for others.

"There is such a feeling of love in his presence. I don't know if love can be seen, but it seems to emanate from Swamiji, in the glow of his skin, and in something so tangible, I can almost touch it. Master's bliss flows through him.

"But it is even more than that. I said to Swamiji, 'It feels like Master is living in the house with us. That he is so overjoyed about this book, he is eagerly running up and down the stairs with you, carrying the pages through your hands for us to read.'

"Quietly, Swamiji said, 'Yes, he is.'"

Long before he started writing the *Gita*, Swamiji was aware that Master had blessed him with a remarkable capacity to remember whatever his guru had said to him.

In *The Path*, Swamiji describes how Master once taught him a few Bengali words. A decade later, when Swamiji went to India for the first time, he remembered them easily. In fact, as Swamiji described it, "I had a clear memory not only of the words, but of the sound of Master's voice saying them."

In 1990, when he wrote *The Essence of Self-Realization: The Wisdom of Paramhansa Yogananda*, Swamiji said, "I wrote that book not only from the notes I had taken during the years I was with Master, but also from my memory of many other occasions when he spoke on the subjects I was writing about.

"While I was working on the book, there was a big snowstorm and for several days, the power was out. I couldn't use my computer; I had to write by hand. In my mind, I could hear Master speaking. Sometimes I had to ask him to slow down. Writing by hand, I couldn't keep up."

Swamiji's remarkable memory encompasses more than just the words of his guru.

"We met with Swamiji to discuss a piece of property we were thinking of buying near Ananda Village," Padma explains. "I had a sheaf of papers in my hand that the Realtor had given me with her business card clipped on top. At one point in the meeting, Swamiji leaned over and glanced briefly at the papers.

"Hours later, we needed to call the Realtor. I was rummaging around in my purse looking for her business card when Swamiji recited her phone number from memory.

"'How do you know her number?' I exclaimed in astonishment. 'You've never called her. You've never even met her!'

"'I saw it on her card this morning,' Swamiji said.

"'But you just glanced at it. You didn't even hold it in your hand,' I exclaimed.

"I didn't *glance* at those papers,' Swamiji replied, 'I *concentrated* on them. It was brief, but it was enough. Awareness doesn't take *time*, it takes *energy*.'"

About writing the *Gita*, Swamiji said, "This must be what Master had in mind from the start. He knew I would end up on my own. That's why he had me there to listen to him dictate the commentary and then gave me the entire manuscript to read. Fortunately, I have a clear memory, and because he asked me to edit, I read with particular care. I can remember what Master said stanza-by-stanza, not every word, but every idea. He must have known that later I would have to write without having seen the manuscript since that time.

"Master can write through me as he wants it *now*. Then I was just a young man without any experience; now I have been a disciple, teaching and writing, for nearly sixty years."

When Swamiji was commenting on that portion of the *Gita* that describes how far the soul can go into delusion, and the suffering that ensues, Pranaba was one of Swamiji's many visitors from America. "When he came downstairs with those pages," Pranaba said, "Swamiji was more subdued than he had been when he was writing other sections of the book. The thought of how much people suffered filled him with compassion. He knew what this book could mean to people, how much it could help them get away from this 'ocean of suffering' as Master called life without God."

Another visitor said, "After the suffering, comes the part in the *Gita* where Krishna says, 'Give me your heart.' When he got there, Swamiji became all love and sweetness. It was like Krishna was living through him."

At the end of the *Gita*, after almost 700 stanzas of profound teaching, Krishna says in essence, "Now that I've given this to you, *do with it what you will.*" In other words, Krishna had total respect for the free will of his disciple.

"When I read that part," Pranaba said, "I told Swamiji, 'This is just the way you have worked with us. This book isn't only the essence of the *Bhagavad Gita*, it is also the essence of Swami Kriyananda.'

"Quietly, Swamiji replied, 'Yes, it is.' I think what he meant was that writing this book has been for him the culmination of a lifetime of discipleship."

It didn't take Swamiji ten years to do the *Gita* commentary. It took eleven weeks—eight weeks of writing and three weeks of editing for a book of more than six hundred pages.

"It was a miracle," Swamiji said simply. "I believe this is the book Master had in mind when he said 'Millions would find God.'"

When the last chapter was done, Swamiji sent out a simple e-mail announcement to his friends.

"I've finished it all! What a historic moment! I am weeping with joy."

with the Gita *manuscript*

He Saw You

Several hundred people came to Ananda Village that weekend to celebrate Swamiji's 77th birthday. Many had been with Swamiji for decades. There was a concert, a festive dinner, Sunday Service, and several smaller gatherings hosted by Swamiji at his home. The culminating event was a garden party at Crystal Hermitage.

Once again, we sang "Happy Birthday" while Swamiji blew out the candles on yet another exquisitely decorated cake. When the refreshments had been served and the entertainment was over, Durga stood at the microphone. Speaking for all of us, in a voice choked with emotion, she expressed gratitude to Swamiji for all he has done to bring Master to us and to help us realize God. The applause went on for several minutes. When it finally died down, he responded.

"If I thought you were celebrating me," Swamiji said, "I would be quite embarrassed. It is not me, however, that we are celebrating. It is all of us and all that we have done together.

"Master told me many times that I had a great work to do. After he died, Rajarsi Janakananda, his spiritual successor, repeated the same words to me, 'You have a great work to do.' Then Rajarsi assured me, 'And Master will give you the strength to do it.'

"Rajarsi was speaking about all of you. *You* are the strength Master has given me. Master saw you, he knew you would come, and that through you, this great work would be done."

~ 7 ~

FOR JOY
I LIVE

"A sad saint is a sad saint indeed!"

St. Francis de Sales

How Are You?

Swamiji had been sick for weeks with a sinus infection and now his heart was giving him trouble.

"How are you today, Sir?" I asked.

"Not well," he said, smiling sweetly, as if what he had just told me was wonderful news. "But what does it matter how I feel now compared to the eternity of bliss toward which we aspire?"

Click. Click. Click. Click

There were no pilot lights on the propane cook stove in Swamiji's dome. At first we used matches to light the burners, then Swamiji bought a device like a pistol that shot a spark out the barrel. You pressed it against the gas ring, turned on the fuel, and pulled the trigger.

Swamiji performed this maneuver effortlessly, but I could never get the hang of it. It took him *one* click. It took me at least a dozen, and still, in the end, I often gave up and used a match. My ineptitude with that thing was a standing joke between us. We often laughed about it, but Swamiji never let me off the hook. He was determined that I learn. I couldn't get away with using a match. His whole house then was just the dome, and wherever he was he could still hear me in the kitchen.

One day when he was in seclusion I came to cook him dinner. He was keeping silence, so he greeted me with folded hands, then went to the sleeping loft to rest until dinner. Everything was fine until I had to put a pot on the stove. With a sigh, I picked up the sparker. Click. Click. Click. Click. Click. Click. Click. Click. It was worse than usual.

Somewhere in the middle of all those clicks, Swamiji came into the kitchen. He took the sparker from my hand and carefully showed me how to use it. As usual, with one click, he lit the burner. I put the pot on the stove and he went back to the loft.

My relief was short lived. A few minutes later, I needed a second burner. I considered changing the menu, looked longingly at the matches, then picked up the sparker.

"Swamiji does this easily," I said to myself. "I'll pretend that I am he." I adjusted my posture to match his straight spine, heart-forward stance. Then, imitating his movements exactly, I lit the burner in one click.

He was in silence, so he couldn't cheer, but from the loft came the sweet sound of Swamiji applauding.

This has been a vivid memory of mine for more than thirty years. I always thought it a charming example of what fun it is to be with Swamiji. But now as I write this, I see he had a serious purpose.

I couldn't use the sparker because I couldn't concentrate long enough to coordinate all the movements. I'd put the barrel to the ring then forget to turn on the gas, or I'd pull the trigger when it was too far away to light. Lack of concentration was a problem in areas of my life that were far more important than cooking. Meditation, for example.

Swamiji couldn't *order* me to concentrate; it was something I had to learn for myself. He didn't want to criticize me directly, he knew I was over-sensitive and easily discouraged. But I did respond well to humor. Because the sparker was a humorous game, I persevered, and eventually I learned to use it, sometimes even in *one* click. It was a small step, but over many years, small steps make a mighty journey.

Pyjamas with Roses

It was late at night, after a lecture, when Swamiji discovered someone had driven off with his car keys. He was on tour, staying an hour out of town. Rather than inconvenience someone by asking him to drive back with the keys, Swamiji accepted our invitation to sleep in the guest room at my in-laws' house where my husband and I were also staying.

None of the men had a spare set of pyjamas to loan him, so I gave Swamiji a pair of mine. I was six months pregnant and a friend had made the pyjamas big enough for me to wear until the baby was born. In fact, I could have carried a three-year old child inside those pyjamas with me. They were huge. The pattern was red roses as big as dinner plates printed on a white background. Very festive.

We had all retired for the night when we heard a gentle knock at our bedroom door. It was Swamiji. "Are you still awake?" he asked in a low voice. "I have something to show you."

When we opened the door, Swamiji sailed in wearing the rose pyjamas, then walked and turned like a runway model showing off his outfit. He knew how ludicrous he looked and hadn't wanted to wait until morning to share the humor with us.

The next day, he also entertained my in-laws with his runway model routine. Then he did his energization exercises and ate breakfast with the family still wearing those ridiculous pyjamas.

My mother-in-law had never met Swamiji before. She was so impressed by his humility and his complete lack of self-importance that she went and found a book of his we had given her as a gift. She had never read it; it had been sitting on her shelf for months. Now she brought it to the breakfast table, and as respectfully as you could speak to someone clad in those rose pyjamas, asked Swamiji to autograph the book for her.

~ From Hridayavasi ~

The Questionnaire

Swamiji does not allow the limitations of his body to define him. When he needed a specialist to do a complicated dental surgery, his usual dentist, Sheri Bernadett, went along to assist.

"First we have to take your medical history," Sheri said. "Do you have heart problems?"

"Yes."

"High blood pressure?"

"Yes."

"Prosthetic surgery?"

"Yes." Both hips had been replaced.

"Other surgery?"

"Yes." Bypass surgery and an artificial valve in his heart.

"Hearing loss?"

"Yes."

"Diabetes?"

"Yes."

"Arthritis?"

"Yes."

On and on it went to the last question. "How would you rate your overall health?"

"Excellent!" Swamiji said. "Just excellent!"

Give Your All

In the summer, Swamiji often invited people over on Saturday afternoons to enjoy the swimming pool at Crystal Hermitage. One afternoon, the men started playing a game of "Horse and Rider." One man would get on the shoulders of another and the two "riders" would wrestle until one or the other was knocked into the water.

Swamiji entered the game as a rider. He is twenty years older than the men he was playing against but he is strong and has enormous will power. Everyone who went up against him was quickly defeated. Of course, the men were a little half-hearted in their efforts. After all, they were fighting against Swamiji.

Then my husband Bharat got into the game. There was nothing half-hearted about the way he played. Bharat loves competition and was determined to win.

I was horrified. It was all in good fun, but pushing and grabbing did not seem to me the way to treat your spiritual teacher. Bharat is strong and he fought hard. It took time for Swamiji to defeat him, but eventually Bharat tumbled into the water, and the game ended with a big splash and then a burst of laughter.

My only comfort was that at least Bharat hadn't won. But I shouldn't have worried. The next day at Sunday Service, Swamiji described the scene in the pool, graciously omitting any reference to who had won or lost. Then he praised Bharat for the determined way he played the game.

"It takes energy to succeed," Swamiji said appreciatively. "If you are going to do something, you should give it everything you've got."

~ From Anandi ~

Handling Pain

One day, when he was living in Italy, Swamiji bit down on a hard piece of bread and broke off a front tooth. The dentist in Gualdo Tadino said, "The break is right at the gum line. It won't do to just glue it back on. I'll have to dig into the jawbone above the gum, kill the nerve, then drill a hole into which I can insert a post, and then glue the tooth onto that post. You'll have to come back four times."

"I don't have that much time," Swamiji said. "Just do the whole job now, without anesthesia."

"It will be very painful!" warned the dentist. "The nerve is alive, and the front teeth are very sensitive."

"I know," Swamiji said. "I've had lots of dental work done this way."

"The dentist," Swamiji told us later, "seemed to want to prove he'd been right. He went at it rather more roughly, I think, than was necessary. When he cut the live nerve and pulled it out, he waved it above me so that two friends of mine, who were in the same room, could see what he'd done and appreciate the full extent of my 'ordeal.'"

Throughout it all, Swamiji remained calm and unmoving. The dentist was astounded.

"Once the procedure started, I thought you would *have* to take anesthesia," he said afterwards. "How were you able to bear the pain?"

"I thought about God," Swamiji replied.

Later, Swamiji said, "I didn't want to explain it to the dentist. He wouldn't have understood. But what I did was simply broaden my reality base. I saw that fleeting pain as just a passing phase in a long life. The chair I was sitting in, and the operation itself, were like mere dots on the panorama of that life. In that way, I didn't focus my reality on what was happening at that moment, but on a longer time span.

"This is the other side of the teaching to 'be here now': Be in the *unchanging* here, and in the *unchanging* now. Live *in*, but not *for*, the moment."

The Electric Parade

When Swamiji went to Los Angeles in 1973 to speak at a "New Age Fair" and give a few other lectures, about a dozen of us went with him to help. When the programs were over, we stayed an extra day to go to Disneyland. Nowadays, Disneyland includes many worldly aspects of popular culture. In those days, it was more simple and innocent. Swamiji loved the child-like spirit and the uncompromising way Walt Disney had carried out his vision.

"He never settled for 'good enough,' Swamiji said, "not even in little things. For example, look at the background characters in those elaborate rides. You see them for just a moment, but the expressions on their faces, their costumes, their antics are all perfect. Someone of lesser vision would have cut corners, but not Walt Disney. And the people who work at Disneyland are always smiling and helpful, true karma yogis."

For his lectures, Swamiji wore his orange robes, and we also wore Indian clothes: sarees for the women, cotton "pyjama" style shirts and pants for the men. For some reason, we decided to wear these clothes to Disneyland.

Swamiji had a definite plan for the day. As soon as one ride ended, he made a beeline for the next. He chose the charming, beautiful, or amusing ones rather than those that were merely thrilling. This was before arthritis made walking difficult for him, and he could go far and fast. It took time for a dozen people to disembark, so it often happened that we were strung out behind him like a family of ducklings as we hurried to keep up. Sometimes we held hands so as not to get separated in the crowd. With our unusual garb we were quite a spectacle. We were having so much fun, however, that people smiled as we hurried past them.

One of the highlights of the day in Disneyland is the "Electric Parade," which happens just after dark. Beautiful floats and costumed characters covered with twinkling lights march down "Main Street." Because there were so many of us, we went an hour early, when the sidewalk was still empty, to stake out our place. We had an hour before the parade started, so we stood quietly watching the hundreds of people from many countries enjoying Disneyland that day.

"Imagine *being* every one of these people," Swamiji said. "Not merely *loving* them, *being* them. That is God's consciousness. And it is Master's."

Then he sat down on the sidewalk and began to meditate. We had been following him all day, so, naturally, we also sat to meditate. As the hour passed, our little group gradually became an island of meditating yogis surrounded by a sea of people gathered to watch the parade. Our inward mood was so deep, however, that we didn't notice. Finally, when the parade was right in front of us, the mood shifted. We opened our eyes, stood up, and finished our happy day in Disneyland.

Fine.

In 1995, Swamiji visited Swami Chidananda in Rishikesh, India. They had met more than forty years before, when both were young monks. Chidananda is one of the best-known disciples of the great yogi, Swami Sivananda. He is also president of the Divine Life Society, one of the largest spiritual societies in India and one of the most well respected in the world.

There is much that is similar in the lives of these two swamis, one Indian, one American. Both became disciples and monks at a young age. To each has fallen the lion's share of responsibility for carrying on his guru's work. Both lead international organizations and are known and revered by thousands of people around the world.

Swamiji describes Chidananda as "The monk I respect most in all of India." The two met occasionally over the years, but not often, and were seeing each other now after a long separation. They greeted each other with folded hands and a long calm look into one another's eyes. They sat down together on cushions placed on the floor with a group of devotees crowded in a semi-circle around them.

Swamiji spoke first. "And how is the Divine Life Society?" he asked Chidananda.

With an amused half smile, Chidananda said, "Fine," as if he were commenting on the comfort of his cushion, rather than the state of his life's work.

Then, with a twinkle in his eye, as if to say, "I've caught the ball and now I'll toss it back," Chidananda asked Swamiji, "And how is Ananda?"

In perfect imitation of Chidananda's response, Swamiji said, "Fine."

Then both swamis began to chuckle, and the chuckle grew into soft, musical laughter.

Suddenly I "got the joke," and felt a rising joy from my heart to my spiritual eye. The swamis had come to a perfect understanding. Your "life's work"? My "life's work"? What does it matter?

What was delightful in them was not so much what each had *accomplished*, but what each had *become*.

with Swami Chidananda

Overcoming Karma

When Swamiji had hip replacement surgery, he did it with a spinal block rather than taking general anesthesia. "I don't like to be unconscious," Swamiji said. "It was a little disconcerting to hear all the sawing and hammering during the operation. I kept expecting to hear the cry, 'Timber!'"

In one of those operations, however, the anesthesia wore off too soon. By the time they were sewing him up, he could feel them stitching.

"I didn't say anything," Swamiji said, "because at that point they couldn't have given me another spinal block; they'd have had to put me under—something I didn't want. Yes, it was a bit painful, but not very. I just thought about other things."

In the recovery room after surgery, the anesthesiologist came in to check on him. "Can you wiggle your toes?" he asked. Swamiji easily moved his whole foot. The doctor paled. A spinal block wears off from the hips down. If Swamiji could already move his foot that meant the anesthesia had worn off while he was still in the operating room.

Moments later, Swamiji happened to see the anesthesiologist leaning over a nearby bed, his face and posture expressive of mental shock.

"What anesthesia does is disconnect the senses from the brain so there is no experience of pain," Swamiji said. "Even without disconnecting the senses, one can rise above pain by simply not defining it as such. Of course, that takes willpower. I'd rather use willpower for such a process, however, than take a drug."

Someone once asked Swamiji, "How can one tell when he has overcome a karma?"

"When one is no longer afraid of it," Swamiji replied.

Most people fear physical pain. Life usually brings only occasional opportunities to face this fear. Thus, the karma lingers. Swamiji tells us about times like these, when he has deliberately undergone painful procedures without anesthesia, to inspire us with the same courage to face our own fears. Few of us have accepted this particular challenge!

Star Player

When Donald [Swamiji] was fifteen years old, he was playing tennis with a fellow student at Kent School in Connecticut.

"I thought I was the better player," Swamiji says now. "To prove it, I put all my energy into what I thought would be a terrific stroke. Unfortunately, instead of keeping the racket level and parallel to the ground, as you are supposed to do, I executed a 'vicious' uppercut. I missed the ball and smashed the racket into my face, hitting my nose so hard I broke it.

"I lay on the ground in some pain, with blood spurting out of my nose. But the situation struck me as so funny I couldn't help laughing at the absurdity of it."

Swamiji appreciates a good joke, even if the joke is on him.

Retirement

Age has not diminished Swamiji's capacity to work. Instead of slowing down, his creative output has increased.

On his 65th birthday, a devotee said jokingly, "Sixty-five? Time for you to retire."

"Yes, time to retire from ego," Swamiji replied.

Eggnog

For the community Christmas Eve party, Swamiji suggested we serve alcohol-free eggnog. I was in charge of the Retreat kitchen, but I didn't know how to make eggnog, so he sent me a recipe (known as "Swamiji's recipe," though he always said he got it from the bulletin board at a supermarket!). Before I came to Ananda, I was a bit of a fanatic about diet. Master recommended a more moderate approach, and Swamiji wanted the Retreat kitchen to reflect Master's guidelines, not the rules I was inclined to impose. I knew Swamiji was right, but sometimes I rebelled anyway.

A key ingredient for the eggnog was Eagle Brand Sweetened Condensed Milk. But it came in a can and was made with sugar. According to my system, these were two strikes against it. So I substituted a thick brew of powdered milk and natural honey, which I thought would be healthier. I didn't take into account how it might taste. In fact, it tasted *awful*. The milk was chalky, and the honey was as strong as molasses.

On Christmas Eve morning it began to snow. Swamiji lived at Ayodhya—over the hill from the main village—and in the late afternoon Seva drove him to the Retreat in her Volkswagen Bug. By then there were nearly blizzard conditions. Swamiji came to the kitchen to see how things were going.

We talked a bit about the party. Then he said, "If the eggnog is ready, perhaps I could have some now?"

"Of course, Sir." I filled a cup for him.

He took a small sip. "Hmmm," he said, "It doesn't taste the way I remember it." Then ever so gently, he spat the mouthful into the sink. "Is this the recipe I sent you?"

"Not quite," I admitted, and explained what I had done.

"Hmmmm," Swamiji said again. "I am not sure people will like it. Perhaps we should think about making it again. Do you have any Eagle Brand here?"

Of course I didn't.

"What do you think, Seva? Would they have it in North San Juan?" North San Juan consisted of a gas station and a mini-market, but it was ten miles closer than the big supermarket in Nevada City.

"Sir, there is a blizzard going on outside," I said.

"Oh, Seva is a good driver, and that VW of hers can go anywhere," Swamiji said breezily. Then, more seriously he added, "She'll be fine."

A minute later, Seva was out the door and on the road. An hour and a half later she returned with everything we needed for the eggnog. Almost miraculously, she had found it all in North San Juan. Swamiji sat in the kitchen and we chatted amiably while I poured the first batch of eggnog down the drain and made it all over again, this time according to the recipe.

After the party, many people thanked me for the eggnog. "It really felt like Christmas," they said.

Swamiji never scolded me or said an unkind word on the subject, but I got the point. "A pure *heart* is the way to God," Master said, "not a pure *stomach*."

Oh, Never Mind

My mouth sometimes gets ahead of my mind and ill considered words get me into trouble. After I had been at Ananda for a few years, I came up with what I thought was a brilliant plan to make myself slow down. Whenever I realized I was talking without thinking, I would stop immediately—in the middle of a sentence, even in the middle of a word. "Oh, never mind," I would say, putting my hand over my mouth.

I was working for Swamiji as his secretary. Every afternoon I would go to his house to deliver the mail. Several others would usually be there, too. We would have tea with Swamiji, give him the news of the day, and talk about many things. In keeping with my new plan, I would sometimes stop what I was saying with an, "Oh, never mind."

This went on for several weeks. One afternoon, Swamiji began to speak to me very seriously.

"I was meditating this afternoon," he said, "and Babaji came to me. He had a message for you."

I had never heard Swamiji say anything like this before. I could hardly breathe.

"Babaji told me to tell you," Swamiji paused, then lifted his hand; just before covering his mouth he said, "Oh, never mind."

I began to laugh and so did Swamiji.

"You did that very well!" I said. "My heart is pounding." Then I asked, "Is it that annoying?"

"Yes," Swamiji said. "Please stop."

If he had told me I was behaving like an idiot, I would have been so embarrassed it would have taken me weeks to recover. But through humor, he knew he could reach me. Of course, I never did it again.

with Asha

Root Canal

"Can we do this with no anesthetic?" Swamiji asked his dentist, Sheri Bernadett. She was going to do a root canal for him.

"We can," she said, obviously reluctant. "I have done it that way before, but not often. I think I'll be more uncomfortable than you will be, but if you can do it, I can do it."

Swamiji had a headset and a small tape recorder. "This is the master tape of my newest album. I want to see if the mix is right," he said.

Sheri said later, "He sat through the whole procedure with the headphones on. He didn't fidget, in fact he didn't move. He hardly seemed aware of what was going on in his mouth. I was close enough to hear the music and it was so beautiful, it calmed me down, too, and I stopped worrying about what he might be feeling."

Attracting a Husband

A woman at Ananda longed to be married, but she couldn't seem to find the right man. A friend said, "To draw the right person, you have to be very specific about what you want."

So the woman made a list of all the qualities she wanted in a husband. The list came to three pages. Later she showed it to Swamiji.

He read it carefully, then said to her, "My dear, you are asking for Jesus Christ to be your husband! And Jesus Christ would not marry you!" Then he added, "And even if he would, you wouldn't be happy with him. You need a husband closer to your own level of consciousness."

She took Swamiji's advice, tore up the list, and wrote, "I want a husband who loves God and has a good sense of humor."

Not long afterwards, a man with these and many other fine qualities came into her life and she has been happily married to him ever since. (Curiously, her husband's birthday is Christmas Day, December 25!)

With Cream, or Without?

On one side of an endless merry debate were those who took tea *with* milk and coffee *with* cream. On the other side were those who took them *without*. Swamiji and I were steadfastly *with*; Jyotish and others were equally steadfastly *without*. There was much merriment as each side tried to prove the spiritual superiority of its own choice.

One day there was no cream or milk in the house. It was time for tea, the nearest market then was twenty miles away, there was no choice: *all* of us had to go *without*. I was sitting quite near Swamiji, and with a great show of reluctance, we lifted our cups at the same time and took a sip of tea *without*.

It was *delicious!* I could see Swamiji felt the same. "Say nothing," he whispered urgently, with a surreptitious smile. "Think of the implications!" With my eyes I assured Swamiji, "I'll never reveal the secret, not even if they torture me!"

The apex of absurdity was reached, however, a few weeks before the wedding of Jyotish and Devi (Spring 1975). It was an ideal match. Swamiji gave them his heartfelt blessings; the whole community was delighted. Jyotish and a few others had come to Swamiji's house for a meeting. As the meeting ended, Swamiji lapsed into silence. He sat staring at the floor, as if trying to decide whether or not to speak. Then, with a deep sigh, he looked sadly at Jyotish.

"I don't see how this marriage can work out," he said. "How can Devi be happy with you? You'll never be able to say to her, "*You're the cream in my coffee*"!

Swamiji didn't speak this line, however, he *sang* it. He went on to finish the verse from the 1920s popular song:

You're the cream in my coffee.
You're the salt in my stew.
You will always be my necessity,
I'd be lost without you.

We were laughing so hard we could hardly hear him. We asked him to sing it again, and he gladly obliged.

with Jyotish and Devi

Walking Laps

After I had emergency surgery for a burst appendix, Swamiji invited me to recuperate in the guestroom at the Crystal Hermitage. He also was recovering from surgery and both our doctors had prescribed walking a certain distance every day to hasten the healing process.

It was the middle of winter, much too cold to walk outside, so we did indoor "laps": Circle the living room, up the stairs, through the dining room, around the kitchen then back again.

I enjoyed this blissful interlude with Swamiji, but I also felt guilty. My workmates were all putting in long hours to meet an important deadline. It frustrated me that I couldn't help them.

"I feel so useless," I said to Swamiji. (I am inclined to think I have to earn God's love.)

With a twinkle in his eye, Swamiji replied, "You *are* useless. Why hide from the truth?"

We both began to laugh. Two near invalids, already staggering as we walked around the Hermitage, and now laughing so hard we could barely walk at all.

The surgery did diminish my capacity to work. That moment with Swamiji helped me accept what I had become. Just because my outer circumstances were different, that didn't have to change my inner joy.

~ From Elizabeth Palmer ~

A Cup of Coffee

It was only 5am and Swamiji was already dressed and ready to go to the airport to catch an early plane to Europe. With my new espresso machine, I was making him a cappuccino.

I was in a hurry and started to remove the container full of used coffee grounds before the steam had dissipated. Swamiji, who had more experience with these kinds of machines, said, "Better not..."

At that moment, the pressure from the suddenly released steam blew the container off the machine, and launched a soggy projectile of hot coffee grounds that hit Swamiji squarely on the chest.

He didn't even flinch, just calmly finished his sentence.

"...do that," he said, without missing a beat.

Cheerfully, then, he gave me the shirt off his back. I quickly washed, dried, and ironed it, and we still made it to the airport in time.

Ringing Mobile

Several hundred people were gathered at the Bristol Hotel, in Gurgaon, India, listening to Swamiji speak. It was March 2005, more than a year after he had moved to India to start Ananda's work there.

The occasion was the first annual International Ananda Convocation in India to celebrate Master's Mahasamadhi. Devotees had come from Europe and America to join their Indian brothers and sisters for the event.

Except for Swamiji's voice, the room was silent, the audience spellbound, hanging on his every word. Suddenly, the inward mood was shattered by the ringing of a telephone. Cell phones—"mobiles" as they are called in India—are ubiquitous there; in public places they often sound incessantly.

Sternly, Swamiji asked that the phone be turned off.

Everyone with a phone checked his or her mobile to make sure it was not the culprit. Still the ringing persisted.

"Would someone please do something about this matter?" Swamiji said again. Then, with a look of sudden comprehension, he reached into his own pocket.

"Oh!" he said. "It is *my* phone."

The room rang with laughter, Swamiji enjoying the joke as much as anyone. Divine Mother, he felt, was playing with him.

Amplified by the microphone, Swamiji's voice could be heard above the laughter. But he wasn't speaking to the audience. They were listening in on a private conversation he was having with Divine Mother. In an intimate tone, in a voice rich with appreciation, he complimented Her.

"Very good," he said. "That was *very* good. One of the best."

Saved by a Nose

I had been living with AIDS for four years, and now I also had spinal meningitis. By the time my friends got me to the Emergency Room at the hospital, my condition was so serious even a trip in the elevator to Intensive Care would have taken too much time away from the immediate need to save my life. Doctors, nurses, admitting administrators, and a crowd of Ananda friends surrounded me as I was wheeled into a small room near the entrance.

The meningitis had caused my brain to swell, creating a pain that was indescribable. I was dehydrated, my blood pressure was non-existent, and I was going in and out of consciousness.

The administrator kept asking for my Blue Shield Insurance card, while nurses poked needles into me again and again in a desperate effort to find a vein that hadn't collapsed so they could start an IV.

Not realizing the seriousness of the situation, a well-meaning friend had brought a bouquet of helium balloons—cheerful faces painted on a red and gold surface. In my delirium, they looked like astral bogeymen hovering on the ceiling, taunting me as I prepared to exit from this world.

Thinking that the end was near, a friend started leading me in a visualization down the tunnel of light into the astral world. Vital signs and hope were dropping.

Every thought echoed good-bye.

At that moment, Swamiji walked in. He sat down on a chair by the bed, wedged in between the doctors and nurses who were frantically working on me. I was able to open my eyes enough to acknowledge his presence.

My extremities had already begun to die. My hands and feet had turned blue, my nose was bright purple, and the color was spreading across my cheeks. I was a frightening spectacle.

Swamiji looked carefully at my face, then he smiled and said, "Happy, you look like Rudolph, the Red-Nosed-Reindeer!"

At these words, the whole room froze, as if someone had pushed a Cosmic Pause Button. Then I smiled, and a surge of energy went through me that allowed me to laugh. Some of the nurses laughed, too, and everyone began to relax, easing into Swamiji's aura of calm, detached acceptance.

At that point, everything changed. The nurse found a vein, the administrator found my insurance card, the IV started, my blood pressure began to rise, and hope returned.

Swamiji taught me many lessons that day. The most cherished among them is the simple thought: The way to overcome negativity and fear is to meet it head-on with joy.

~ From Happy Winningham ~

Home Sweet Home

"Swamiji's house" refers to three places on three continents. In America at Ananda Village, it is *Crystal Hermitage*. In Europe near Ananda's retreat in Assisi, Italy, it is *Seva Kutir*. (A *kutir* is a cottage, and *seva* means "selfless service to God.") In India in Gurgaon, a city just south of New Delhi where Ananda's work is centered, it is *Guru Kripa* (Guru's Grace).

Although these houses are referred to as "Swamiji's," it is a principle of his not to own property. "I am a monk," he writes in his *Last Will, Testament, and Spiritual Legacy*, "and therefore possess no personal property of any kind, having given to God everything I own, and indeed my entire life." The copyrights to all his books and music are held in a trust created for that purpose. Crystal Hermitage is owned by Ananda Village; Seva Kutir, by an individual in that community. The title to Guru Kripa is in Swamiji's name, but only until a proper trust can be established, then Swamiji wants the title transferred to the trust.

Crystal Hermitage started as a single dome. (The story of its evolution from humble beginnings to its present spacious beauty is the subject of the book, *Space, Light & Harmony*.) In 1968, a friend of Swamiji's from New York City came to visit Ananda. There he had a vision in which Master told him, "Build Kriyananda's home." He was a skilled carpenter and offered his services. The original dome cost $5000, including furnishings.

Fifteen years later, after both his parents died, Swamiji used most of the inheritance he received to build Crystal Hermitage as it is now. The original dome is the living room of the Hermitage.

"During his lifetime," Swamiji said, "my father never donated any money to Ananda. I believe that by the end of his life he was impressed by what I had accomplished, but he never understood what I was doing, or why. He definitely did not approve of the fact that I never accumulated any money of my own. Everything I earned I put back into Ananda. Once I had to appeal to him for help to avert a potential health crisis. In exasperation he responded, 'You simply *must stop* giving all your money away.'

"I don't think his soul would have rested in peace if I had used his money for Ananda. And my soul wouldn't rest in peace if I didn't. The solution was to build Crystal Hermitage and the gardens that surround it. I have an apartment there, so it is my home. It also serves as the spiritual center of the community. In this way it satisfies both my father and me."

To Swamiji, the garden is the heart of Crystal Hermitage. "Give my love to the garden," is how he sometimes ended his phone calls from Italy when speaking to the friend who took care of the Hermitage grounds.

Even during the early years when he was building Ananda in America, Swamiji also traveled and lectured in Europe. In the mid-80s, when Ananda began a retreat center there—first in Como, then in Assisi, Italy—Swamiji began staying in Europe for several months at a time. In June 1996, he was having lunch at the Ananda Retreat in Assisi, when a woman visiting there for the first time sat down across the table from him.

"Why don't you come settle in Italy?" she asked Swamiji.

To her surprise, he replied, "That's a good idea. I think I will."

The decision was not so sudden as it appeared. For some time, the thought had been growing in Swamiji's mind. Her question merely confirmed what he already felt to be Divine Mother's will. Soon after, she also moved to the community, and in time received the spiritual name Premi.

"Those were the first words I ever spoke to Swamiji," Premi said later. "Now he jokes, 'I moved to Italy because Premi asked me to.' I am happy to take the credit, but it was Divine Mother who asked him through me. I was astonished when I heard the words coming out of my mouth."

There was no suitable place at Ananda Assisi, however, for Swamiji to live. Most of the housing is rented from a neighboring landlord. Whenever Swamiji came to visit, someone would vacate his home so that Swamiji would have a place to stay.

Hours after Premi suggested he come live in Italy, a devotee in Germany called Swamiji. "It is important that you move to Europe *now*," she said emphatically. "I can't afford to give you money, but I can loan you what you need to buy land and build a house for yourself near the community."

"The work in America is going well," Swamiji explained, when he announced that he was moving to Italy. "Those who are in charge of our communities make the same decisions I would. My presence in America, even at The Expanding Light retreat at the Village, doesn't have that much impact on how the work goes.

"On the whole continent of Europe, however, I am the only direct disciple of Master who is teaching and available to the public. When I am at our retreat in Italy, people come from many different countries to see me. If I live there, Master's work will grow all over Europe."

There were other reasons as well. Swamiji had long since turned over to others the responsibility for running Ananda Village. For years before, however, he had been at the heart of everything that happened there. As long as he continued to live at Crystal Hermitage, people would continue to ask for his input on personal and community matters. It was a hard habit to break, even for Swamiji.

"I want to help people," Swamiji said simply.

His apartment at Crystal Hermitage is completely private. Looking out the window, all he sees is a vast expanse of national forest and the Yuba River in the canyon below. From inside the apartment, he can't hear anything that is going on elsewhere in the Hermitage. The community facilities, however, are just a few steps outside his door, so even when he is alone, he is still surrounded by the vibrations of Ananda.

"Ananda Village is important," Swamiji said, "but it is only one part of the work Master has given me to do. What I feel Master wants from me now is, through my writing, to reach out to the whole world. In order to do that, my consciousness has to be free from any limiting influence, even the influence of the community I myself founded. The solution is for *me* to move."

The community in Italy had developed without Swamiji's direct involvement, so they didn't have the same habit of seeking his advice on so many matters. He could spend most of his time alone writing and then be available to guests and residents on the weekends.

An isolated piece of land was found about a half mile from the retreat. It was close enough for the community to provide the friendship and support Swamiji needed, and far enough away to give him the freedom to think in new ways. The loan from Germany would cover the cost. It was more land than he needed, and the extra portion could be subdivided and sold to help pay back the loan. The land was purchased in the name of an Ananda member. Swamiji paid back the price of both the house he built and the land it sits on within a year.

For years, Swamiji had been interested in houses made from pre-fabricated kits as a way for Ananda to build quickly and economically. In his travels around the world he had seen several beautiful models. No one, however, had taken up the idea. This was his chance to try it out. The core of Seva Kutir is a kit based on a design developed in Sweden.

The house isn't large; Kutir is an apt name for it. Upstairs, there are three rooms radiating off a cozy living room. Downstairs, there is a meeting room large enough to hold several dozen people, and a spacious office where Swamiji writes. Ananda builders came from all over the world. With the help of the kit, the house went up in record time.

Seva Kutir proved to be just the sanctuary Swamiji had hoped for. It is well off the main road, surrounded by woods and open fields. Even the phone rang only occasionally, and then it was usually a call from America. In this quiet haven, he wrote some of his most profound books, including many with a notably universal appeal, such as *Hope for a Better World, The Promise of Immortality, The Hindu Way of*

Awakening, a new edition of *Out of the Labryrinth,* and *Conversations with Yogananda,* among others.

His secluded life at Seva Kutir, however, ended abruptly in October 2003, on the very day he completed *Conversations with Yogananda.* When he was a young disciple, Master said to him, "Write down what I say." The understanding was that someday Swamiji would write about his guru.

"For fifty years," Swamiji said later, "the notebooks in which I recorded Master's words were my most cherished possession. I looked after them the way a father would attend to a sickly child."

Some of the contents of the notebooks appeared in his auto-biography, *The Path,* and also in *The Essence of Self-Realization: The Wisdom of Paramhansa Yogananda.* Much material remained, however. *Conversations with Yogananda* offers the rest of what was in those notebooks.

When he was in the last stages of writing *Conversations,* Swamiji felt an inward call from Master to go to India and complete the work he had had to leave unfinished forty years earlier when he was expelled from SRF. One hour before friends from India and America converged at Seva Kutir to discuss plans for that work, Swamiji finished the last page of *Conversations.* A few weeks later, in November 2003, he left Italy to live in India.

"How long are you going to be in this country?" Indian devotees asked Swamiji.

"For the rest of my life," Swamiji replied. "India is my home now."

"Even though I told them I intended to stay," Swamiji said, "I could see they didn't believe me. One way to prove that we weren't going to leave was to buy a home of our own. In India, people live in the same house for generations. The Indians needed to see that we were committed before they would be willing also to commit themselves."

Devotees all over the world were as eager as Swamiji to get Ananda going in India and willingly donated the money needed to buy a house there. It is called *Guru Kripa* because it is a gift from Master to serve the work in India.

The harsh climate and the stress of starting a new work at his age had already taken a toll on Swamiji's health. It was no longer practical for him to live alone. Fortunately, Guru Kripa is much larger than Seva Kutir or than his apartment at Crystal Hermitage. Six people live there with him. They include Dharmadas and Nirmala, the leaders of Ananda's work in India.

"The house was brand new and had to be completely furnished," Dharmadas said. "It was a spiritual lesson in itself to see how Swamiji did it."

Most people, when they shop, like to look around before making a selection. Swamiji goes by intuition. Even if he has never been in a store before, or has nothing particular in mind when he walks in, he usually goes directly to the item he will buy.

Even for a large purchase like a new computer, Swamiji uses the same method. One day he went into a huge electronics store and walked right to the model he wanted. It took less than five minutes. Swamiji knows very little about computers and relies entirely on the expertise of his secretary, who wasn't with him. Later, however, his secretary researched the options and confirmed that Swamiji had intuitively picked out just the model he himself would have recommended.

In furnishing Guru Kripa, Dharmadas said, "Swamiji was involved in almost every aesthetic decision. There were so many choices, yet he always seemed to know exactly what was needed—clear, beautiful colors, and fabrics and fixtures that reflected light, like brass, silk, and crystal. I came to appreciate just how much Swamiji lives in a world of color and light."

In *The Path,* Swamiji describes himself when he was a child. "Beautiful colors thrilled me almost to ecstasy," he wrote. "I would cover a table down to the floor with a colorful American Indian blanket, then crawl inside and fairly drink in the luminous colors. At other times, gazing into the prism formed by the broad edge of a mirror on my mother's dressing table, I would imagine myself living in a world of rainbow-colored lights."

Swamiji would only go to stores where the vibrations were uplifting and he was treated like a friend, not merely like a customer. Even if there was good merchandise at a better price somewhere else, friendship and the quality of the energy were more important to him.

One store in particular won his loyalty. The owner attributes the success of his entire business to the blessing of having Swamiji shop there. Even now, the manager personally makes any deliveries needed at Swamiji's home in order to have his *darshan.*

For the shared rooms in Guru Kripa, Swamiji chose a soft golden color, enlivened with touches of burgundy and cherry red. There isn't enough land around Guru Kripa to have a proper garden, so Swamiji brought the garden inside in the patterns of many of the curtains and carpets.

In the main living room, the sheer curtains that give privacy in the daytime are covered with hand-painted flowers. The heavier drapes, drawn in the evening, are made of silk and reflect the lamplight in such a way that the whole wall seems to glow. In his office, the curtains are embroidered with flowers in shades of blue and white. In his bedroom, over a large curved window, the drapes are a lavender jacquard with a pattern of irises. At night, the streetlight glows through the fabric and, from inside the room, the curtained window looks like a wall of luminous flowers.

In *Space, Light, and Harmony,* Swamiji makes the point that it is helpful to keep a sense of humor about your home as well, at least in some area. Ananda Village is nearly 200 miles from the ocean. At Crystal Hermitage, therefore, at the bottom of an internal stairwell, Swamiji created his his own private "beach," with a photomural of the ocean and a sandbox with sand and shells from Hawaii. To complete the effect, he added a recording of surf that goes on and off with the light switch.

In Guru Kripa, Swamiji installed a fake fireplace in an upstairs sitting area. The temperature hovers around 100 degrees for months at a time, so a fireplace can only be a joke. The impression of "glowing logs" is created by colored lights and paper.

When Swamiji and the group from Ananda first moved to India, someone asked him, "Ashrams in India are often quite austere, sometimes just bare concrete rooms with straw mats. That is not how we live in America or Europe. What is appropriate for us here?"

"We should be ourselves," Swamiji said simply. "Everything we do, including the way we live, should be a sincere expression of our consciousness. Even if it is different from what people are used to, they will feel our sincerity, and what we do will feel appropriate to them."

And so it has proved. A friend remarked, "You could entertain the prime minister of India, or the simplest sadhu from Rishikesh, and both would feel equally at home in Guru Kripa."

On another occasion, Swamiji said, "India is too important to the world to remain impoverished forever. There is a new consciousness emerging in the country now. Master's teaching is not a new *religion*. It is, however, a *new expression*. We are not here for those who look to the past. It is the *forward*-looking people of India we have come here to reach."

Even though Swamiji describes Guru Kripa as "one of the most beautiful houses I have ever lived in," he relates to it with the same detachment he felt for both Crystal Hermitage and Seva Kutir.

"I could walk away in an instant and never look back," Swamiji said. This is no idle comment. Already he has done it twice, first leaving Crystal Hermitage for Italy, then Seva Kutir for India.

"Detachment does not mean lack of *commitment*," Swamiji said. "You have to say 'Yes!' to life and the only way to do that is to give yourself completely. Every night, though, give back to God all your thoughts and feelings, and whatever little bit of this world He has made you responsible for during the day. Whether you live in a palace or in a cave, spiritually the only thing that matters is that you remain inwardly free."

~ 8 ~

THROUGH
ALL TRIALS
I SING
THY NAME

"Where there is dharma [right action],

there is victory."

Indian saying adopted by Swami Kriyananda
as a guiding principle

Tapasya

When Sant Keshavadas, a well-known spiritual teacher from India, came to visit Ananda Village in the late 1970s, he was given a grand tour of the community. Impressed by what had been accomplished in such a relatively short period of time, he exclaimed, "Creating this community required a great deal of *tapasya*."

"Yes," Swamiji said quietly.

Tapasya is a Sanskrit word usually defined as *austerity*. It is equally true to say that *tapasya* means *devotion*.

"Some Christians believe that God demands suffering in exchange for his blessings," Swamiji explained on another occasion. "This is not true, nor is it what Jesus taught. To accomplish anything in this world, however, does require sacrifice. You have to renounce lesser desires—even real needs—in order to focus your energy on achieving the goal you set for yourself.

"Others may define such renunciation as suffering. To the devotee, however, if his attitude is right, it is not suffering at all. It is joyful self-offering to God. That is why *tapasya* can be defined as both austerity and devotion.

"The scriptures and epics are filled with heroes and devotees who do 'penance,' as it is called in the West, to strengthen themselves and draw the grace of God. You don't have to go out looking for *tapasya*, though. It also comes of itself.

"Whether you call it Satan, the dark force, human jealousy, or human ignorance, any effort to do good in this world sets in motion a counter force that tries to keep that good from manifesting. Sometimes God Himself puts obstacles in the way of the devotee in order to test his sincerity and to help him build the inner strength he needs."

Peter Caddy, one of the founders of the Findhorn community in Scotland, came to visit Swamiji. Just a month earlier, the brand new temple at Findhorn had been burned to the ground by an arsonist. Peter told the story of this recent loss without a hint of self-pity.

"To be attacked in this way is a sign of success," Peter said. "The more good you do in the world, the more people try to stop you. In fact, if you aren't being persecuted, it means you are slacking off and need to work harder."

"If you measure success in terms of how much opposition you face, then Ananda, too, is a *huge* success," Swamiji said with a smile.

Peter and Swamiji laughed with delight at their mutual "good fortune."

"I get so many brickbats," Swamiji said once, "I can't keep track of who has styled himself as my enemy. The simplest answer I've found is just to treat *everyone* as my friend."

Ananda was besieged for a time by a series of petty acts of vandalism. When I described to Swamiji the latest incident, he reassured me cheerfully. "We have to expect opposition," he said. "After all, we are trying to transform all of society and naturally it will take a little time."

A Prayer and a Fall

The crisis descended on the Ananda community in Assisi, Italy, just a few weeks after Swamiji had left that country to start a work in India.

Some months earlier, a disgruntled ex-member had filed a lawsuit against the community. This was only one of many lawsuits this man had filed over the years against former employers, landlords, and even members of his own family.

The man alleged that Ananda was a dangerous cult that had brainwashed him, then forced him to work hard for low wages. Under Italian law, "enslaving" someone of "weak will" for "financial gain" is considered "criminal activity." These are serious charges. It put Ananda in the same category as the Mafia.

As "evidence" that his claim was true, the man included allegations from an equally scurrilous lawsuit that had been filed against Ananda in America. Without conducting further investigation, the local prosecutor concluded that a world wide criminal organization was operating right in her neighborhood.

The Ananda leaders in Italy thought of the lawsuit as more of a nuisance than a threat. Ananda had already been through it in America. There was no basis for the allegations in either lawsuit and they knew it would eventually be straightened out (as in fact, for the most part, it has been).

Only in the middle of January 2004, when eighty armed policemen descended on the community at 5am to search for evidence, did the Ananda community understand how serious the situation had become.

When Swamiji left Italy, he had no inkling of what was about to happen. It looked, however, as if he had "fled the scene before the roof collapsed." As the "Capo" of Ananda, Swamiji was first on the list of the "accused."

A few weeks later, in early March, seven people from Ananda, the "ringleaders" according to the lawsuit, were arrested and taken to jail. In Italy, if the charges are serious, the "accused" can be imprisoned to keep them from fleeing the country or interfering with the investigation. The judge released them after five days, but at the time the "accused" were arrested no one knew how long they would be imprisoned.

The arrests were national news. In response, thousands of people all over Europe rose to Ananda's defense. Swamiji wanted to return to Italy immediately.

"I am the leader of Ananda," he said. "It is me they really want. If they can question me, they'll see that the charges are false."

Ananda's Italian lawyers said it would be folly for Swamiji to return. "You Americans don't understand how much power the police have here," one lawyer said. "Swamiji could be picked up at the airport and taken straight to prison. At the very least, he would be put under house arrest for who knows how long."

"I am not a coward," Swamiji replied.

If he were imprisoned, however, Swamiji knew he wouldn't be able to help with Ananda's defense, his main reason for going. Furthermore, the consternation it would cause to have him in jail would take energy away from the defense effort. Reluctantly, Swamiji agreed that it was better for him to stay in India.

In fact, he wasn't physically strong enough to make the trip back to Europe. Ever since coming to India his health had been poor, and he had recently been released from the hospital after a near fatal episode of double pneumonia.

To dispel any thought, however, that he was "hiding" in India, Swamiji went to the Italian consulate in New Delhi where he presented medical evidence of his inability to travel. He then authorized the lawyers in Italy to speak on his behalf and offered to have his deposition taken at the consulate where it could be videotaped and sent to Italy.

Swamiji prayed to Divine Mother, "If there is anything more I can do, I offer myself willingly."

In his bathroom in India, a marble sill, four inches wide and four inches high, with a curtain above it, was all that divided the shower area from the rest of the room. Soon after the arrests, while the "accused" were still in jail, and not long after his prayer to Divine Mother, Swamiji lost his balance and fell backwards so hard across that sill that his back arched over it.

The resulting pain was excruciating. At first the doctors thought it was only a bad bruise. Only weeks later, when the pain had not abated, did a more careful examination reveal that a rib had broken and was now detached from the spine. It took months to heal.

To a few of his closest friends, Swamiji said, "I prayed. Then later I fell. I hope the pain helps matters in Italy."

My Only Cause

In *The Path*, Swamiji describes Daya Mata as he knew her during the years when they both lived in the ashram of their Guru.

"Kindness," he wrote, "was the hallmark of her personality. I looked upon her as my model in the ideal spirit of discipleship that I was striving to acquire."

Considering how harshly Daya Mata treated Swamiji in later years, his generosity toward her in his autobiography, which he wrote during those later years, has always astonished me.

"Her worst persecution," I said to Swamiji, "came after 1990, with the lawsuits she, through SRF, filed against you. But even in 1976, when you wrote *The Path*, you had already been expelled from SRF, and she'd shown herself to be anything but charitably disposed toward you. Yet you don't even hint at that side of her character. Instead, you helped create the image of Daya as Master's ideal disciple. Only a few know her personally, others take their cue from what people like you say. Because of what you wrote, many people later sided with Daya, not with you. In your autobiography, you worked against your own cause."

"*Truth* is my only cause," Swamiji said. "What I wrote is how I experienced her at the time. Subsequent events did not change that. In *The Path,* I chose to emphasize a reality in her toward which she herself is striving, and which I still see as her deeper reality."

I Choose To Love

A woman had a consensual affair with a married man at Ananda Village. When the man, urged to do so by Swamiji, decided to stay with his wife, this woman left Ananda in a rage, claiming now that she had been sexually harassed. She took her complaints to SRF, where she met with Daya Mata and other members of their Board of Directors. With the help of an SRF attorney, she pursued a lawsuit against Ananda. She claimed Ananda was a "sham organization" set up by Swamiji for the sole purpose of "exploiting women." The charges were preposterous. Ananda refused to settle so the case went to trial.

"I was in the courtroom one day during the trial," Pushpa, an Ananda member said later. "The judge hadn't come in yet. I was sitting near the center aisle and had a clear view of Swamiji sitting alone at the defendants' table, and also of Ananda's accuser and one her supporters, seated on the plaintiff's side.

"The two women were taunting Swamiji, jeering and pointing at him like school girls, then giggling at their imagined cleverness. Their faces looked quite evil.

"I was appalled. How could they be so mean to a fellow disciple, and a *direct* disciple of Master? I wanted to shield Swamiji from their taunting. I thought, 'How vulnerable I would feel, sitting all alone as he is.'

"Then I looked at Swamiji. He was so relaxed; he could have been sitting in his living room at Crystal Hermitage. When they jeered at him, he didn't turn away. He didn't even flinch. In fact he smiled, and in his eyes, there was only kindness.

"Swamiji has endured years of persecution from SRF, without ever becoming angry or bitter toward them. I have often heard him say 'I choose to love them, because I myself am happier when I love.'

"I thought of that passage from the Bible, 'Love your enemies, bless them that curse you, do good to them that hate you, and pray for them which despitefully use you, and persecute you.' This was the first time I had ever seen that kind of love actually practiced.

"Several years later, I went to India, where I met Master's nephew, Harekrishna Ghosh, who is also a direct disciple. 'What do you remember most about Master,' I asked him.

"'His kindness,' Harekrishna said, 'and his love. Master loved everyone.'

"Immediately, I thought of that day in the courtroom. 'I never met Master,' I thought, 'but I understand what Harekrishna is saying because I have seen that kind of love in Swamiji.'"

with Harekrishna Ghosh

Bicentennial Liberty Committee

In the early years, when the Ananda community was just getting started, the only dwellings many of the residents could afford were teepees they sewed themselves out of heavy canvas. When the local newspaper heard a rumor about what was going on out on the "Ridge" where we lived, it printed an article about the problem of "tent cities" springing up "all over the county" without proper supervision by the local authorities.

Swamiji knew that Ananda was the only thing in the county that fit that description. The day after the article appeared, he went to the county offices.

"I'm here to answer your ad," he said.

In fact, Ananda was already under county jurisdiction as a "church camp" supervised by the Health Department. Once a year, the Fire Inspector came to make sure our extinguishers were working and that our brush clearing was adequate. Two or three times a year, the Health Officer came. He had worked for years in impoverished countries overseas, however, and had no problem with the rather primitive conditions in those years at Ananda—no electricity or indoor plumbing. As long as we were safe and sanitary, he didn't object.

Being a "church camp" allowed us to live permanently in all kinds of "temporary structures": trailers, teepees, and the equivalent of tarpaper shacks, which was all we could afford at the time. The handful of proper buildings we did have we had been allowed to construct without permits or inspections. It was a godsend. If we had had from the beginning to meet the stringent planning and building requirements imposed upon us later, Ananda literally would never have gotten off the ground.

In 1974, when we acquired an additional 365 acres of land on which we planned to build a new Retreat (now The Expanding Light), we went as usual to the Health Department to talk about our plans. To our surprise, the Health Inspector told us that he no longer had jurisdiction. From now on, he said, Ananda would have to answer to the Planning Department.

A group of us, including Swamiji, had a meeting with the Planning Director. We had never met her and she had never been to Ananda, so we explained in some detail the ideals behind Ananda, how the community functioned, what we had accomplished so far, and our vision for the future.

When we were done, she reached over to a nearby bookshelf, pulled out a thick volume of regulations, and thumbed through it until she found what she wanted. Pointing to the proper paragraph, she announced decisively, "So, you are a condominium." A condominium is an ownership arrangement for an urban apartment complex. It bore no resemblance to what we were doing at Ananda.

The Planning Director had started as a secretary and risen through the ranks to the top job in the department without ever receiving the specialized education and training needed to do the job in a fair and professional manner. There was no real system of checks and balances in place, so she was able to wield her power according to her own perception of things with very little outside interference.

A planning problem as complex and unusual as Ananda was simply beyond her capacity to solve. As a cover for her own incompetence, she decided that Ananda itself was the problem. Her solution was to make things as difficult as possible for us until, she hoped, we would give up and go away.

She started by imposing a moratorium on all new building at Ananda pending the submission and approval of a proper Master Plan for the development of the whole community. By late 1975, we were on our third version of the Master Plan. The two previous versions had been rejected, because, *after* we submitted them, the Planning Director issued a new set of guidelines that made what we had done unacceptable.

Now the Planning Director tried to force us to remove all "non-conforming" structures before she would even consider the next version of the Plan. Just about everything on our land fit her definition of "non-conforming." This demand would have put us out of business. Only after we hired an attorney did she back down.

The rest of us were too inexperienced to see the handwriting on the wall. Swamiji, however, knew we were in big trouble and the only solution was to get the Planning Director replaced. We weren't the only ones being hurt by her capricious ways. She had caused great hardship for many citizens in the county. Some had even lost their property because of the unreasonable standards she imposed. Swamiji knew that Ananda, as one of the few organized groups in the county, had the capacity to create change in a way no individual would be able to do.

The coming year, 1976, was the bicentennial celebration of the founding of America. Swamiji saw it as the ideal rallying point for the campaign he had in mind—a county-wide movement reaffirming the principles of freedom and personal responsibility upon which this country was founded. He called it *The Bicentennial Liberty Committee.* He started with a petition describing the principles and intentions of the *BLC,* as it came to be called.

"Two hundred years ago," the petition said, "our forefathers fought for the right to be represented in government by people who were responsive to their needs, rather than to rules and restrictions insensitively imposed from afar. In this Twentieth Century, increasing centralization of power has raised again the threat of insensitive legislation, originating similarly from afar, where the needs of the individual are ignored in favor of mass uniformity.

"We, citizens of Nevada County, feel that with the approaching celebration of our country's bicentennial it is time to affirm with some of the revolutionary zeal of our forefathers the need for personal liberty and self-direction. We call upon our governments in Washington, Sacramento, and especially in Nevada County to pay heed not only to the rules that are imposed on us from above, but also to us, the individuals who must live by those rules.

"Particularly we demand the right to live our own lives as we choose to live them, so long as we do not infringe on the freedom and rights of others; and to develop our own properties and build homes thereon according to our own tastes and inclinations, provided only that we show sensitive regard for the land we live on, and that we not endanger the health and safety of others."

Swamiji's plan was first to get a hundred local businesses to endorse the petition. Then we would reprint it with all those names on it.

Teams of people would then take those petitions out to the local shopping areas and gather individual signatures. He knew individuals would be more willing to sign if they saw that the businesses were already behind it.

Within the Ananda community, however, the idea of the petition, and the whole Bicentennial Liberty Committee, went over like a lead balloon. "The great majority of responsible people at Ananda opposed it," Swamiji wrote later.

Most thought it was foolhardy to risk antagonizing the local government. "Don't you realize the Planning Department could shut us down completely?" was the gist of their argument.

"We won't even *have* a community if we don't do *something*," Swamiji responded. He alone understood that our survival was *already* in jeopardy.

Others protested that the whole idea was "goofy" and not at all in tune with Ananda's apolitical nature. Some even said it was spiritually wrong for us to get involved in a project like this.

"What I propose to do isn't immoral," Swamiji responded. "Indeed, it's *super* moral. The officials we are dealing with have been appointed to their positions and have a duty to listen to public opinion."

Few at Ananda were persuaded.

"Rather than spending all your energy trying to win over those who oppose you," Swamiji has said, speaking of how to be an effective leader, "give your energy to those who are with you. Generally speaking, negativity has little cohesive power compared to the magnetism generated by those who put out positive energy, and who set good examples."

Swamiji knew if he could create even a small nucleus of support for the BLC within Ananda, he could build from there. That nucleus turned out to be me. As Swamiji himself described it years later, he got my support by appealing to my lively sense of humor! It was a serious situation, but, at the same time, it was so far out of the ordinary flow of Ananda life that it had a certain quality of madcap adventure about it, which he knew would appeal to me.

I knew Swamiji well enough to know that he wouldn't launch such a bold and public campaign without a strong sense of inner guidance. He was confident, and that was enough for me. Besides, the way he presented it, it seemed like a lot of fun. And it was.

My enthusiasm was the spark that soon convinced others from Ananda to help. We took the petitions into town and in just a few days had the endorsement of almost a hundred local businesses. After two weekends at the shopping centers, we had thousands of individual signatures, plus a bulging file of stories of how citizens had been mistreated by the local government.

Swamiji was chairman of the BLC; I was the secretary. We didn't hide the Ananda connection, but nor did we advertise it. He used his American name, J. Donald Walters. (Later, in order to reach a wider public in America, he published many books under that name, but at the time it was relatively unknown.)

Editorials and articles appeared in the local paper speculating about this "Committee" which seemed to have sprung out of nowhere.

When curiosity was at its height, Swamiji called a public meeting at a large hall in Nevada City, the county seat.

Ananda people came "incognito," about a hundred in all. They arrived by ones and twos and pretended not to know each other, to swell the numbers without tipping our hand. Many from Ananda were still skeptical, some even predicted disaster, but all were as curious as anyone else in the county to see what would happen next! In all, the crowd numbered several hundred, an impressive turnout, duly reported the next day in the local paper.

Swamiji presided over the meeting as "J. Donald Walters, Chairman of the Bicentennial Liberty Committee." For the occasion, he had written a pamphlet he called *Your Freedoms Are Like Old Friends: Don't Take Them For Granted.*

Of the four hundred pieces of music Swamiji has written, *one* is a political song—*Salute the Nice Paper Flag.* Obviously, this was the time to sing it. The song satirizes the passivity that comes when people rely too much on the government to take care of them and the ruin that descends on any country that encourages that dependency. The crowd loved it. Nevada County was founded by gold miners, and that independent, rough-and-tumble spirit is still very much alive there.

Swamiji spoke of the widespread discontent with local government, as evidenced by the thousands of people who signed the petition in just a few days. He urged county officials to be more compassionate and responsive to local needs. Other speakers shared personal stories of mistreatment at the hands of local officials. The whole meeting was designed to fan the flames of controversy and it succeeded beautifully.

A few days later, an editorial in the local paper attempted to defend the county against the charges raised by the BLC. At Swamiji's instruction, I responded with a series of letters to the editor. The intent was to make the officials feel that the whole county was under siege. I systematically targeted, not only the Planning Department, but also the Building Department, the County Counsel's office, and others as well. I included specific examples from the bulging file of stories we had collected. My letters prompted a host of other letters from county residents, almost all in sympathy with the BLC.

I appeared on local radio talk shows and became a "regular" at meetings of the Board of Supervisors. I was fair minded and stuck to the issues and gradually I won the respect of most of the Supervisors, even those who didn't agree with what I had to say. At the right moment, I presented to them our impressive stack of signed petitions.

"They wouldn't have listened to us alone," Swamiji said. "County officials hold their jobs by public appointment. I had to make them see that there was widespread public opposition to their behavior. I wrote that petition very much in earnest. And the large number of people who signed it constituted a significant force."

When Swamiji finally publicly declared his connection to Ananda, he did it as a peacemaker, seeking to smooth the troubled waters with the voice of reason. It was amazing to see him calming a controversy he himself had stirred up!

In what he called *A Special Plea to our Supporters,* Swamiji wrote, "It is common, these days especially, to conduct civic protests in anger. But anger assumes bad faith on the part of those one opposes. Such assumptions are not always fair. Surely most of us in Nevada County would *prefer* to believe in the good faith of our public servants. In fairness, then, to those who have devoted themselves to serving us truly and well, let us assume the best of intentions in them all. Let us go even further: Let us offer friendship to those, even, whom we may be forced eventually to oppose. Let our struggle be not against *them*, as individuals, but against the uncivic attitudes for which they have chosen to stand. If they change those attitudes, there is no reason why we should not continue to give them our fullest support."

The Grand Jury investigated the Planning Department and rec-ommended that the Planning Director be fired. Her replacement was a competent, trained professional who soon got Ananda's planning process back on track.

A side effect of the whole thing was that when it came time to elect a new supervisor from our district, I had gained a certain amount of notoriety and there was a movement to draft me to run for the position. It was nothing I wanted to do, but for Ananda's sake I was willing to consider it.

I was greatly relieved when Swamiji said, "We have accomplished our objective. There is no point in 'flexing our muscles' any further. It wasn't power we were after; it was simple survival, so that we might continue in the way of life to which we are dedicated."

After it was all over, I asked Swamiji, "Did you know when you started how it would turn out?"

"Not exactly," Swamiji said, "although I am not surprised. I knew intuitively it would work and just took it a step at a time."

Master says that by the time a soul reaches the advanced state of spiritual realization that Swamiji has achieved, he has drunk the cup of worldly power to its dregs. Master himself was a king and a warrior many times before. Swamiji has made references to several such incarnations of his own.

He has a unique way of discussing current events. To him, the decision makers on the world stage are not names one reads about in the newspaper. He regards them as colleagues, and discusses their decisions not in the gossipy way most people do, but as if he were at the table of power with them, and had as much right as they to direct the course of history.

"Everyone is just a child of God," Swamiji says simply. "I feel no trepidation or exaltation at meeting even the heads of nations."

When he was in India working on behalf of SRF in 1961, Swamiji felt that the way to get Master's work established in that country was to build a temple in the capital city of New Delhi. The only available land where Swamiji wanted to build, however, was part of the "Green Belt." By government decree, virtually no building was allowed in that sector. More than two thousand charitable and religious societies had tried to get land there; all had been denied.

"The only way you will be able to build in that area," Swamiji was assured by those in the know, "is to get permission from Prime Minister Nehru himself."

"Then I will do so," Swamiji resolved.

"It never occurred to me," Swamiji said later, "that Nehru was out of reach merely because of his position. It had to be done, so I would do it."

From a chance meeting on a train, Swamiji had made the acquaintance of a highly placed government official. This man had been well impressed with Swamiji and was willing to recommend him to another highly placed person. One led to others, and soon a handful of officials were willing to back his proposal, *if* he could get Nehru to agree.

Encouraged by Swamiji's success so far, a friend was able to get him an appointment with Nehru's daughter, Indira Gandhi. It turned out they had attended separate schools in the same small village in Switzerland. In French, a language Swamiji learned as a child, they discussed their attendance there. At the end of their meeting, she agreed to recommend Swamiji to her father.

Prime Minister Nehru spent forty minutes with Swamiji. Some heads of state got only five minutes from him. Nehru agreed to walk the land Swamiji had requested, and, in the end, gave him permission to build the temple.

It was a triumph for Master's work in India. Incomprehensible though it may seem, the SRF Board of Directors, ten thousand miles away in Los Angeles, California, saw the whole thing in a very different light.

On the nine-person Board of Directors, there were eight women and Swamiji, the only man. For years the women had viewed his expansive spirit and never-ending flow of creative ideas as a threat, rather than a benefit, to the future of Master's work. Now this "presumption," as they saw it, of daring to confer with the Prime Minister of India, was the last straw.

Swamiji had acted with the approval of Daya Mata. When she saw, however, how the other members of the Board felt about what

Swamiji had done, Daya made it seem as if Swamiji had acted entirely on his own. To them, his bold move was nothing but an attempt to gain power for himself by taking away from Daya Mata the control of SRF's work in India.

Nothing Swamiji said could change their minds. They absolutely refused to have anything to do with the land Swamiji had worked so hard to obtain for them. Even though he complied with their request to drop the project completely, from that point on it was a downhill slide. A year later, in July 1962, Daya Mata summoned Swamiji to New York City and expelled him from SRF.

Considering his background in this life, and in incarnations before, Swamiji was unimpressed when I expressed admiration for how skillfully he had orchestrated the whole campaign with the Bicentennial Liberty Committee.

"A tempest in a teapot," Swamiji called it.

"It may have been," I said. "But it is the teapot where we live. Thank God you had the foresight to save the day."

Stand Unshaken

One of the worst days of the Bertolucci trial was when Swamiji's most virulent opponents testified against him. Many of his closest friends couldn't even be in the courtroom with him. As "designated witnesses" scheduled to testify later, we weren't allowed to hear anyone else's testimony.

I know Swamiji to be a powerful spiritual person. He can take care of himself and all of us as well. Still, when the courtroom door closed behind him, I felt as if we were sending a lamb to the slaughter. For the next several hours, we sat in the hallway praying for Swamiji, just waiting for it to be over. When he finally emerged, we were so relieved we swarmed around him like bees around a flower.

Almost in tears, someone asked, "How are you, Sir?"

To understand what happened next requires a little explanation.

One of the lasting legacies of the two years Swamiji spent as a student in an English boarding school is his life-long affection for the humorous stories of P.G. Wodehouse. To our everlasting delight, he has passed that enthusiasm on to us by often reading stories aloud to the community. In every Wodehouse tale, some good-hearted, but usually inept, hero finds himself enmeshed in preposterous circumstances, from which he invariably emerges unscathed.

Swamiji has also enjoyed the adventures of James Bond, Ian Fleming's "Agent 007," who also wins out every time against impossible odds. Now, standing in that miserable hallway outside the courtroom, it was "007" who provided Swamiji's answer to that tearful inquiry.

"*Stirred!*" Swamiji replied, with the accent and attitude of a suave super-hero, "*but not shaken!*"

The "plot" of the Bertolucci trial was as preposterous as any Wodehouse tale or James Bond thriller. Yet, like the heroes of those adventures, Swamiji had emerged unscathed.

Our tension evaporated in a burst of appreciative laughter.

"When a battle can't be avoided," Swamiji said on another tension-filled lawsuit day, "you have to find your joy in doing battle."

~ From Elizabeth Palmer ~

Victory

When Swamiji was on vacation with a few friends, one of his companions simply took charge of the daily program, without consideration for his preferences. Swamiji quietly went along with whatever she wanted to do.

Later, the woman's job changed and she began to work closely with Swamiji in matters where the future of Ananda was concerned. When she tried to boss him around as she had done before, to her surprise he responded forcefully.

"When we were traveling together," Swamiji told her, "I went along with whatever you wanted for the sake of my own humility. If I were to go along with you now, however, it would not be humility. It would be abdicating my responsibility to Master's work, and *that I will not do*."

A man at Ananda, who tended to be guided by his personal desires, sought to justify his uncooperative nature by comparing himself to Swamiji.

"I have always admired your independence," he told Swamiji.

"My independence is not based on personal desire," Swamiji replied. "It is based on doing what is right."

"Nowadays people equate strength of will with aggressive scowls and hostile posturing," Swamiji said on another occasion. "My willingness to go along with others when nothing is at stake but my personal convenience, and my seeming passivity even in the face of personal attack, gives some people the impression I am easy to defeat, that they can simply run roughshod over me. They misunderstand.

"I rarely dispute with others. It has never been my way to fight *against* anything. I simply find a way to go forward according to what I believe to be true, no matter what other people think. I will not allow others to impose their will on me when principles are at stake."

Anandamayi Ma, a great Indian saint, said, "Let come what will."

A devotee questioned her. "Does that mean you would go along passively with something that was wrong?"

Ma responded, "Let them try, and see what happens!"

"When Bertolucci's lawyer vowed to destroy me," Swamiji said, "I didn't respond on his level of argument and accusation. Beyond answering what was legally required of me, I didn't defend myself at all, not even mentally, because I was untouched inwardly. I surrounded myself with a psychic wall of inner freedom, which for him proved impenetrable. In the end, all his efforts against me came to nothing.

"Even in the face of seeming defeat," Swamiji went on to explain, "I've turned every setback into another kind of victory—a victory of new opportunities and new directions, of guidance to do something broader and better."

One secret of prosperity, Swamiji has said, is *creativity*.

"*Poverty consciousness* means to be locked into a single way of thinking," he explained. "If that way doesn't work out, you are defeated. *Prosperity consciousness* means also to have a wealth of *ideas*. If one way of doing things doesn't bring the results you want, you keep trying other alternatives until one of them finally succeeds.

"When the Bald Mountain Association refused to let me build on my own land, I bought land elsewhere and built there. For years, I held Ananda back, out of a wish not to compete with SRF and in the hope that, eventually, we would reconcile. When SRF still refused to work with us, and even filed a lawsuit, I came to understand that Master wants us to be separate organizations. I stopped holding back and the result for Ananda has been glorious."

I Had Work To Do

The founding of Ananda coincided for Swamiji with the onset of arthritis in both hips. Before that, he had been a fast runner, a good skier, and a tennis player of what he calls "mild ability." Soon arthritis made all that impossible. Much of the time, walking or even standing was painful for him.

He didn't like to give in to the pain, or to draw attention to his difficulty, so he continued to stand while lecturing or giving Kriya initiations, sometimes for two hours at a time. Only after fifteen years was he willing to sit down for some of these public programs.

"I don't think you're hearing a word I'm saying!" a friend complained once to Swamiji during an afternoon walk. His inattention had offended her and Swamiji felt he owed her an explanation, so he spoke more frankly than usual.

"I'm sorry," he said. "You are right. It is taking every ounce of my willpower just to put one foot in front of the other. I see to the end of the block and tell myself, 'You can get that far.' When I reach that goal, I set myself another one. In that way I manage to keep going."

"How were you able to bear it?" I once asked him.

"I had work to do," Swamiji said. "I couldn't allow the pain to interfere. I related to it impersonally as just one of the many obstacles I had to overcome. You can't imagine how much willpower it took to get Ananda going."

Only after twenty years, when Ananda was secure and the arthritis had progressed to the point where it threatened Swamiji's ability to serve, did he finally put his attention to it. Something had to be done or he would end up crippled. In two operations several months apart, Swamiji had both hips replaced. He was a new man.

"Hello, fellow athletes!" he said to those who came to see him in the hospital. He wore a tee-shirt that proudly announced, "Watch my smoke!"

"In all my years," the surgeon said to Swamiji, "I have never seen hips in such bad condition! On one side, a full two inches of bone had been worn away."

"I did limp a bit," Swamiji admitted.

"I don't know how you walked at all!" the surgeon replied. "You should have been in a wheelchair, or bedridden."

The surgeon was delighted with Swamiji's quip after the second operation: "Hip, Hip, Hooray!"

Bullies

As a boy, Donald [Swamiji] never started a fight, but if a fight sought him out, he never ran away—especially if a bully tried to intimidate him. Even if the bully was much stronger and could beat him physically, Donald never gave in mentally, and in this way refused to give the bully the victory.

When Donald was eleven years old, he was a student at the Downs School in England. One day, an upper class boy, big enough to intimidate his own classmates, met Donald upstairs as he was coming out of the art room. Finding no one else about, he gave Donald a shove. Perfectly aware that he stood no chance against this bully, but nevertheless undaunted, Donald shoved him back.

This was all the excuse the bully wanted. He threw Donald to the floor, sat on him, and began pummeling him fiercely. "Do you give up?" he demanded.

"No!" Donald replied.

So the beating continued until the bully tired of administering it. From then on, though, he carefully avoided Donald's company.

Years later in America, when Donald was in boarding school at Hackley in Tarrytown, New York, an older and much stronger boy baited Donald for weeks. The bully weighed 230 pounds; Donald weighed 104. Still, Donald refused to be intimidated. This so infuriated the bully that one day he came into Donald's room and pinned him to his bed. There was nothing Donald could do, so he lay there quietly while the bully pummeled him. Between blows, the bully whispered fiercely, "I'd like to throw you out the window!" (They were three floors up from the ground.) Finally, the bully tired himself out, and left the room, panting with rage.

"Why didn't you call for help?" one of Donald's friends asked later. Other students were in nearby rooms, and would have answered his cries.

"Because I wasn't afraid," Donald replied.

After the beating, Donald treated the bully with the same calm reserve as before. From then on, however, the bully gave Donald a wide berth, and never again threatened him.

Another time at the Downs School in England when Donald was twelve, he was in the sick rooms with a boy named Taylor, who was unpopular with his classmates. Sneeringly Taylor hurled the epithet at Donald, "Dirty foreigner!" (Donald was the only American in the school.)

"Well, maybe you're a dirty Englishman," Donald replied conversationally. This wasn't meant as an insult, only a question of how recently each of them had bathed!

Taylor, however, enraged, leapt angrily at Donald. This time, however, Donald was the stronger of the two. In such cases, his method was simply to wrestle his opponent to the floor and sit on him until he calmed down. Repeatedly, Taylor spat up at Donald's face, never quite reaching it. Finally, recognizing himself powerless, Taylor stopped writhing and spitting, and admitted he'd been bested. Donald calmly stood, allowing Taylor to leave. Thus, the matter was dropped.

Bald Mountain Association

The first land Swamiji bought for Ananda is the area known as the Meditation Retreat, six miles from the Village. He purchased the land in 1967 in conjunction with four other men. It was strictly an economic arrangement. They had no interests in common except that each wanted a secluded piece of land as a place of retreat, and they could get a better deal if they went in together.

Richard Baker, who was at that time the head of the San Francisco Zen Center, was the one who put the deal together. The others— two poets, Gary Snyder and Allen Ginsberg, and an attorney, Dick Wertheimer—were his friends. Swamiji didn't know any of them before he joined with them to buy land.

Richard had found one large undivided piece that they could get at half the going rate if they bought the whole thing. When Swamiji went to see the land he felt the Masters had already blessed the Eastern portion of it, and that he was meant to buy it.

The agreement was that Richard would purchase the land with the money the others gave him, and register it in his own name. He would then subdivide it into seven 24-acre parcels and give each man title to the one parcel he wanted. Then the partnership would end.

Swamiji was the fourth person to come in. Richard had a little more than a year to find buyers for the remaining three parcels or the whole deal was off. Ten months later, only one of the three parcels had been sold. Swamiji was concerned that Richard wouldn't be able to find buyers for the last two and they would lose it all. So he offered to buy the parcels himself.

"It is a lot of money and more land than I need for myself," Swamiji explained to Richard. "But I also want to start a community. I have a friend who would donate money for that purpose.

"It isn't ideal. The land is too remote. And a community is not what you had in mind when you included me. I could start there, however, and then, after, say, five years, move the community to another location."

Richard was not enthusiastic, but he didn't want to risk losing the land either, so he reluctantly agreed. However, when Swamiji began to develop the community, Gary Snyder raised a hue and cry against it. Gary and Swamiji were the only two owners actually living on their land.

Instead of standing by his word, Richard sided with Gary, and so did the other two owners, who were Richard's friends. Richard then told Swamiji not to do anything more until they all agreed on how the land should be used.

Richard had not yet carried through on his promise to give each man title to his portion. He was still the sole owner of the entire piece.

"You are a guest on *my* land," Richard told Swamiji. "If you go to court, you'll be evicted." Then he added, "I could consider the money you paid as rent."

Since it was four against one, a lawsuit was Swamiji's only option. The very idea of a lawsuit, however, was anathema to him.

"I would never sue you," Swamiji said.

As Swamiji explained later, the dispute was just about land and money. No eternal principle was involved. And land and money were of no importance to him compared to *ahimsa*—nonviolence, or, more accurately, harmlessness. In fact, now that Richard had made his position clear, Swamiji had no intention of disputing anything they asked of him. He would build the community elsewhere.

Assured, now, that there would be no lawsuit, Richard scrapped the original purchase agreement. Instead of each buyer owning and controlling his own land, it was now decided that they would own and manage all the land together under what was called the Bald Mountain Association, after a prominent local landmark.

Forty percent of the total acreage belonged to Swamiji. He owned three times as much land as any of the other men. But the Bald Mountain Association was set up to be one man, one vote. The four of them were united against Swamiji on every issue. They had taken control of his land.

"The *Association* feels that the land is held in common," Gary Snyder declared. "The intention is to establish ground rules for land use."

Earlier it had been agreed that each owner could have one hermitage with two residents per acre of land. Swamiji was still well below that limit. Now Gary told Swamiji, "Our original estimate for development was much too high. The permanent structures you have already built amount to full land use." Then he added, by way of explanation, "We should all be able to learn and change our ideas as we go along."

Gary then proposed population and development limits that left no room for what Swamiji had intended to do when he bought the land. He had no choice, however. He had to go along.

"I'll sign anything you want," Swamiji told Richard, "as long as you don't *destroy* what I have created so far."

That was in 1973. Swamiji had already moved his home to another part of Ananda, and now he also withdrew his creative energy. Until then, Swamiji had played a leading role in the planning and development of that property. Since then, he has left it entirely in the hands of others.

Swamiji had worked hard to pay off all the land so the community could start debt free. When Gary and Richard objected to any community being started there, Swamiji bought another piece of land for it, six miles down the road. He didn't have the money so he took on a debt of $250,000.

Later, when Richard and Gary objected even to the presence of the Meditation Retreat on what was now "their" land, Swamiji added an additional $350,000 of debt to get other land for the Retreat as well.

"If they had made any effort to work *with* me," Swamiji says, "I would have been happy to cooperate with them."

Swamiji encouraged those who were in charge of the Meditation Retreat to comply with the guidelines of the Bald Mountain Association. Considering the circumstances, though, he felt it was sufficient if they complied with the spirit of the agreement. The population remained low and development was kept to a minimum.

Gary, however, insisted that every provision be followed to the letter and he kept constant watch to make sure it was done. Any violation, no matter how small, he took as *proof* that Swamiji could not be trusted to keep his word.

Gary made no secret of his disdain for Swamiji. He broadcast his views throughout the county and beyond. He even wrote a poem ridiculing Swamiji and Ananda, published it in one of his books, and presented it at poetry readings. Of his own part, and that of Richard and the others, in taking the land from Swamiji in the first place, Gary made no mention.

It is largely because of Gary's insistence that Swamiji "cannot be trusted" that many of our neighbors are suspicious of Ananda. Even those who moved to the area long after these events took place, accept as true the commonly held belief that Swamiji "violated the Bald Mountain Association agreement."

"I don't care about my own reputation," Swamiji says. "I am here to get out of my ego, not to defend it."

When the issue of the Bald Mountain Association comes up, his usual response is, "Richard Baker promised to give me title to the land that I paid for and he never did." Then he leaves it to his listeners to put the pieces together from that one clue.

"Why fight with them?" Swamiji says. "It just isn't worth it. It is unfortunate, though, that Ananda has had to bear the brunt of it all these years."

A Choice

"Maybe this book will be the one that finally convinces SRF that we need to work together," Swamiji said. He was referring to his work-in-progress in February 1990, *The Essence of Self-Realization*, a collection of sayings by Master.

When Swamiji speaks of "SRF" in this way, I know he means the handful of direct disciples who lead the organization, the ones with whom he lived and worked closely when he was part of SRF, the very ones who later expelled him and have maintained toward him ever since an attitude of unrelieved hostility.

Despite this separation, Swamiji maintains a positive attitude toward them. They are his *gurubhais*—his brothers and sisters in the guru's family. To respond with hostility, Swamiji feels, would be to betray not only his friendship for them, but also his relationship as a disciple to his guru.

"I have a peculiar 'quirk' to my nature," Swamiji says. "The way I feel about others has never been influenced by the way they treat me. Once I give my loyalty, I never take it back. I may alter my *behavior* in response to what others do, but not my friendship.

"As Master said, if you reach out your hand to someone and he keeps knocking it away, after a while you just put your hand in your pocket. That doesn't mean, however, you have closed your heart."

I know all this about Swamiji, so when he speaks in this optimistic way about SRF, I usually keep my doubts to myself. This time, however, I felt he had to be more realistic.

"I think the effect of this book on SRF will be to make matters worse," I said to him. "The more inspiring the book, the more unhappy they will be with you."

Very quietly, and *very* seriously, Swamiji answered me. "I simply can't afford to think that way." Simple words, but spoken with such conviction. Clearly, the discussion was ended.

I was taken aback, embarrassed to realize that I'd been wrong to think him naive. His positive attitude is not based on present realities, but on his hope for the future. Swamiji has the same commitment to helping SRF that he has to helping Ananda.

"I *choose* to love," Swamiji has often said.

That day, I caught a glimpse of the will power, faith, and patient endurance it has taken for Swamiji to hold firmly to that decision.

~ From an Ananda devotee ~

Quick Change

It was Swamiji's idea to incorporate Ananda Village as a California city. As a municipality, we would have control over our own land use, planning, and zoning. This would get us out from under the county approval process, which had proved to be cumbersome, expensive, and gave our neighbors too much influence over internal community affairs.

Many of our neighbors had come to the area to drop out of society. It was almost a principle with them to oppose *all* organized groups and strong leaders. Many objected, also on principle, to the population density and some of the land use inherent in having a community. We were not indifferent to their needs, but most of their opposition was not based on anything we had done, or planned to do, but on the fear of what we *might* do if they did not keep a close watch on us.

In fact, the community is quite self-contained. Most of what happens within the borders of Ananda has no actual impact on those who live nearby. Filing for incorporation was like filing a declaration of independence. Even if we didn't succeed, we felt it was time to stand up to our neighbors and at least bring the controversy out into the open.

Incorporation proved to be a long and complicated process. After a year-and-a-half of hard work, it culminated in a series of public hearings, then a vote by a seven-member council called LAFCO, the Local Agency Formation Committee. Each hearing drew more people, went on longer, and was more contentious than the one before.

Before the public hearings started, the members of LAFCO seemed to favor our application. We didn't look like a city, we looked like a farm, but we met the legal requirements for a municipality, and that was all that mattered.

LAFCO was forbidden by law to decide our application on the basis of religion. Even to discuss religion in relation to the incorporation, or to let the subject come into a public hearing, was a violation of our rights. The fact that "Ananda City" would be both a spiritual community and a municipality was like a shadow lurking in the background that could never be brought into the light of day.

The LAFCO members visited the community, met Swamiji, and also met many of the residents. They liked what they saw and for a time it looked like our effort would succeed.

The opposition of our neighbors, however, was our undoing. They were determined, well organized, and came out in droves for the public hearings. We were largely unsuccessful in getting anyone outside of Ananda to speak in favor of incorporation. Gradually the LAFCO members began to side with what appeared to be the majority view: to deny our application.

At the end of the final hearing—which lasted seven hours and was attended by 800 people—only one LAFCO member voted in favor of our application. In that hearing, though, and in several leading up to it, LAFCO allowed extensive testimony from our neighbors about Ananda's religion and how it would affect the municipality. We protested repeatedly, but to no avail.

The incorporation effort attracted statewide media attention. After LAFCO voted down the application, I and another Ananda spokesperson vowed in front of the TV cameras to get the decision reversed on appeal, because testimony about religion had been allowed in.

Later, another television crew came to the Village to interview Swamiji. I met them at the community and rode in their car the three miles up the dirt road to Swamiji's house.

The entire time they plied me with questions about what we planned to do now. I was emphatic that this was just a temporary setback. Our rights had been violated. The process was compromised. This is America. We have not yet begun to fight.

In previous incarnations, no doubt I have been part of more than one revolution, probably including the American Revolution, so this kind of rhetoric comes naturally to me.

When we arrived at Swamiji's house, he said to the television crew, "I don't know how much time you were planning to give me, but if you let me have a full five minutes to read a statement I have prepared, I have a special scoop for you."

I turned to a friend who was there when we arrived and asked him, "*What* is Swamiji talking about?"

My friend paled, then said, "You don't know?" He refused to say anything more. The filming was just about to start and I couldn't ask Swamiji myself.

A few minutes later, in front of the camera, Swamiji started reading the first page of his prepared statement. Immediately I saw that he was speaking of the project in the *past* tense. That was the scoop. It was over. We weren't going on.

According to the law, Swamiji explained, LAFCO had acted improperly when they let religion come into the debate. But the fact is religion *is* the central question. Separation of church and state is one of America's most cherished principles. Even if "Ananda City" conducted itself in an honorable way—which we have every reason to believe it would, Swamiji hastened to add—to allow Ananda to incorporate would set a bad precedent. LAFCO made the right decision.

The moment Swamiji finished speaking the crew turned the camera on me. I had to improvise on the spot all the reasons why I agreed completely with what Swamiji had just said. Of course, I was contradicting everything I had said off-camera just a few minutes earlier, but these crews interview a lot of politicians and it didn't seem to bother them.

I then took the television crew back to the community, talking all the way about the wisdom of the Founding Fathers and how much we support the basic premises of American life. As soon as they left, I made a beeline back to Swamiji's house.

"Why didn't you tell me what you were going to do?" I asked him. I described the scene in the car, how I gave the crew one story on the way over and another story on the way back. "Fortunately, I think fast on my feet." By this point, we were both laughing. The situation was so ludicrous.

"I'm sorry, Asha," Swamiji said. "It was a surprise to me, too. When I sat to meditate this morning it just came to me that it was not right for us to go on. It was already too late to reach you." There were almost no phones at Ananda in those days. Swamiji didn't have a phone, and neither did I.

"Why didn't that revelation come to me?" I asked Swamiji. "*I'm* the one who has been working on the project all this time."

"Probably because you didn't ask," he said.

"No," I said honestly, "I didn't. I just went on as if the guidance for today would be the same as the guidance for yesterday. A serious oversight on my part."

"Yes," Swamiji said. "It is not wise to presume. You have to be open, and continuously ask Master, 'What do you want me to do?'"

"I only want to do God's will," I said to Swamiji, entirely reconciled now to what had happened. "I threw myself into this project because you asked me to do it and I felt it was right. If you feel it is God's will that we stop, that's fine with me."

Then I added, "I don't mind losing. I have to admit, however, that our neighbors have been so unkind, in fact at times so downright nasty, that I don't like the idea that they have *won*."

"It is not a matter of likes and dislikes," Swamiji said. "It doesn't matter if we lose face, or even if people think we were foolish for having tried in the first place, or for having vowed to go on and then pulling back so suddenly. The only thing that matters is truth."

"Ahh…. Yes," I said with a smile, "Where there is dharma there is victory." Then jokingly I added, "Dharma has served us well so far. No point in changing horses in midstream!"

"Even though we didn't become a city," Swamiji said, "I think in the long run our neighbors will respect us more for standing up to them. That's how they operate and we have to show them we are not pushovers. We can also play their game."

After that, our neighbors still spoke against most of our proposals, but some of them had been so appalled by things that had been said in the heat of the moment at public hearings that they resolved not to let emotion take over like that again.

Swamiji paused for a moment during our talk, then went on. "Working on this has also been good for you," he said. "At the beginning, when you spoke in public, you were inclined to tell your listeners what they wanted to hear, rather than tuning in to what needed to be said. Having to stand up to all that opposition at the public hearings has lessened this tendency in you. Now you will be a better minister. That's the main reason I asked you to do it."

Because the incorporation had been such a public event, Swamiji wanted to inform the whole county of Ananda's decision and the reasoning behind. What he'd written was too long to be printed as a "Letter to the Editor," so Swamiji bought advertising space in the local paper and printed the following statement:

April 16, 1982

A representative group of us at Ananda met yesterday and decided to go to court over the decision of the Local Agency Formation Commission (LAFCO) to deny our petition to be granted incorporation status as a municipality. Next week this matter would be taken to the entire community for discussion and final decision. Our legal counsel feels we have a good chance of winning.

The issue, from our own point of view, is clear-cut: We want the freedom to develop, according to law and to the broader interests of Nevada County, but without the restrictions of bureaucratic red tape, and without the all-too-frequent, basically emotional opposition of our neighbors. Our (to us) perfectly reasonable wish has aroused unprecedented, and unprecedentedly emotional, opposition. Ananda has been vilified; my own character publicly slandered. I have repeatedly expressed my desire to work for harmony, and for the general good of all, including the good of our neighbors as much as our own. The press, instead of quoting these statements, has tried to fan the controversy by quoting people who would make me out to be another Hitler, or Jim Jones.

For myself, I am interested in the truth. Lies, whether public or private, are still lies and simply don't claim my respect. I have consistently affirmed that only two arguments could persuade me not to proceed with our efforts to incorporate: One, that incorporation would not give us the one thing we want from it: greater freedom; and two, that incorporation would actually (as opposed to theoretically) hurt our neighbors. During the LAFCO hearings, no one in the opposition addressed these two issues in such a way as to convince me of the justice of their cause.

Rather, they expressed fears which, our legal counsel assured us, were groundless. They said we might, if incorporated, annex their property. Legal counsel told us they would have plenty of recourse in the event of our wanting to, a thing we would never be interested in doing anyway. They said that as a religious community we would be in conflict with the church-state separation guaranteed by the United States constitution. But the legal decision from Sacramento on this issue was that to deny us on these grounds would be to deny *our* rights as U.S. citizens. County counsel advised the LAFCO members to reject testimony against our bid on these grounds as invalid. Part of our suit against the county would certainly be based on the evident fact that religion was in fact admitted as a major part of the testimony, and could not but have influenced the final decision against us.

I have always said that truth is my guide—not opinion; not likes or dislikes; but truth. I am not interested in winning, or in saving face. In the present issue, I am only interested in the rights and wrongs of it. I feel that within the limited context of what Ananda's needs are, and of our contribution, past and future, to Nevada County we were right.

However, last evening, after the meeting at which we decided to appeal, I sat down and read reports on this issue in the national press. As a result I have come to appreciate the problem in the broader context of America as a whole. And I have come to feel that the church-state issue, despite the official pronouncement on the matter from Sacramento, *is* at the heart of the matter. At stake is not the question of whether I would abuse my power as leader of this religious community. I have never done so. Nor is the issue whether I might do so. I think those who know me are quite certain that I would not. The real issue, however, is whether I *could* abuse this power. And there we have to say, There are no guarantees that human nature will not express any of its hidden potentials, whether for good or for evil.

Our constitution was written with a clear eye to history, and to the evils that have occurred in the past when any group of people whose interests drew them together for one reason allowed those interests to dictate their decisions in other matters. One of the saddest periods in the history of Christianity was, in my opinion, when Christian teachings became widely enough accepted to become mixed up with national policy.

If, for example, Minneapolis were to become a wholly Christian city, and St. Paul (its sister city) a wholly Jewish one, to the extent that their definition as legal entities became rooted in their respective religious beliefs, I can see the possibility of persecution, perhaps decades down the road.

As long as Ananda was a local issue, our bid for corporate status revolved around land use, self-government, etc. I believe strongly, moreover, and said so at the last LAFCO hearing, that what Ananda stands for in a sociological sense—namely, cooperative effort at a time when our nation is becoming all-too-fragmented—needs to be encouraged, not discouraged.

This very fragmentation, however, that I see taking place on a national level might also be *strengthened* if religious groups like ours were permitted the status of legal entities. I foresee a time of great stress for this country, when groups will be pitted against one another in an ideological struggle. At such a time, I feel, religion will need to speak out on religious, not political, grounds if it is to be effective for the truth.

In the broader context of America's history and future directions, I think the LAFCO decision not to grant us corporate status was a wise one. This does not mean I think we were wrong, for what we wanted was valid. This does not mean I think LAFCO's *reasons* were necessarily right. But it does mean I think there were higher forces at work here, and that the truths that our neighbors intuited were valid, and a valid reason for concern.

I shall make my recommendation to our Ananda community that we drop the issue.

Sincerely,

Swami Kriyananda
(J. Donald Walters)

A Cheerful Patient

When he moved to India in November 2003, the transition was hard on Swamiji's body. He took several bad falls, had a near-fatal case of pneumonia, persistent dehydration, and several episodes of congestive heart failure. His friends were deeply concerned, but Swamiji accepted it all cheerfully.

Once, when he was recovering in the hospital, a swami from Rishikesh visited. "I am so sorry to find you unwell," the swami said sympathetically.

"Don't worry about me," Swamiji replied with a smile, "this is just *tapasya* to help get my Guru's work going in India."

The Bertolucci Lawsuit

A married man had an affair with an unmarried woman. At the time, they both lived at Ananda Village. His name: Danny; hers: Annemarie Bertolucci.

When Swamiji heard about the affair, he urged them to end it, and supported Danny when he made the decision to go back to his wife and daughter.

Annemarie refused to accept Danny's decision as final. She made it clear to Swamiji that she was determined that Danny should leave his wife and marry her. "I would make a *good* mother to his little girl," she insisted. The child was not developmentally normal and needed special care.

"I will not let you stay here and destroy that family," Swamiji told her firmly. Later, Swamiji said, "I didn't hesitate. I knew intuitively, however, that, in thwarting her desires and abiding by dharma, I would be faced with a difficult test."

To Annemarie he said, "You must move to another Ananda community." She pleaded to be allowed to stay, but Swamiji was unyielding. "You must live as far away from him as possible. That will make it easier to break the attachment." He suggested she go to Ananda Italy, or, as a second choice, to Ananda Seattle. She rejected both in favor of Ananda Palo Alto, where she had lived before. Swamiji did not dispute her choice.

"She appeared to cooperate," Swamiji said afterwards, "but underneath I could see she was seething with rage. Not at Danny, but at me. She was certain that if I hadn't intervened, she could have gotten him back. She once told Danny, 'I *always* get what I want.'"

It was no surprise when, a few months later, she left Ananda altogether. Her dispute with Ananda became her entrée into SRF. She visited SRF headquarters in Los Angeles, was given lunch by Daya Mata, and met with several other members of the SRF Board of Directors. Even longtime SRF members rarely get to see Daya Mata. For a newcomer to be received so royally was, indeed, exceptional.

Soon after, she filed a lawsuit against Danny, Swamiji, and Ananda. She claimed, among other things, that she had been brainwashed, coerced, and sexually harassed. At the time, the lawsuit said, she may have *thought* the relationship with Danny was consensual. Now, she alleged, *nothing* she had done, in the abusive atmosphere of Ananda, had been of her own free will.

When Swamiji heard about the lawsuit, he said simply, "This is not about Danny. It is SRF trying to destroy me."

The SRF lawsuit took twelve years to resolve. By 1994, however, when the Bertolucci lawsuit began, SRF had already lost 95% of their case. The next eight years were mostly repeated attempts on their part to get the judge's rulings reversed. SRF took its appeals all the way up to the United States Supreme Court, which refused to hear the case.

In 1994, SRF still had one possible way, apart from reversal on appeal, to retrieve what it had lost. It was a legal concept called "tarnishment." If SRF could prove that Swamiji and Ananda were morally corrupt, and that any association in the mind of the public between SRF and Ananda would "tarnish" SRF's reputation, then the judge could impose restrictions on Ananda that would diminish that association.

Even though the court had dissolved SRF's copyrights, trademarks, and publicity rights to Master's name and teachings, through "tarnishment" they might have those exclusive rights restored. Swamiji had told us to be ready for just such an attack from SRF.

Most of us referred to "Lawsuits" in the plural—meaning Bertolucci and SRF. They were legally separate, filed in different courts—SRF's in federal court in Sacramento, Bertolucci's in state court near Palo Alto. Swamiji, however, never referred to them in the plural. To him, it was just "The Lawsuit," since it was obvious to him that SRF was behind them both.

Just as Swamiji had predicted, SRF soon filed a motion in federal court, describing the Bertolucci lawsuit, and asking for relief on the basis of "tarnishment." We countered with the charge that SRF had "unclean hands."

"SRF can't be permitted to both *create* a scandal and then *benefit* from that scandal," our attorney argued. He had considerable evidence to back this up, starting with the way Bertolucci had been received at SRF headquarters just weeks before she filed the lawsuit.

He went on to list other convincing facts. Bertolucci's attorney was a prominent member of SRF. (Later he became the lead attorney in

SRF's federal case as well.) A major SRF donor had been fraudulently passed off as a paralegal so as to be able to attend Swamiji's deposition in the Bertolucci case.

Swamiji had never met the man, but when he saw him sitting there Swamiji said to our attorney, "That man is an SRF member. What is he doing here?" Bertolucci's attorney insisted that he was a paralegal. It was impossible at the moment to disprove his claim.

Not long after the deposition, SRF transferred to that donor a large and valuable property for the sum of $1. The donor was already a client of Bertolucci's attorney and our assumption is that he was the conduit through which SRF financed the Bertolucci case.

On the basis of this and other evidence, we demanded the right to question Daya Mata about SRF's involvement in the Bertolucci lawsuit. SRF waged a fierce battle to prevent us from questioning her. Their efforts to do so did not, in the end, help their cause.

"Your very reluctance to allow her to be questioned tells me you have something to hide," the judge said when he ordered Daya to submit to a deposition.

"It is not right for fellow disciples to be fighting each other in court," Swamiji had written to Daya more than once since the SRF lawsuit began. He urged her to accept his invitation to meet together and find a way to settle the case. Always she had refused.

Now, faced with the prospect of having to answer questions about SRF's involvement in the Bertolucci lawsuit, Daya contacted Swamiji and for the first time appeared eager to settle.

At the settlement conference, however, as a condition for even beginning the discussion, Daya demanded that we give up the right to take her deposition. Naively, we agreed.

Settlement negotiations dragged on for months. SRF expected us to cede back to them all the exclusive rights to Master and his teachings that the court had taken away. They negotiated as if it were they who had won, not we.

By the time it became clear that settlement was impossible, the window of opportunity to take Daya's deposition had closed and could not be reopened. Later, we were forced to conclude that Daya had initiated the whole settlement process for the sole purpose of escaping the deposition.

SRF did, however, withdraw its "tarnishment" claim.

The Bertolucci lawsuit proved to be exactly what Swamiji expected: a vicious personal attack on him. The linchpin of Bertolucci's case was the "coercive, cult-like atmosphere of Ananda." Without that, it was just an affair between two consenting adults. An abusive cult cannot exist without an abusive cult *leader*. Danny soon became an "also-ran," almost incidental to Bertolucci's case—at times even a sympathetic character, because he, too, was presented by her attorneys as a "victim" of the "abusive cult leader."

Swamiji and Ananda were not the first spiritual group or spiritual leader to be sued by Bertolucci's attorneys. By the time they got to us, they had perfected a method for destroying reputations and winning huge out-of-court settlements.

The first step in their system was to write the lawsuit and supporting declarations to be as lurid and shocking as possible, with an eye to how they would play in the media. The second step was to court the media like an ardent suitor.

Accusations in a lawsuit are exempt from the laws that usually govern libel. No matter how false they may later turn out to be, the accusations can be repeated and reprinted in all forms of media without fear of retribution.

Scandal sells newspapers. The same day the lawsuit was filed in court, it was also released to the media. From then on, Bertolucci's attorneys argued the case in the press as much as they did in the courtroom.

The lawsuit was so extreme as to be almost a parody of itself. It read as if the lawyers kept a boiler-plate, anti-cult lawsuit in a file drawer and just pulled it out as needed. Perhaps it is not so far from the truth to say that they simply inserted the names "Ananda" and "Swami Kriyananda" whenever a specific reference was needed.

Human nature tends to think, "Where there is smoke there is fire." Or, between two conflicting points of view, "The truth must lie somewhere in the middle." Few people are discerning enough to know when they are being taken in by a daring ploy that Hitler called the "Big Lie." This is something so outside of reality as to have no foundation in truth at all.

With this understanding of human nature, and by skillful use of the media, the reputation of a spiritual leader can be destroyed by accusation alone.

Nothing in the lawsuit reflected Ananda or Swamiji as we know them to be. It was the "Big Lie."

At Ananda, women are in charge of half the departments. Still, in the lawsuit, the community was described as an environment "hostile to women" in which they are "second-class citizens," forced into drudgery, mere sexual playthings for "the Swami" and his male minions.

Swamiji was described as a ruthless dictator, indifferent to the welfare of anyone but himself, obsessed with power, pleasure, and money, who routinely took advantage of vulnerable young women. According to the lawsuit, Ananda was nothing but a "sham religious organization" set up primarily to keep "the Swami's harem stocked."

When she filed the lawsuit, Bertolucci did not accuse Swamiji of abusing her. She alleged only that he was responsible for creating the atmosphere in which abuse could occur. To bolster that claim, the lawsuit included declarations from a few women, former residents of Ananda, now all affiliated with SRF, who claimed that in the past they had been subjected to coercive sexual advances from Swamiji.

The most recent was alleged to have occurred thirteen years before the suit was filed in 1994, the most distant was twenty-eight years earlier. None of these women were plaintiffs in the lawsuit, but these declarations proved to be the core of the campaign to destroy Swamiji's reputation.

The third step in the method used by Bertolucci's attorneys in their attack on spiritual groups and their leaders, is, gradually, over the course of a lawsuit to uncover more and more abuse, and thus draw into the lawsuit an ever-increasing number of plaintiffs. Eventually, the sheer magnitude of the case against the "cult" and its leader forces them to pay whatever is needed to avoid a trial and the risk of an even greater loss of money and reputation.

Four years passed from the time the Bertolucci lawsuit was filed until the trial ended. During that time, Bertolucci's attorneys sent letters, made phone calls, held public meetings, and at one point even dropped leaflets from an airplane onto Ananda Village, all in an effort to uncover further abuse and draw more clients for their case.

These efforts were entirely unsuccessful. There was no abuse to uncover. The only ones who spoke against Swamiji at the end of the case were the same ones who were there at the beginning: a few SRF-affiliated women.

Dozens of Ananda women did come forth, however, to testify and file declarations on behalf of Swamiji.

"Women have an instinct for these things," one woman wrote. "They can sense when a man has sexual intentions. I have worked closely with Swamiji for more than two decades. He has been a guest in my home. I have been a guest in his. I have traveled with him. I have worked alone with him late into the night. Not once, in hundreds of hours of close association, have I felt from him, or observed in his interactions with other women, even the slightest expression of sexual interest. Not even an appreciative glance or a remark with sexual overtones. Nothing. Sometimes I think he doesn't even notice the gender of those around him."

Another woman said, "To speak of Swamiji as 'coercive' is like saying the sun rises in the west. The truth is, when you are with him, you have to be careful not to express preferences that might interfere not merely with his convenience, but with his real needs.

He is nothing less than heroic in his willingness to sacrifice his own well-being for the sake of others."

"I've been discussing Ananda personnel issues with Swamiji since the community was founded twenty-five years ago," a woman wrote. "I don't even want to think about how many meetings I've attended. I can't recall a single instance in which a decision was made on the basis of gender. That kind of bias just doesn't happen at Ananda."

In the "discovery" phase of the lawsuit, Swamiji was subjected to *eighty hours* of deposition. Bertolucci's attorneys videotaped the entire proceeding. Each day, in an attempt to unnerve Swamiji, the camera was moved a little closer to his face. Bertolucci's attorney was deliberately lewd and insulting in the hope of embarrassing Swamiji or, better still, enraging him and capturing it all on video.

Less than a year earlier, Swamiji had had open-heart surgery. His physician, Dr. Peter Van Houten, was present for the deposition to monitor Swamiji's condition and call a break in the proceedings whenever he felt Swamiji needed a rest.

"Bertolucci's attorney knew about the surgery," Dr. Peter said later. "Still, he was completely unconcerned about Swamiji's well-being. I think he could have pushed Swamiji to the point of a heart attack if I hadn't been there to prevent it. Even when Swamiji asked to be excused to go to the bathroom, the attorney would say, 'Just one more question.' Then he would go on with the deposition as if the request had never been made. If Swamiji reminded him of the need for a break, the attorney would say again, "Just one more," until Swamiji would simply get up and leave anyway, with the attorney calling out questions even as Swamiji walked out the door."

Later, Swamiji said, "I am so accustomed to microphones and cameras. It meant nothing to me to have the video even inches from my face. As for the attorney's attempt to bully and insult me, I saw no reason why his rudeness should affect my inner peace."

Hour after hour, Swamiji calmly answered all the questions they put to him.

During that time, in conversation with a few close friends, Swamiji shared some of his personal history that he had never talked about before.

"At my first meeting with Master," Swamiji said to us, "he asked me, 'Of the three major delusions—sex, wine, and money—which ones attract you?' Wine and money have never been issues for me. I had no wish to get married, but I did experience sexual desires and I told him so. He made no comment.

"At the end of the interview, Master initiated me as a disciple and also as a monk. I took that for his answer and resolved to do my best. It was a struggle. Once I said to him, 'I would commit suicide rather than fall into temptation.'

"'Why speak of suicide?' Master replied. 'This is not deep in you. Keep on trying your best. You *will* overcome it.'

"On another occasion I asked him to whom I might go for counseling on this issue after he was gone. I was astonished when he replied, 'Speak of it to no one.'

"'Not even Rajarsi?' I asked.

"'No,' Master replied firmly. 'No one. You have a great work to do and no one must know.'"

Swamiji was twenty-two years old when he became a monk. For the first fourteen years, he lived within the protected environment of the SRF monastery. When he was expelled from SRF in 1962, he found himself suddenly, at the age of thirty-six, all on his own.

Most monks and nuns who, for whatever reason, find themselves suddenly no longer in the monastery, have usually gotten married shortly thereafter. Swamiji was determined to remain a monk, even without a monastery to support him.

In India, a solitary swami is a common sight and people relating to him understand his position. In America, there is no such tradition. Many women still considered him "fair game." Some even found him more attractive because of his commitment to be a monk.

Swamiji maintains a certain detachment from his own feelings. That detachment, however, does not diminish the depth and sensitivity of those feelings. Only a few, even of his closest friends, have been able to appreciate how deeply he has been hurt by the way SRF has treated him. All these years he has not had the company of even one fellow monk. Instead, he has been vilified and relentlessly persecuted by fellow disciples, some of whom were, at one time, his closest friends.

It was only natural that Swamiji would long, as most people do, for a small haven of emotional intimacy as a bulwark against so much hurt and betrayal, especially when that comfort was freely offered.

"When I took my vows as a monk, and then a few years later, as a swami," he later wrote, "it was not a declaration, 'I am free!' Rather, it was an affirmation, 'I will do my utmost to become completely free in this life.'"

Swamiji struggled valiantly against a lingering desire for human love and intimacy. Mostly he succeeded. A few times he did not. Always it was consensual. It is not in Swamiji's nature to impose his will on anyone.

Mentally, however, he himself never gave his full consent, but acted always in obedience to Swami Sri Yukteswar's advice quoted in *Autobiography of a Yogi*: "Even when the flesh is weak, the mind should be constantly resistant."

"A slip is not a fall," Swamiji often says to encourage a person to cling to his aspirations even if, for a time, he fails to live up to them. Master said, "A saint is a sinner who never gave up."

When Swamiji started the community a few years after he was expelled from SRF, he had no choice but to mix freely with both men and women. If he had remained aloofly protective of his monastic vocation, Ananda would have failed.

"I made the decision to risk even my own salvation," Swamiji said, "in order to do the work Master had given me to do."

Later he wrote, "I could see no alternative but to go on, hoping for the best, clinging with faith to Master's power, believing that he would take me eventually out of delusion. To me personally, the risk was agonizing. Meanwhile, I never pretended to myself or to anyone else that it was *not* a delusion, or that it might be in some way justifiable. I always saw, and spoke of it, as a fault. At last, as it happened, I discovered that Master's blessings had been with me always."

During the time of the depositions, in that conversation with his close friends, Swamiji went on to say, "Bertolucci's lawyers tried to make it seem like sex was something I reveled in. That is not true. It was always something from which I wanted to be freed.

"There was no point, though, in running away from it or doing all those other extreme things people do in an effort to kill the impulse within them. Quite simply, I'd tried that and had found it didn't work. I realized I just had to live through it, maintaining as much mental detachment as I could.

"To maintain detachment in this way is a form of Tantra yoga. Many people think Tantra is about *enjoying* your desires. That is entirely wrong. The teaching of Tantra is to *withdraw* the feelings, by an act of will, from sensory enjoyment, not to indulge them.

"The follower of Tantra trains himself to keep the thought, 'Even in the midst of enjoyment, I myself am not the enjoyer.' The goal of this practice is eventual inner freedom. By maintaining mental detachment even while experiencing apparent 'fulfillment,' one gradually comes to see that desire itself is a delusion.

"Tantra can be dangerous, however, and the masters do not recommend it. I would not have chosen even this one practice for myself if my situation had not forced it upon me.

"It complicated things for me that Master had told me not to talk about it. Of course I would follow his guidance, there was no question about that. If he hadn't guided me that way, however, I would have talked about it easily. I have done my best and I am proud of the life I have lived. Sexual desire is, after self-preservation, the most powerful instinct there is. It is nothing to be ashamed of."

Bertolucci's lawyers offered to settle, but Swamiji refused even to consider it. "It would," he said, "be tantamount to admitting an untruth—a whole series of untruths, in fact."

The Bertolucci trial turned out to be a travesty of justice. The judge was biased against us from the start. He told Bertolucci's attorneys what arguments to make and what motions to file so he could rule in their favor. He put Ananda's spiritual practices on trial. He issued a ruling that prohibited us from offering *any* defense against the fulcrum issue in the case: the allegation that Swamiji was a "sexual predator."

When it came time for the women who had filed declarations against Swamiji to testify against him, *they knew in advance* that we'd been prohibited from cross-examining them. They could perjure themselves without fear of exposure. Some of their testimony contradicted what they had said in their own declarations and depositions, but there was no way we could bring even this fact to the attention of the jury.

The jury was *never informed* about the prohibition imposed on us by the judge. They observed, without any explanation, that we offered no defense. They drew the obvious conclusion that we had no defense to offer, and considered the issue proved.

The attorney we worked with from the beginning to the end of the SRF lawsuit is a brilliant lawyer, an honorable man, and has become a dear friend. But he is not a litigator. So we had to hire another attorney to work with him for the trial.

Swamiji was in Europe when this litigator was hired. He was a well-known defense attorney, who, we found out later, specialized in defending guilty criminals. His contribution to justice was to be sure that the criminals, although guilty, received a fair trial.

When Swamiji came back to California a month or two later, they met for the first time. The litigator had apparently decided he needed to make it clear from the start who was the boss. He treated Swamiji as if he were a guilty criminal who needed to be bullied into telling the truth.

Afterwards, Swamiji said, "He is the *wrong* attorney for us." It wasn't personal. It was just obvious to Swamiji that such a man could never tune in to him or to Ananda and therefore would have no idea how to defend us.

Swamiji's remark was met by a hailstorm of reasons why we had to keep working with that lawyer.

"We've paid him a big retainer."

" He's done a lot of work already to prepare for the trial."

"He has a reputation for winning."

"We don't have time to bring someone else up to speed."

Again Swamiji stated emphatically, "He is the wrong attorney for us." When the hailstorm began again, Swamiji made no further effort to persuade us.

Throughout all life's challenges, Swamiji's first thought has always been, not, "How to win?" or "How to succeed?" but, "How to maintain the right spiritual attitude required by the highest principles of dharma."

Even in a matter of such importance, if we were not receptive, it was contrary to dharma for Swamiji to *impose* his will on us.

"I knew this attorney would be a disaster for us in exactly the way he proved to be," Swamiji said later. "When I couldn't get you to listen, however, I accepted it as God's will."

The irony is that the man was hired to defend Swamiji against the charge, among others, of being a dictator. Even though the consequences for Swamiji personally were enormous, he let us go forward as we preferred and let God determine the outcome.

So we went to trial represented by an attorney who didn't believe in our cause, who believed still less in Swamiji, who never understood the case, and who refused all our helpful suggestions. As a result, insofar as he was allowed to present a defense at all—given the judge's prohibition—his defense was so weak that in many ways it strengthened the case against us.

We continued to affirm victory right up to the end, but it was no surprise when the jury ruled in favor of Bertolucci. Afterward, we consulted with several attorneys about filing an appeal.

"Even without considering all the other improprieties in the way the judge conducted the case," one attorney assured us, "the prohibition against your presenting a defense to the key issues is enough in itself to *guarantee* that the verdict would be overturned on appeal. That verdict has the shelf-life of an *apple*."

To our dismay, however, we found out that even if one wins an appeal, all he gets is the right to a new trial, sometimes even in front of the same judge. The first trial had lasted three months, cost us hundreds of thousands of dollars, and for the entire time, thanks to Bertolucci's attorneys, and our own lawyer's refusal even to let us talk to the press, we were raked over the coals by the media.

No thank you, we decided. We'd had quite enough of this so-called "justice."

"Where there is dharma there is victory." What does it matter how we are judged in the courts of man? All that matters is how we stand in the eyes of God.

Even in the worst hours of the trial, Swamiji said later, "I felt inwardly free. My constant prayer was, 'Divine Mother, they can take everything away from me, but they can never take away from me my only treasure: my love for You.'"

Bertolucci's attorneys very nearly succeeded in taking from Swamiji the copyrights to all his books and music, the fruit of a lifetime of work. Only by putting Ananda for a time under the protection of the bankruptcy court were we able to prevent that from happening.

In the end, the trial proved to be a great blessing for Swamiji. "Since then," Swamiji said, "I have not felt the faintest stirring of attraction toward human love."

It seems an inescapable conclusion that those women who helped Swamiji in achieving his ultimate victory also reaped for themselves, in time, some of the good karma of that victory.

Speaking to a group of friends, all of whom happened to be married couples, Swamiji said, "I don't mean to hurt your feelings, but Master told me something that I didn't understand at the time, but I do understand now. He was speaking of the attraction between the sexes. 'Once you have overcome that desire' Master said, 'you will see it is the greatest delusion.'"

Persecution has been the lot of many great souls throughout history. St. Teresa of Avila was called before the Inquisition. St. John of the Cross was cast into prison. One of John's persecutors was even there at his deathbed interviewing the nuns who nursed him in the hope of finding evidence of misconduct to use against the saint.

In his Christmas message to the community the year of the Bertolucci trial, Swamiji wrote, "We have so much to be grateful for. I wouldn't trade anything God has given us this year for some imaginary 'better deal.' Spiritual growth comes as much through divine tests as through overt blessings—so much so that I'm inclined to say, 'What tests?'

"What we want from life is to grow closer to God. Nothing else—absolutely *nothing* else—matters. Speaking for myself, and I think for all of you, my love for Him is deeper than ever. So also is my faith."

~9~

GRACE

"The deeper the Self-realization of a man,
the more he influences the whole universe
by his subtle spiritual vibrations."

Paramhansa Yogananda

Darshan

The minister of the Church of Religious Science in Reno, Nevada, was a friend of Swamiji's and invited him to address the congregation there. As a guest in someone else's church, Swamiji was careful not to draw his listeners away from the path they were on, but urged them to follow wholeheartedly the inspiration they felt from within.

There was power in the air that night. Swamiji seemed to be speaking with the voice of the Divine, and the audience sensed it. Afterwards, almost everyone present lined up to greet him.

Usually, at such times, Swamiji is quite informal. He shakes hands with people, laughs and talks with them—often speaking, if it is an international crowd, in several languages. This evening was different. Swamiji didn't say much. He greeted people only with his eyes, standing very still, hands folded in *namaskar*, which means, "The soul in me bows to the soul in you."

I stood a little to one side, watching a scene I felt had been repeated many times before. In other bodies, in other lifetimes, these same souls had stood before the spirit that is Swamiji to receive a touch of his consciousness.

For Swamiji, it was an act of pure giving. None of these people would ever be part of Ananda. It was a different spiritual family, but in some way, Swamiji felt a responsibility to inspire them. They were souls seeking the light, and he felt he had to give them what he could.

Darshan means the blessing that comes from the sight of a saint. In India, they say "One moment in the company of a saint will be your raft over the ocean of delusion."

I don't think many in that audience knew the word *darshan*, and probably none had heard that Indian saying, but they all seemed to know that something out of the ordinary was happening, as they waited patiently and reverently for the moment when they could stand in front of Swamiji.

Midnight Blessing

Right after Swamiji had hip replacement surgery, those of us in the community with medical training took turns staying with him in his hospital room, so someone would always be on hand to help him if he needed it.

I used to be a nurse, but then trained as a chiropractor. I was just starting my new practice and was quite nervous about it. It was around midnight of the day Swamiji had his operation—hardly the time to discuss my personal problems. But Swamiji knew what I was doing and must have sensed my anxiety, for he started talking to me about the practice.

"Think of your work as your sadhana, your way of serving Divine Mother. She is in the suffering bodies you serve. When you relieve that suffering, you are helping Her. Serve joyfully, with complete faith in what you are doing, and you will have plenty of energy.

"Don't think of what Divine Mother can do for you. Think only of what you can do for Her. Work for God Alone. That is the way to succeed."

Then he asked me to stand right next to his bed. He was weak and in pain from the surgery, but he lifted his hand and blessed me at the spiritual eye.

I had come to help him, but it was Swamiji who helped me.

~ From Kent Baughman ~

Healing Touch

From childhood I carried a deep sadness. Even as a little girl, I knew it came from a past life in which I had experienced the traumatic death of a beloved spouse. It was a kind of "post-traumatic stress syndrome" that spanned more than one incarnation.

Sometimes, when I was a child, the grief was more than I could bear and I would weep uncontrollably. As I grew older, and especially after I got onto the spiritual path, I made progress in resolving it, but much grief remained. I didn't know what else to do except pray, and accept that the grief might be with me for the rest of my life. I could feel the karma as a knot of energy lodged in my spine just behind my heart.

One evening, after I had been living at Ananda Village for many years, I went with my husband to a community musical event. The concert was a birthday gift for Swamiji. As part of the program, a group played selections from his album *Secrets of Love*. The music uplifted me and at the same time made me aware of my inner grief. I didn't want any unhappiness to mar the evening for Swamiji, so I prayed to Divine Mother, "Please don't let my sadness touch his joy."

During the intermission, Swamiji came to where my husband and I were sitting with a group of friends. He stood between us, with one hand on my husband's shoulder, and the other hand on my spine. His fingers were right where the karma was lodged.

I felt a tremendous pressure from his hand and enormous energy going into me. Swamiji didn't make a point of what he was doing; the whole time he chatted casually with the others. He didn't, however, speak to me, but let me receive his energy in silence.

A few minutes later, Swamiji took his hand away. The knot of energy was gone, and with it the sadness I had known all my life. Every once in a while since then, a shadow of it has crossed my consciousness, just enough to make me continuously grateful to Swamiji for taking that karma away.

~ From an Ananda devotee ~

Sarcoidosis

Sarcoidosis is a serious disease that causes inflammation of the body tissues. Bharat had it in his lymph system, surrounding his heart. For three years, he suffered from debilitating weakness and almost daily bouts of fever. Finally, the fever abated and his strength began to return. But his lungs had been affected, and he coughed almost constantly, sometimes for five minutes at a time.

Swamiji was recovering from open-heart surgery, but he asked Bharat and his wife Anandi to come over briefly to discuss a certain matter. Sarcoidosis is not contagious, but on the way to the Hermitage, Anandi said, "Perhaps you shouldn't expose Swamiji to your cough. You could wait upstairs while I go down to his apartment to see him." Bharat agreed.

When they arrived, Swamiji sent word that he wanted both of them to come down. Bharat went too, therefore, but he stood a little away from Swamiji and let Anandi do the talking.

As they were about to leave, Anandi explained, "Bharat has been coughing for six months."

Swamiji looked at Bharat, and in a strong but matter-of-fact way said, "Bharat doesn't have a cough."

At that moment, the cough stopped and never returned.

"Swamiji's blessing lifted me over the last karmic hurdle of that long illness," Bharat said.

Touched on the Heart

It was always hard for me to be on this planet. Awareness of my own imperfections, and how those imperfections hurt others, caused me to suffer intensely. I had been diagnosed as clinically depressed. It was a cyclical thing and sometimes I had to take prescription drugs for it. Because of the depression, I've had some pretty serious problems in my life.

I always felt I wasn't okay, that somehow I needed to justify my existence. Before I came to Ananda for the first time, I worked for a nonprofit organization, where I thought I could really do some good in the world. The job became my purpose for being on Earth. But then one of my depressions hit. It affected the way I worked and I got laid off.

Eventually I got over the depression and off the drugs they'd given me to cure it, but I felt like I'd lost everything. I was into yoga, and had been meditating on and off for years, so I decided to take the Yoga Teacher Training Course at Ananda Village. I didn't know much about it, but a friend had taken the course and said it was great. So I registered and sent in my money.

After that, I stumbled onto a website that described Swami Kriyananda as a terrible person. I was shocked and scared. My yoga teacher had also recommended the course, so I asked her, "What about all these stories?"

She had never met Swamiji, and didn't know any more about him than I did, but she offered this reassurance: "Don't worry, he lives in Italy now."

Soon after I arrived at Ananda, I bought Yogananda's book *Scientific Healing Affirmations*, with his picture on the cover. I put it on my nightstand where I saw it every morning and evening. I was intrigued, and wanted a better picture of him. So one afternoon, about two weeks into the program, I decided to walk over to the boutique at Crystal Hermitage and get one.

I got lost, and eventually bumped into two people I'd never met before. Although I didn't know it at the time, one of them was Swami Kriyananda, who had just returned from Italy. He directed me to the Hermitage and I got my picture.

On my way back, just outside the Hermitage gate, I ran into him again. By now I had figured out who he was. This time, he asked me a few questions. "Where are you from? Are you enjoying Ananda?" That sort of thing. He was very kind and very gentle. Not at all like the man described on the website.

Then he asked, "Have you ever meditated in the Crystal Hermitage chapel?"

I told him, "No, I haven't."

"I think you should," Swamiji replied.

I said something noncommittal and started to walk away from the Hermitage.

"I really think you should meditate now," Swamiji said. His voice was light and there was twinkle in his eye, as if to say, "It is just a suggestion; you decide."

So, to be polite, I turned around and went back to the chapel. There was no one else in there. I sat down to meditate. After about ten minutes, I suddenly felt a finger touching my heart, *inside* my body. It was palpable and I knew it was Yogananda.

At the same time, I was lifted into the light, and flooded with the knowledge that it is okay to be on this planet. It didn't come to me in words, it was just the feeling that I don't have to justify my existence, I don't have to work for the organization that fired me, I don't have to *do* anything. I can just be who I am and that is enough.

In that moment, a cloud lifted from my life and it has never come back. The cycle of heavy depression ended. It was gone.

Easter was a few days later, and Swamiji gave the service. He was so inspiring, it threw me for a loop! I couldn't reconcile all the stuff I had read on the internet with Swamiji as I was experiencing him.

One thing he said really impressed me. He referred to the enormous debt Ananda had accumulated defending itself against the SRF lawsuit, which was still threatening Ananda's future.

"In the long run, though," Swamiji said, "it is not all that important whether or not Ananda survives. What is important is how we handle ourselves through whatever tests God sends us."

There was so much integrity in the way he said it. He was talking about his life's work, and he was ready to let it go rather than give up dharma.

I thought to myself, "I can't know what happened in the past. I have to go by my own experience. I trust this man standing in front of me and I am willing to accept him as my teacher."

Soon after, I became a disciple of Yogananda, and eventually moved to Seattle and joined the Ananda community there. When Swamiji came to visit, I told him about the healing I had received from Master in the chapel.

"If you hadn't suggested it," I said, "I would never have gone into the chapel to meditate. I was already walking away when I saw you."

"I remember," Swamiji replied. "I didn't know what it was, but I felt something in you."

I shudder to think what my life would be like now if I hadn't listened to him.

"Thank you, Swamiji," I said to him. "You were a perfect instrument of Master. It was pure grace."

~ From Carolyn Denslow Riffle ~

Light of Prayer

On the altar in his meditation room, Swamiji keeps a list of all those who have asked for his prayers. When he meditates, he asks God to bless these souls, and all those who have appealed to him for help.

A chronically ill man, whose name was on that list, took several treatments from a gifted psychic healer.

"Suddenly, in the middle of a session," the healer said, "I saw a powerful white light within him. I had never encountered anything like it before. Somehow I knew it was the light of Swamiji's prayer."

Later it was confirmed that the time of the treatment was the same time that Swamiji was in his meditation room, meditating and praying.

A Marriage Saved

I was with Swamiji and a big crowd of Ananda people in a very public place when I had the sudden intuition that my husband was infatuated with another woman. I turned my back to the crowd and walked away sobbing. Swamiji knew what was happening, and after a few minutes he came over to where I sat crying.

He made no attempt to console me. "Remember, it is all just Divine Mother's *lila*," he said. *Lila* is a Sanskrit word meaning "the play of God."

"I know, Swamiji. I know." Intellectually I understood, but my heart was breaking.

Swamiji made no reply. I sensed, however, a wordless transfer of power from him to me. Suddenly I felt as if I were standing at the top of a five-story building looking down on the scene playing out before me. From that perspective I could see that my little "tragedy" was just a single thread in the vast tapestry of life. This image of looking at life from the top of a tall building is something I have used many times since whenever attachment and emotion threaten my inner peace.

That night, because of the consciousness Swamiji put into me, my husband and I were able to talk in a way I wouldn't have believed possible. Swamiji had changed me from a child ruled by emotion into a grown-up who could talk impersonally about truth and dharma, even in a matter that concerned me deeply.

"Is it wrong to love somebody?" my husband asked me, referring to the "other woman." Swamiji has often said sympathetically, "One can't always control the feelings of the heart," and I remembered that now.

"Of course not," I said. "It is never wrong to love."

The "other woman" was also a friend of mine, and she, too, was married. I went on, "The question, however, is not about love. It is about dharma. What is right for all of us in this situation?"

I was so grateful to Swamiji for not offering me any false reassurances. All marriages end eventually, in death, if not before. Only consciousness endures. From then on, I worked much harder at my sadhana.

Later I was even able to meet with the "other woman." Through her tears, she assured me she had never intended to hurt anyone. Amazingly, I was able to discuss with her as calmly as I had with my husband, what might be right for all of us.

Time passed, and the situation was still unresolved. I began to grow impatient. "How long do I have to wait for him to make up his mind?" I finally asked Swamiji. "I don't even think he respects me."

Very seriously, Swamiji responded, "If it is true that he doesn't respect you, you should leave him."

Swamiji has often stated that the cornerstone of marriage is not love, as most people think. It is respect. Over the course of a lifetime, love may wax and wane. If there is respect, however, there is always a basis for cooperation and friendship. When respect is lost, it is very difficult to go on together.

Swamiji's statement terrified me. I didn't want the responsibility for ending the marriage. If a decision had to be made, I wanted my husband to make it. Swamiji was pushing me to face my fears.

I couldn't think what else to do, so I just repeated to my husband what Swamiji had said.

"I don't know how you could possibly think that I don't respect you," my husband said. He seemed genuinely shocked at the mere suggestion.

That was the beginning of our reconciliation. Swamiji had shown me the bottom-line condition for continuing the marriage and my husband was able to rise to the occasion. He resolved to renounce his infatuation and that opened my heart to him again. The marriage began to heal.

We are so grateful to Swamiji. Without his wise counsel I don't think our marriage would have survived.

The whole time our marriage was in jeopardy—a period of several months—I lived in a state of awareness higher and calmer than my normal way of being. I would almost call it a state of grace. It began when I was crying and Swamiji transferred energy to me. It ended practically at the very moment it was clear our marriage would survive. I think Swamiji projected a sustaining force that I tuned into. I was able to see my life in the rhythm of eternity, rather than the passing moments of pleasure and pain.

"To all who received him," it says in the Bible, "to them gave he power to become the Sons of God." I had the good karma to receive for a time. After the crisis passed, I wasn't able to do it in the same way. I am a different person, however, and a far better devotee for the experience. And it certainly whetted my appetite for the day when I can live always in that state.

~ From an Ananda devotee ~

Electric Embrace

I was a newcomer and had only seen Swamiji in large public gatherings. When I heard he was returning from a trip to Europe and would spend a few days at Ananda's San Francisco center, I drove four hours to the city to see him.

When I arrived at the ashram, I was disappointed to see that about 40 other people had gotten there before me and it wasn't possible even to sit near Swamiji. I felt excluded, alone, and increasingly morose, certain that I'd never be able to penetrate the circle around him. After dinner, Swamiji was heading out with a small group to see a movie. I was sitting in another room, talking with a friend. Suddenly, I felt a hand on my shoulder. I turned around, and Swamiji was there.

With a deep and earnest gaze, he looked at me for what seemed like a long time. Then he opened his arms and embraced me like an old friend. A surge of electricity passed from him into me. I felt as if my body was on fire, but without the heat. Thought stopped, and I was filled with a profound sense of peace and comfort.

It was in fact just a brief embrace. Then Swamiji stepped back, smiled warmly, doffed his cap, and went on his way without speaking a word to me. For the next fifteen minutes, I was vibrating with energy as the electricity continued to move through me. I felt elevated, buoyant, light as a feather. I had been feeling so left out, but God had heard my thoughts and sent Swamiji to show me: Don't be fooled by appearances. We are all equally children of God and equally loved by Him.

~ From an Ananda devotee ~

The Wart

For years, I had a noticeable wart on my hand. I tried all sorts of medicines, and the usual array of alternatives. But the wart stubbornly remained.

One day, I happened to be with Swami as he was walking to his car. He was a little shaky on his feet and rested his arm on my shoulder for support. I put my hand on his back to help steady him. The walk was all of two minutes, sweet, but otherwise uneventful.

The next day, I happened to glance at my hand, the hand that had touched Swamiji's back. The wart had vanished without a trace.

~ From an Ananda devotee ~

Taming a Tamboura

It was the middle of a concert when Swamiji picked up the tamboura to accompany himself while he sang. A tamboura is an Indian instrument that easily goes out of tune. It was dreadfully off-pitch and no matter how much Swamiji tried, he couldn't tune it. Finally he gave up and began to play it as it was.

I was near him on the stage and every time his fingers went across the strings I cringed at the dissonance. With his sensitive ear, I don't know how he kept singing, but he did. Gradually, the dissonance waned. By the time Swamiji was half way through the song, the tamboura was perfectly in tune and it stayed that way for the rest of the concert.

Patanjali's *Yoga Sutras* describe the practice of *ahimsa*. "Non-violence" is how it is usually translated. Swamiji calls it "harmlessness" and has dedicated himself to that practice. The fruit for one who practices *ahimsa* perfectly, Patanjali says, is that in his presence, no disharmony can arise. Wild animals are tamed, ferocious criminals subdued.

Some people may disagree, but I have been playing musical instruments since I was a child and I know they have personalities that respond to human consciousness. I think, in the presence of Swamiji's *ahimsa*, the tamboura simply couldn't hold on to its disharmonious "attitude." Swamiji's harmonious vibrations tamed it.

~ From Bhagavati ~

Twice Blessed

I had an accident that caused a blow to my skull so great I started to exit from my body. I traveled down a tunnel of light and was greeted by friends and relatives who had passed away years before. I came into the presence of a "Being of Light" who enveloped me in pure unconditional love.

Thoughts of unworthiness and shame for things I had done in the past made a brief, futile effort to invade this aura of love. Faster than the thoughts could arise, they evaporated. It was more than being forgiven. The "Being of Light" communicated to me that I, too, am made of light, and in that light there is nothing to forgive.

This was 1976. No one then was talking about "Near Death Experiences," so it wasn't until years later that I had an explanation for what had happened to me. All I knew at the time was that my life had been changed forever.

A few hours after the experience, a voice inside my head said, "Why do you continue to live in the same way? I have given you the key to life. I have given you yoga."

I had already been studying Hatha Yoga for about six months. From then on, I made it the center of my life. Two years later, I met Swamiji, and soon after had a private interview with him. At the end of the interview, I asked if I could touch his feet.

This was no small thing for me. My father had died ten years earlier, when I was fourteen. (He was one of those who greeted me in the tunnel of light.) Since then, I had been very headstrong and refused to take advice from anyone—until I met Swamiji. Now I wanted to bow down in front of him and put my life in his hands.

In India, touching the feet of a spiritual teacher is a common gesture of respect. Swamiji, however, has never encouraged that kind of outward show, but he must have sensed how much this meant to me, so he gave his permission. He was sitting in a chair and invited me to kneel in front of him.

Reverently I placed my hands on his feet and bent over until my forehead was almost resting on the backs of my hands. After a moment, I felt Swamiji gently lifting me by the shoulders until we were face to face. He closed his eyes and touched me at the spiritual eye. I closed my eyes to receive his blessing.

A horizon line formed before my closed eyes, illuminated from below, as if the sun were about to rise. Beams of white light streamed from the hidden sun. I was bathed in luminescence. I forgot myself. I forgot that Swamiji was blessing me. All I knew was light, peace, joy, and what I can only describe now as a state of utter "desirelessness." In that moment, every imaginable fulfillment was mine already.

Then Swamiji removed his touch and the light went away. I looked into Swamiji's eyes, which were now just inches from mine, and saw there a quality of impersonal, yet unconditional love that I had never seen in anyone else before.

Only later did I link the two experiences. Twice I'd been touched by the light. The first time, I had to leave my body and go into another world to experience it. The second time, the light came to me, when I was willing to bow in humility and reverence before its pure channel: Swamiji.

~ From Krishna Das ~

My Name is Gratitude

If I were to choose a spiritual name for myself, it would have to be Gratitude.

I started drinking in my early teens. Drugs came later, in the '60s, just before I turned twenty. All my friends drank, and everything that happened after sundown involved drugs and alcohol. So we were more inclined to play loud music than to play chess. Drinkers hang out with other drinkers. It's tidy that way, no unpleasant images in the mirror—everyone looks like you.

Whatever we were having, I consumed more of it than my friends. It always took more to get me to the edge of contentment, and the edge was as close as I could ever get. In a typical evening, I would drink a six-pack of beer, a substantial amount of hard liquor, and use whatever drugs were at hand.

I never got mean, never got in fights, never fell down, but from my early teens, I was drunk every night of my life. In those early years, I had a couple of auto accidents, but nothing after that, even though, if it was dark, driving or not, I was drunk.

I never drank during the day. In fact, I couldn't imagine why anyone would want to be dull while it was still light. During the day, I went for stimulants, but, come nightfall, nothing could stop me from drinking. Stimulants during the day meant more alcohol to come down at night, then more stimulants the next day to push away the effects of the previous night's drinking: truly a vicious and deadly cycle. I also smoked quite a lot of marijuana, occasionally took mushrooms, and used cocaine. My friends either kept up, or they fell away. Some died, many ended up permanently damaged.

I was married in the early '80s, but my habits didn't change. I merely couched them now in transparent respectability, more evenings out drinking good wine, or at home drinking good scotch and premium beer. Cocaine replaced the cruder stimulants. But the truth is, I would have drunk cheap gin, if that were all I had.

My wife drank only moderately, just an occasional glass or two of wine with dinner. It is unusual for a non-drinker to marry someone who is already wedded to this habit of nightly oblivion, but then, she never knew me any other way. We didn't discuss it. I figured it was just part of the package she had chosen. She clearly saw something in me beyond the man she married, and she knew the power of prayer.

We bought a house and built a business. At one point, though, she expressed enough concern for my overall health that I agreed to have a "routine" physical. The doctor stated unequivocally that I was on my way to an unpleasant, and perhaps lingering, death.

He said it would be dangerous for me to try to quit drinking on my own. The withdrawal symptoms would be so severe I might even have seizures. He wanted me to go straight from his office to the hospital.

To bolster his argument, he called in another patient, an ex-alcoholic, who, he said, just happened to be in the waiting room. This gentleman, in a glib and self-important voice, rambled through a fragmented assessment of my future unless I followed the good doctor's advice. But he was so cognitively damaged it was easy for me to brush off both him and his counsel. I genuinely felt I would rather drink myself to death than wind up like him.

The meeting with the doctor was such a disaster neither my wife nor I ever mentioned it again.

In the middle of all of this, sometime in the early '80s, we started going to Ananda classes and services. In 1986, when Swami Kriyananda announced he was leading a pilgrimage to Southern California to see Master's shrines—Mt. Washington, Encinitas, the Lake Shrine, and the crypt—we decided to go along.

The first evening in Encinitas, at the Sanderling Hotel, Swamiji held a Discipleship Initiation. I sat in the back of the room, watching people go up and kneel before him. He blessed each one by placing his finger at their spiritual eye, the point between the eyebrows. After a moment, he would remove his hand. The person would then rise, bow to Swamiji with folded hands, and return to his seat.

I just couldn't identify with the ritual. I was strongly drawn to Master, and I had great respect for Swamiji, even though I had spoken to him only a couple of times. I wasn't sure it was the right time for me to become a disciple, or if, in truth, Master would want me.

So I just watched, like a stone gargoyle peering down from a cathedral roof. Then, somehow, I found myself kneeling in front of Swamiji. I don't recall why I decided to do it. In fact, I don't remember deciding to do it at all, but there I was.

When he touched me at the spiritual eye, there was no spark of light, no uncontrollable trembling, no sound of crashing waves. As I recall, I didn't feel anything.

But after the blessing, I stood up, bowed respectfully to Swamiji, and walked away a different person.

That was two decades ago. Since that moment I've had not a hint, not a longing, not a whisper of unnamed or unfulfilled desire for drugs or alcohol. I went, as they say, cold turkey on a twenty-five year habit without a single unpleasant symptom.

I rarely tell anyone with a drinking or a drug problem about my experience. I have seen how terribly difficult it is for them to quit. I want to help; I love them for their courage, but they need inspiration that is within their reach: something as close, as tangible, and as obtainable as the substances and the mental state they crave.

I do not believe it would inspire someone in the throes of the struggle with addiction, to hear that God, without even being (consciously) invited, came and lifted my burden, leaving nothing behind but gratitude. It would be too far beyond hope, leaving them feeling even more isolated and unworthy.

I often hear the statement, "I am a recovering alcoholic." Those who use that phrase have earned the right to say it. They have fought hard, and for most of them it is a lifelong struggle.

My life, however, was changed in an instant. What I can and do say, with humility and endless gratitude, is, "I am the disciple of a Great Avatar, and the loving student of a Great Teacher who can, with his touch, channel the Master's transforming grace."

~ From an Ananda devotee ~

I Need Your Help

For 29 years, I was afflicted with a terrible addiction. Not merely a habit, but an addiction, something I needed every day. I tried therapy, 12-Step programs, affirmations, will power. Nothing worked.

When I got on the path, I read everything Master said about overcoming temptation and changing habits. Still the addiction was unbeatable, stronger than anything I could throw at it.

When I confided to an Ananda friend, she responded, "Have you asked Swamiji to help you?"

"I wrote to him several times," I said.

"Just writing to him isn't enough. What I'm asking is: Have you opened your heart to him? Have you asked him to give you the strength to overcome this? Have you *prayed* to Swamiji?"

I hadn't done any of those things so I decided I would try. That night in meditation when it was time to pray, words came to me with such intensity I felt that they were praying me.

"Dear Swamiji," I said, "I can't do this alone. I need your help. *I know you can help me.*"

For the first time I understood what Jesus meant when he said, "Pray believing." I *knew* that Swamiji could help me.

A few days after I began that prayer, 29 years of addiction ended. The desire completely disappeared. In the years since then I haven't had a single symptom, not an urge, not even a temptation.

About six months later, I greeted Swamiji after a Sunday Service and thanked him again for the help he had given me. He held my eyes with a penetrating gaze. When he spoke, I felt as if a surge of electricity came into me, bathing me with his protection and courage.

"Don't ever give up," Swamiji said. "Keep at it with every ounce of your being. Know that Master is blessing you."

~ From an Ananda devotee ~

Meet It at the Crest

For seven years, the man had struggled to resist an attraction to a woman in the community who was not his wife. Finally he said to Swamiji, "I am too unhappy, I can't go on this way."

"Let me tell your wife," Swamiji said. "It will be easier for her that way."

"He has done his best to overcome this," Swamiji said to her, "but he can't. It is something he has to live through." She was devastated, but she took it bravely.

When the news came out that the man was leaving his wife for another woman, some people reacted judgmentally. "What about his obligation to the community?" one said to Swamiji. "This will reflect badly on all of Ananda."

"He gave seven years to the community," Swamiji said. "I think that is long enough. He did his best. You can't ask more than that of anyone."

The day after the couple separated, Swamiji asked the two women to come to his house and cook dinner together for him and a few guests, including the husband.

"Sir! Are you sure that's a good idea?" a woman exclaimed when she heard the plan. "Don't you remember what happened yesterday?"

"Of course I remember," Swamiji said. "But they have to get over it sooner or later. If they wait until some future lifetime they won't even remember why they dislike each other, and it will be much more difficult to overcome. When a wave of karma hits, raise your energy and meet it at the crest! That's the way to make spiritual progress!"

Later, the wife described what happened that evening. "I wanted to give in to my grief and run away," she said, "but Swamiji wouldn't let me. He had more faith in me than I had in myself. It wasn't easy to summon up the courage, but I did my best, and divine grace did the rest. The whole evening, I felt nothing but love for them. Even though circumstances had changed, the underlying friendship was untouched.

"Afterwards, I wasn't always able to maintain such a high state of consciousness, but I had done it once, so I knew I could do it again. Because I followed Swamiji's advice, I believe I saved myself years, perhaps even lifetimes, of suffering."

A Fistula

"You have a serious medical condition called a fistula," the doctor said to me. "The only remedy is surgery."

I had come to Italy to visit relatives and take care of some business obligations there. As soon as I arrived, I started feeling something very painful in my lower back. Within three days, it was so bad I couldn't walk, and I had to go to the hospital. A fistula, I found out, is an abnormal opening or connection between two internal organs, or from an internal organ to the surface of the body. Mine was inside.

"We have to operate as soon as possible," the doctor said, "otherwise you won't be able to stand the pain."

I agreed, and the next day I had the surgery. The fistula, however, was so large and so deep the surgeon was unable to repair it completely.

"You'll have to wait a few weeks until the first surgery heals," the doctor said. "Then I'll operate again and finish the job."

Oddly enough, the doctor tied one end of a string to the spot where he stopped working, and left the other end dangling outside my body, so he could easily find his way back in. (Shades of Theseus in the labyrinth!) It was disconcerting to see that string hanging there.

After the surgery, I had to stay in the hospital another five days, still in great pain, which the doctor said would continue until after the second operation. Swamiji happened to be visiting Italy at the time, and he sent me a beautiful big bouquet of flowers. It caused quite a stir. In Italy, so many flowers are given only to mothers with newborns.

When I was released from the hospital, I was still gasping with pain and hardly able to move. That very day an Ananda friend called to tell me that in two days, Swamiji was coming to visit me. I couldn't say no, but I also couldn't imagine how I'd be able to see anyone.

The next day, I was still in excruciating pain. The day after, however, I woke up feeling quite a bit better. When I got up and started to make the bed, I was horrified to see the surgical string lying there on the sheet. It had fallen out of my body! Immediately, I went to the hospital. The doctor inspected the site of the surgery. He was strangely silent. Then he said, "I see nothing there at all. Everything looks perfect. I can't find any sign of the fistula." It was obvious to me, too, that something had changed, for now I had only a little bit of pain.

I was stunned by this sudden turn of events, and delighted that I would be well for Swamiji's visit. We met at 4pm, and at his suggestion, went for a walk together. The day before, I would have been in too much pain. Now I walked easily. My wife knew about my remarkable healing, but I didn't mention it to Swamiji, or to anyone else.

Suddenly, without warning, Swamiji stumbled and nearly fell to the ground. For no apparent reason, he suddenly had an intense pain in his hip, and, being unable to put weight on his leg, could hardly walk. Fortunately, we were not far from the home of one of my relatives, and I half-carried, half-dragged him there. Thank God I was well enough to do it! Swamiji lay down on a bed, and for the next several hours could hardly move because of the pain. Finally, it began to lessen, and I was able to get him back to his hotel. The next day, he was fine.

I thought deeply about what had happened: my mysterious healing, and Swamiji's sudden collapse. I believe he suffered to protect me from suffering. This is something only a saint can do. I will never forget what Swamiji did for me.

~ From an Ananda devotee~

Divorce

I went through an extremely painful divorce. One particularly awful day coincided with a huge public event. I held myself together until late in the afternoon. Ironically, it was a compassionate look from a dear friend in the middle of a roomful of people that started me crying again.

"I'm going to take you over to Swamiji," my friend said. Swamiji was standing just a little distance away. I made a feeble protest, which my friend simply ignored.

"Hridaya is having a terrible time today," my friend said to Swamiji. I collapsed against his shoulder and he held me while I cried and cried. "I am so sorry," he said. "I am so sorry."

When I finally gained some little bit of control over myself, I stood back and looked into his eyes. Swamiji is no stranger to disappointment. God has tested him over and over again. In his eyes I could see compassion born of experience. But there was also something else. He wasn't willing to meet me on the level of shared pain. His eyes invited me to join him on the level where human suffering is just something we offer up to God as a way of growing closer to Him. Sad as I was, I was also thrilled by that look and the promise it held.

Swamiji then blessed me by touching me on the heart and on the spiritual eye. My tears stopped completely, and from that point on I started getting better.

~ From Hridayavasi ~

Blue Moped

For many years, the only way to drive to Crystal Hermitage, Swamiji's home at Ananda Village, was over two miles of unpaved road, deeply rutted and littered with potholes.

For years also, Swamiji's only car was a big blue Chevrolet, purchased for him from a government auction of used automobiles. Two cars, exactly alike, were bought at the same time—one for Swamiji to drive, and the other to provide spare parts to keep the first one running. Each cost $75. On the door of Swamiji's car could faintly be seen the words, "U.S. Air Force," put there by one of its previous owners. Naturally, the car became known as "Air Force One," an amusing title for this ancient vehicle.

One summer, Swamiji decided it would save wear and tear on the car if he got a moped for the dirt road and used the Chevrolet only for trips outside of Ananda. Several friends warned Swamiji that dirt roads could be treacherous on a motorcycle, but Swamiji was unconcerned. When a blue moped came up for sale, Swamiji bought it.

In that season, his everyday outfit was sandals, Bermuda shorts, and a sport shirt (often a bright Hawaiian print). For some weeks he cut quite a colorful figure in his flowered shirts, sitting straight upright rather than hunched over in typical motorcyclist fashion, and waving cheerfully to passersby. He appeared always serene, driving at moderate speed and calmly smiling.

Then disaster struck.

The dirt road includes a long, steep hill, which, on a small motorcycle, must be taken at just the right speed. Too fast, and one may lose control; too slow, and one may lose traction. Swamiji had safely negotiated the hill before now, but this day something went wrong. His speed was inadequate and the moped lost traction and began to slip. Swamiji gunned the motor, but it was too late. The moped tipped over, pinning him beneath it.

The machine wasn't heavy, but the hot exhaust pipe fell right against the inside of his bare calf, burning into his skin. To get out from under it, Swamiji had to roll over on the ground, which caused the wound to become filled with dust and dirt.

Fortunately, someone was driving not far behind Swamiji and was able to pick him up and take him home. The closest medical care was twenty miles away in Nevada City, and Swamiji didn't think the injury warranted the journey. He had no telephone, but somehow the word spread. Soon people began showing up at Swamiji's door with ideas of how to treat the burn. Over the course of the next several hours he received three or four different treatments. Unfortunately, none of them helped much. The wound did not get cleaned properly, and none of the ointments and salves was appropriate. After a few days the wound became infected. Only then did Swamiji consent to go into town and have it treated medically.

It was a bad burn, and looked even worse: some six inches long and three inches across, inflamed and full of pus. The doctor assured Swamiji, however, that with a little care it would heal fine.

The following Sunday, Swamiji was holding an afternoon satsang in his home, as he often did. He sat in his usual chair in front of the big triangle window that looked out at the river valley and the forested hills beyond. He was wearing Bermuda shorts and, in accordance with the doctor's orders, had his leg propped up on a footstool before him. The wound was unbandaged to let the air reach it freely, so we all got a good view of how awful it looked. About a dozen people were present.

Suddenly, a man named Ram Lila burst into the room. Ram Lila lived in San Francisco, but often visited Ananda. Before becoming a devotee he had belonged to a rough motorcycle gang called the Hell's Angels. By now he had given up most of the worst habits associated with that lifestyle, but he still looked like a "biker," and still drove a big Harley-Davidson motorcycle.

Ram Lila was powerfully built—not tall but very thick, somewhat on the lines of a Sumo wrestler, though by no means obese. His biceps were bigger than the average man's thighs. The astrological bangle that is worn by many Ananda members, made to go around the arm above the elbow, was worn by Ram Lila dangling from a string around his neck. It would have taken at least two bangles to accommodate the circumference of his upper arm. He had a black beard and thick, curly hair, which hung to his shoulders. Heavy boots and a leather vest completed his "biker" outfit.

He looked fierce, but his nature was that of a child. Swamiji had given him the name, "Ram Lila," which means, "God's divine play."

"I laughed when the name came to me," Swamiji said. "It was so appropriate!"

Ram Lila was devoted to Swamiji in an extravagant, adoring way, like a child. He wanted Swamiji to take him on as a bodyguard. Swamiji declined because, he said, "I don't need one." Ram Lila never quite accepted that this was true, and when he was in Swamiji's company he always kept alert, "just in case."

On this day, Ram Lila came straight in and threw himself at Swamiji's feet. "I should have been killed!" he said with deep feeling. "The truck came out of nowhere. BAM!" He slammed one fist into the other open hand to show the force of the impact.

"I wasn't wearing a helmet. I went flying over the handlebars and bounced on the road. BAM! BAM! BAM!" Again he illustrated with fist to hand. "My side, my head, my shoulders, my back: I thought, 'This is it! I'm dead!' Finally I stopped. I checked everything. Man, not even a broken bone! I walked away. I should have died, and I WALKED AWAY!"

What he was describing was serious, but he told the story with such enthusiasm and drama that we were laughing with delight. Ram Lila didn't seem to mind.

"I'm so glad you didn't die, Ram Lila!" said Swamiji, and patted him lovingly on the head.

Now that he'd told his story, Ram Lila noticed for the first time that Swamiji was injured.

"What happened to you?" he asked. Perhaps Swamiji did need a bodyguard after all!

Swamiji didn't answer. "You tell him," he said to me.

"He fell off his moped," I explained. "The exhaust pipe landed on his leg and burned him."

Ram Lila was so shocked he could barely speak. He stammered out a question: "W-w-when did it happen?" I told him the day and the time of the accident.

"O my God! O my God! O my God!" he cried. "That was just before that truck slammed into me. You did it! You saved my life!

I couldn't figure out why I didn't die. Now I know." He knelt before Swamiji and began to sob.

After the accident, Swamiji never touched his moped again. A few weeks later he gave it away.

Paula

Paula checked herself into the hospital because of severe bronchitis, but I think she knew the cancer had returned for the third time. The doctors tried one more procedure, but in the middle, she went into convulsions and for a few moments her heart stopped. After that, the doctor said, "There is nothing else we can do."

She lived three more days. It was one long going-away party, with constant phone calls, a steady stream of visitors, and a crowd of friends and family camped out in her hospital room. She was much loved and would be sorely missed.

It was impossible to be sad, however, for Paula was obviously in a state of grace.

She had a little unfinished business with a few people, but by afternoon of the third day, it was all done. The transition came suddenly, in the middle of a conversation about coffee. (Paula loved coffee.) She stopped talking, gazed upward, then closed her eyes. An even deeper aura of holiness descended and we fell silent.

Paula began to murmur ecstatically, "Swamiji, Swamiji, Swamiji, Swamiji." From then on, there was a subtle shift. Paula continued to relate to the people around her, but her attention was no longer on this world. She was focused now on the world beyond.

To one of her Ananda visitors she said, "You must listen to Swamiji. You must help him, and do everything he asks of you. You don't know what you have in him."

Around midnight she organized a ceremony. Nothing solemn, that wasn't Paula's way. She was dying the same way she lived—light-hearted, happy, almost child-like in her devotion. From Master's book of prayers, *Whispers from Eternity,* she picked a few of her favorites and asked that they be read aloud. Then with her own hand she gave each person a flower. After that, she disconnected the supplemental oxygen she had been using, and lay down as if to sleep.

We all went to sleep, too, in her room, in the hallway, or in empty rooms nearby. The hospital staff let us take over the whole wing. About 4am, Paula woke up from whatever state she had been in and started waking up the others in her room.

"Please, everyone, come in here *now*," she said.

Her husband sat on the bed next to her and put his arm around her, as he had often done in the last few days. Always before she welcomed his embrace. Now she said, quite impersonally, "Don't touch me. I can still feel it." We knew the end had come.

At her request, we began chanting AUM. After a few minutes, Paula said, "This is very hard. You have to help me." For the next few minutes, she was silent and we continued to chant. Then, with great feeling, she said, "God! Christ! Guru!" Those were Paula's last words. For the next half-hour, we kept chanting, and she kept breathing. Then her breath stopped.

Suddenly, I felt power pouring over me as if a mighty angel were passing by. I was astonished to find myself sobbing with joy.

Paula was a spiritual leader at Ananda. Among other accomplishments, she helped develop the Portland community and successfully managed two retail businesses. But she never called attention to herself, and most people thought of her as just one devotee among many. So it came as a surprise at her memorial service a few days later, when Swamiji said, "I believe Paula may have been liberated. Only a person of true realization could die the way she did."

On her last day, Paula spoke to Swamiji on the telephone. "I hope you don't have to come back to this world," she said. "I hope I don't have to come back either. But if you come again, I'll come and help you."

~ 10 ~

IN SACRED JOY
I MELT

"From Joy I came,

For Joy I live,

In sacred Joy I melt."

Paramhansa Yogananda

Master (Paramhansa Yogananda)

One Last Question

A devotee was marveling at Swamiji's many accomplishments. "In one lifetime you've done the work of ten men!" she said.

"Perhaps you're right," Swamiji said quietly. "Nothing I have done is important, however, except to the extent that it has helped people individually to deepen their love for God.

"At the end of this life, the only thing that will matter to me is 'Have I been a good disciple?'"

Every word of this book was written as
a prayer of gratitude, lovingly offered at the feet of my
divine friend and guide, Swami Kriyananda.

This book is dedicated to the fulfillment
in all souls of this prayer by Master:

May Thy love shine forever
On the sanctuary of our devotion,
And may we be able to awaken Thy love
In all hearts.

In *The Path: One Man's Quest on the Only Path There Is*, Swamiji describes his childhood in Europe, his teen years in America, and the intellectual and then spiritual seeking that led him, in 1948 at the age of 22, to the feet of his Master. Part II begins after his initiation as a disciple. *The Path* is a unique, first-hand account of life with a great guru.

In *A Place Called Ananda*, another autobiography, Swamiji begins after Master's passing in 1952, and describes the outer events and inner understandings that led to the founding of Ananda.

The Life of Swami Kriyananda
by Devi Novak

Faith Is My Armor: The Life of Swami Kriyananda was written by Devi Novak, one of Swamiji's closest friends and co-workers. You see the magnitude of Swamiji's accomplishments and the unending stream of challenges he has faced and overcome.

In *Autobiography of a Yogi,* Master describes growing up in India, and his years of spiritual training with his guru, Sri Yukteswar. In chapters like *Kriya Yoga, The Law of Miracles, Babaji: the Yogi-Christ of Modern India,* he explains the principles and divine power behind the teachings of Self-Realization he brought to the West. First published in 1946, this book helped launch, and continues to inspire a global spiritual revolution. (The original 1946 edition, available through Ananda, is free of the many editorial changes made after Master's passing.)

The Essence of Self-Realization is a collection of Master's words on many subjects of supreme importance to the truthseeker, carefully recorded by Swamiji when he was a young disciple at the feet of his guru. Chapters include *The Soul and God, The Law of Karma, The Need for a Guru, How to Pray Effectively.*

Conversations with Yogananda includes the rest of the notes Swamiji took during those early years. Topics cover the heart of the spiritual path and also range in fascinating detail into questions like the nature of evolution, science and religion, life on other planets, to name just a few.

ABOUT THE TEACHINGS
OF SELF-REALIZATION

The Essence of the Bhagavad-Gita describes the nature of the spiritual path and how to follow it successfully to Self-realization. Every page radiates hope and affirms the divine promise of the *Gita*, "Even a little practice of this inward religion will free one from dire fears and colossal sufferings."

The Promise of Immortality is a commentary on the Bible, and also shows the parallels between Biblical passages and verses in the *Gita*.

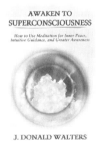

Awaken to Superconsciousness explains how spirit descends into material form, and how, by certain techniques, actions, and right attitudes, the human consciousness can raise itself from matter back to oneness with Spirit.

Meditation for Starters is a how-to manual for anyone who wants a simple, practical way to access the inner world of higher consciousness.

The proving ground of spiritual attainment, a great saint averred, is not only the silence of meditation but the "cold light of day." Swamiji has specialized in making spiritual truth practical.

Cities of Light describes the vision and the principles of cooperative spiritual living that define Ananda. For centuries, to renounce home and family has been considered essential for whole-hearted dedication to God. Formal renunciation will still be for many their chosen way to God, but Master's ideal of "world brotherhood colonies" also gives couples and families a way to live a God-centered life.

Expansive Marriage: A Way to Self-Realization is a guide for couples who seek, as Swamiji puts it, "to become saints together."

Education for Life uses the principles of Self-realization to create a system for educating children.

Material Success Through Yoga Principles, a year-long home-study course, explains how to use the power of Self-realization to serve your fellow beings by manifesting prosperity and success in the world. In his autobiographical writing, Swamiji explains *what* he has done. In this course, he explains *how* he has done it, in a way others can replicate.

Ananda: Past, Present & Future

The early days at Ananda

In 1967, Swamiji started Ananda as a single rural community, the first step toward fulfilling Master's dream of "world brotherhood colonies." In the beginning, only a handful of people were willing to join him. Gradually, however, the inspiration spread.

Now Ananda is a worldwide spiritual network of communities, meditation groups, and individual devotees spanning sixteen countries on six continents, the result of the cooperative efforts of hundreds of willing workers drawn by Swamiji to serve Master in this way. Books by Swamiji are available in 100 countries in 28 different languages.

The original Ananda community, located just outside Nevada City, California, has become Ananda *Village*. Several hundred residents live on 1000 acres of land. There are homes, businesses, *Living Wisdom Schools* for the children, plus a meditation retreat called *The Expanding Light* where visitors come from around the world.

The Expanding Light

The four urban communities—Seattle (Washington), Portland, (Oregon), Sacramento and Palo Alto (California)—serve the areas in which they are located through their teaching centers, Temples of Self-Realization, Living Wisdom Schools, East-West bookshops, and other businesses. Ananda East in Rhode Island is a small rural retreat.

Ananda Europa, located in the country-side a few miles outside of Assisi, Italy, is both a thriving community and a retreat. Hundreds of people visit every year from North and South America, Europe, Asia, Africa, and Australia. Programs are conducted in three languages—English, Italian, and German, with other translations provided as needed. In the dining room, one often hears a dozen languages or more.

The Temple of Light near Assisi

"Brotherhood is an ideal better understood by example than precept!" Master writes in his *Autobiography of a Yogi*. "A small harmonious group may inspire other ideal communities over the earth.

"'World' is a large term, but man must enlarge his allegiance, considering himself in the light of a world citizen. A person who truly feels: 'The world is my homeland; it is my America, my India, my Philippines, my England, my Africa,' will never lack scope for a useful and happy life. His natural local pride will know limitless expansion; he will be in touch with creative universal currents."

From West to East: Ananda India

In 2003, at the age of 77, Swamiji responded to an inward call from his guru, and moved to India to help complete Master's work there.

Swamiji meeting with the President of India, 2006

Every Indian is familiar with the basic truths of Master's teaching. Still, his message of Self-realization and Kriya Yoga is a new *expression* of these truths—a spiritual revolution for India just as it is in the West.

Soon after he moved to India, Swamiji started a daily television show that is now seen by millions in India and a dozen nearby countries.

These TV shows, plus publication of his book, *Conversations with Yogananda,* in 2003, and Master's commentary in 2006, *The Essence of the Bhagavad Gita explained by Paramhansa Yogananda, as remembered by his disciple, Swami Kriyananda,* have already made Swamiji one of the best-known and most highly-regarded spiritual teachers in India today.

"A Way of Awakening," Swamiji's daily television show

"There are so many receptive souls in India," Swamiji has said, "that in time the work there will dwarf everything else Ananda is doing."

Ananda classes are held all over India

India is the point of greatest expansion for Ananda and also the point of greatest need. In order to put the work on a firm foundation and set a clear direction for those who come later, Swamiji has determined to build a Universal Temple of Self-Realization, establish a community and a Living Wisdom School for children, open a university level Yoga Institute of Living Wisdom especially to train teachers in the Education for Life methods of Ananda. A hospice for the elderly, an orphanage for the young, and a manufacturing plant for an innovative solar energy device are also in the plans.

A worldwide spiritual revolution

All of this Swamiji has resolved to do as his final offering in this lifetime of service to his guru.

Many Hands Make a Miracle

The remarkable success of Ananda is the result God's grace, and the day-by-day, prayer-by-prayer, dollar-by-dollar dedication of all those around the world who embrace Master's ideals as their own. In the beginning there were few; now there are thousands of Ananda *Sanghis*, as we call ourselves. *Sangha* means fellowship and *Sanghis* are those who have joined in.

Prayer-by-prayer

Ananda colony leaders

Perhaps after reading *The Way of Ananda Sanghis*, you will feel that this cause is also your own. The essence of Ananda is described in the prayer and seven principles which follow.

The Way of Ananda Sanghis

*"May the Divine Light awaken and purify my heart,
and bring enlightenment to all beings."*

1) We believe in a single, blissful, eternal consciousness, *Satchidananda,* which pervades the entire universe, unifying it and all

creatures in a bond of mutual service. This blissful consciousness is the underlying reality of all existence; it precedes the very manifestation of the universe.

2) We believe that man's highest duty is to realize himself as an expression of all-pervading *Satchidananda.*

a) We embrace the way to this Self-realization through the inner silence, above all, of daily communion with the infinite Self.

b) We embrace, for ourselves, the need to embody this realization in our own lives by daily performing at least one specific, conscious, personally selected act of service to our fellow beings.

c) We embrace—again, for ourselves, since we seek not to impose our understanding on others—the need to honor all, whether friends or self-named foes, as manifestations of the eternal *Satchidananda,* and to see them as our brothers and sisters in that

Supreme Consciousness which is variously called God, Ishwara, Allah, or Jehovah. We recognize all names for that Supreme Being as designating our one, common Progenitor.

d) We embrace the need to give back to our Supreme Source by offering up every ego-attachment and self-limiting identity in daily acts of service to others.

e) We seek as our primary goal in life the state of actual, conscious union with *Satchidananda*.

f) We aspire to make our own lives works of art, whether through music, through the visual arts, or through the simple deeds of our daily existence, with a view to expressing the bliss that is latent in our deeper selves.

g) We seek to make our every thought and action a radiation outward from the center of our being, and not to allow ourselves to become superficial reflections of the thoughts and actions of others.

3) We seek never to convert anyone to our specific cause

except, in love, to inspire all with the desire to reclaim the bliss of their own being.

4) We seek fellowship with others

willing to join hands with us in this loving labor for universal upliftment. Thus, by our united efforts, our hope is to share inspiration with ever-increasing effectiveness.

5) We recognize that, whether or not others join us

consciously in this labor, all human beings, each one individually, serve the Eternal Purpose, doing so by the simple act of seeking, whether ignorantly or wisely, the bliss of their own being. We condemn no one, therefore, for ideas he may hold that are different from our own, but embrace all as fellow seekers of Ultimate Bliss.

6) In token of our dedication to these principles, the assumption of which is our guiding rule in life, we undertake at formal  functions of our Order to wear a color expressive of our hearts' ardor, of the purity of our aspiration, and of the humility of our intentions. We wear that color not to set ourselves apart from others, but simply to remind ourselves to remain focused on our true purpose. The color is a warm hue of yellow, reminiscent of the sun and symbolic of the joy of our own being. By donning this color, we demonstrate our willingness to cooperate with others equally dedicated to this lofty ideal. The color yellow may be worn in any shape: a tie, a scarf, a shawl, or even a handkerchief tucked into the breast pocket of a man's jacket.

7) We recognize that the way of Ananda Sangha is primarily *inward*, not outward; that it leads one by the universal pathway of the spine to the high state of communion with God at that point in the forehead which lies between the eyebrows. We follow this path by the daily practice, after receiving it, of the nonsectarian science of *Kriya Yoga,* as it was named by its reviver in the nineteenth century, Yogavatar Lahiri Mahasaya of Varanasi. The aim of Kriya Yoga is to withdraw one's energy and consciousness from the senses to the spine, and  to lift the awareness to conscious union with the Supreme Reality: *Satchidananda.* Those who practice this sacred science are known as *Kriyabans.* The Kriyabans of Ananda Sangha offer special respect, honor, and reverence to those who inspired the promulgation of Kriya Yoga in modern times: Jesus Christ, Mahavatar Babaji (who was, as he has informed his close disciples, Bhagavan Krishna in a former incarnation), Lahiri Mahasaya, Swami Sri Yukteswar, and Paramhansa Yogananda, ambassador of Kriya Yoga to the West and promoter of the underlying oneness of Hinduism, Christianity, and, consequently, of all the great religions of the world. Kriyabans revere the great saints of all religions, but give special reverence and obedience to the line of gurus on whose lives and teachings we pattern our own lives.

Mahavatar
Babaji

Lahiri   *Jesus*   *Swami Sri*
Mahasaya *Christ* *Yukteshwar*

Paramhansa
Yogananda

For more information about the Ananda communities and schools, how to participate wherever you live, join *The Way of Ananda Sanghis*, or help with the work in India, please contact the Ananda Sangha at one of these centers:

Ananda Village
14618 Tyler Foote Road
Nevada City, California
95959 USA
phone:
530.478.7560
www.ananda.org
sanghainfo@ananda.org

Ananda Europa
Via Montecchio, 61
I-06025 Nocera Umbra (PG)
ITALY
phone: +39 0742-81.36.20
fax: +39 0742-81.35.36
www.aananda.it
info@ananda.it

Ananda India
B-10/8, DLF Phase I
Gurgaon (HR) INDIA 122002
phone: +91-124-405 9550
or +91-98992 67698
fax: +91-124-410 3386
www.anandaindia.org
ananda@anandaindia.org

Crystal Clarity Publishers is dedicated to providing books, music, and other resources filled with inspiration, practical wisdom, and true spiritual principles that have been tested and proven true not only through the ages, but also in the modern day "laboratory" of the personal experience of our authors and staff.

For a complete catalog, or to place an order, please contact us.

Crystal Clarity Publishers
14618 Tyler Foote Road
Nevada City, California 95959
USA

800.424.1055 or 530.478.7600
(fax) 530.478.7610
www.crystalclarity.com
clarity@crystalclarity.com